THE
STONEHAM CATALOGUE
OF

BRITISH STAMPS
1840 – 1979

includes
GREAT BRITAIN
JERSEY, GUERNSEY
ISLE OF MAN

1980 EDITION

STONEHAM PUBLICATIONS LTD
EASTLEIGH, HAMPSHIRE, SO5 3HT
ENGLAND

£3.95
(U.K. ONLY)

First Edition:	February 1978
Second Edition:	November 1978
Third Edition:	September 1979

STONEHAM PUBLICATIONS

ISBN 0 906400 01 5
ISSN 0142–615X

Published by Stoneham Publications Ltd, Eastleigh, Hampshire, SO5 3HT

Photoset and Printed by Printwise, High Street, Lymington, Hampshire, SO4 9AN

INTRODUCTION

We were told by our friends in the philatelic trade that the second edition of a new stamp catalogue is the critical test of its acceptance. By this standard, the Stoneham Catalogue has passed its test and all the evidence shows that it is increasingly being accepted as the dealers standard reference for British stamps. Our belief in the collectors' need for a single volume comprehensive GB catalogue is confirmed and now we can proceed with some confidence to make those improvements and additions which are desirable.

It would be simple to enlarge the catalogue very considerably by the inclusion of controls, cylinder blocks, booklets, abnormals, varieties, and errors – such as missing colours and missing phosphor bands, but all these additions together would increase the price very considerably. We prefer to bring such additions to the catalogue in a phased and gradual way.

In this third edition there are major further aids to the collector – the line engraved Alphabets illustrated in full, – the guides to the identification of the different printings of both the Seahorses and Castles, which we believe will assist our readers in a very practical way.

As those collectors who purchased our previous editions are aware, this is a reference work, we do not sell stamps, and we emphasise again that it IS NOT AN OFFER FOR SALE.

We acknowledge with our sincere thanks all those in the philatelic trade who have so generously given their knowledge and experience in the compilation and particularly the establishing of really up-to-date market prices.

John Tracy
Editor

MARKET MOVEMENTS

A great deal of discussion has taken place during the past year about investment in stamps, not only in the stamp magazines but also in the national press and on television. All this extra publicity has had an accumulative effect on market prices, especially on the high values prior to George VI. Very high prices have also been realised by auction houses thoughout the world.

It has become increasingly difficult to purchase better grade material, whether unused or used, and price changes in this edition reflect these trends. Condition has become of paramount importance when setting prices, unmounted or mounted, centring, good perforations or blunt or clipped ones, postmarks, – fine circular or heavy, parcel cancelled etc. etc. All these factors plus the colour and freshness of appearance are now applied to the overall assessment. The price differential can therefore vary considerably between say, heavily mounted and never hinged, or superb and average used. A catalogue would need 10 columns of differing prices to be really accurate all the time. However, the Stoneham Catalogue cites the mean average when pricing the two grades of used stamps, giving the collector a very good guide to the price they would have to pay.

It is most interesting to note that the increased prices of many stamps, which have not been selected for investment, are showing a similar rise to those which are regularly purchased by investors. This, in our opinion, is indicative of the strength of a market where demand, and demand alone, creates price rises. The George V and George VI sections are perfect examples of this trend, where collectors have appreciated the true scarcity of shades and watermark varieties. The current Queen Elizabeth definitive issues also fall into this category, providing a wealth of interesting material for the specialist collector at relatively low cost.

It is very difficult, at the time of writing, to foresee what will happen in the coming year. With a change of Government and a world oil crisis, it looks as though inflation will once again stay in double figures. When our economy weakens stamps gain in value more than at any other time, and it does appear that we are on our way to a similar situation as we experienced in 1977/78.

To sum up the past year's movements, approximately 90% of all stamps have increased in value, which indicated the strength of British stamps in a world wide market. The forthcoming LONDON 1980 International Exhibition will also have an effect on prices in the coming months, as dealers try to build up their stocks for this, the largest and most prestigious exhibition ever to be held in Great Britain.

STOP PRESS!

VAT INCREASE –
The market prices in this catalogue were based on a VAT rate of 8%. The new rate of 15% announced by the Chancellor of the Exchequer on 12th June will inevitably increase prices for UK buyers by approximately 5 – 7%.

CONTENTS

EXPLANATIONS AND ABBREVIATIONS

PRICES   This catalogue is priced in English pounds.
Whole pounds, generally ten pounds or over, are shown thus: £10.
Less than ten pounds, the amount is shown in decimal form, without the £ sign.
e.g.: 9.50 = Nine pounds 50 pence.
      50 = 50 pence.

The market prices shown are strictly related to the condition of the stamps, and these are specified at the beginning of most sections. Older issues of stamps in exceptional condition will always command a premium.

SETS OF STAMPS   Where these are quoted the set price includes the stamps with values in heavy type only.

FIRST DAY COVERS   for commemorative issues are priced as being illustrated covers with circular "First Day of Issue" handstamps or special illustrated postmarks. Plain covers are worth up to 60% less.

The only exceptions are the commemorative issues of George V where illustrated covers are very rare.

From the 1964 Shakespeare issue, plain covers have no greater value than the equivalent value of the used stamps.

PAPER AND GUMS   Whilst certain variations in paper did apply to earlier issues, and these are catalogued when significant, the Machin decimal issues have provided a whole new area of study for collectors. The various paper and gum combinations are shown separately in this section under the conventional abbreviations.

These are:

GA   =   Gum Arabic. The original type of gum, with a more or less shiny surface.

PVA   =   Polyvinyl alcohol gum, colourless with a matt surface.

PVAD =   Polyvinyl alcohol gum with dextrin added, matt surface but with a greenish tinge.

OCP   =   Original coated paper, slightly creamy to white, but does not fluoresce under ultra violet light.

FCP   =   Fluorescent coated paper, generally whiter than OCP, and fluorescent under ultra violet light.

PHOSPHOR BANDS   The position of the bands are described throughout in the following abbreviated form:

CB   =   Centre band
SB   =   Side band
SB (L) =   Side band at left
SB (R) =   Side band at right
2B   =   Two bands, one at each side.
AOP   =   All over phosphor.
1 BAR =   One bar (centre)
2 BARS =   Two bars (one at each side)

There are different coloured phosphor bands, which re-act in different manners under an ultra violet light. These were applied to the Wilding issues, but are not within the scope of this catalogue.

SCREENING   Many of the low value Machin decimal issues have been printed, at different times, with both 150 and 250 screen density. These are recognised by very specialist collectors, but are not separately catalogued in this edition.

COLOURS AND SHADES   The colour and shade descriptions for the older (classic) issues may not be considered very accurate by modern colour/shade standards, but they are traditional and have become recognised and accepted over many years.

In the modern issues, the Post Office descriptions are used where they are known.

Throughout this catalogue, colour/shade descriptions have been abbreviated where necessary, and in the following manner:

bis.– bistre, bl.– blue, blk.– black, brn.– brown, brz.– bronze, car.– carmine, chest.– chestnut, choc.– chocolate, cin.– cinnamon, emer.– emerald, grn.– green, ind.– indigo, mag.– magenta, mar.– maroon, myr.– myrtle, och.– ochre, ol.– olive, or.– orange, pur.– purple, pr.– prussian, redd.– reddish, sep.– sepia, scar.– scarlet, sl.– slate, tur.– turquoise, ult.– ultramarine, ver.– vermilion, vio.– violet, yel.– yellow, multi.– multicoloured, bt.– bright, dp.– deep, dk.– dark, dl.– dull, lt.– light, pl.– pale.

OTHER ABBREVIATIONS   horiz.– horizontal, inv.– inverted, vert.– vertical, wmk.– watermark, perf.– perforation, photo.– photogravure, litho.– lithograph, typo.– typograph, (P)– plain (gutter pair), (TL)– traffic light (gutter pair).

ILLUSTRATIONS   Definitive issues are full size, and commemorative issues are generally three-quarters size. The large definitive stamps of Jersey, Guernsey and Isle of Man are two thirds actual size. Booklet panes are half size.

ISSUED DATES   are expressed in the British style, i.e. day/month/year – 1/11/00 denotes 1st November 1900.

FINE USED STAMPS AND THEIR SCARCITY

QUEEN VICTORIA – LINE ENGRAVED AND SURFACE PRINTED

It is important for collectors to realise that from 1840 and certainly in the succeeding 50 years cancellations were designed to completely deface the stamps and in fact were called "obliterators". The Maltese Cross and later the Barred Oval of 1844 were the first to be used and it is only when one of these has not been centrally applied to the stamp, i.e. Queen Victoria's profile left clear, that the term fine used is applied. In reality the even greater use of superlatives is applied to stamps that exist in this condition, and it is why of course on imperforate issues this condition with four clear margins can command a considerable premium.

On Surface Printed issues the Duplex cancellation, which came into use in 1853, appears most prevalent, but it was still intended to be an obliterator, and was supposed to be applied so that the number in bars defaced the stamp whilst the adjoining CDS (circular date stamp) was left clear on the left hand side to be read by postal clerks. It is therefore an exception to find these stamps with a CDS and is due either to misapplication of the handstamp or they originated from small rural Post Offices.

Most higher values (2d to £5) were used on overseas mail, parcels, registered packages and international telegraphs, plus internal Post Office accounting. In the latter case once the stamp has been removed from the "form" it is impossible to be sure how it was used and these are now accepted by collectors. The use of registered packages and parcels, both inland and overseas, meant that a high proportion of these stamps suffered very heavy and often smudgy cancellations and the incidence of a fine CDS is small, highly collectable and of course worth a premium.

KING EDWARD VII

The majority of low values, i.e. ½d and 1d are found with CDS having been used by both rural and larger post offices to cancel the colossal volume of mail in the form of postcards which was at its peak in the Edwardian period. The Duplex cancellation was still in use and with it a squared circle, and in 1902 a machine cancel with the wavy lines also came into use.

Higher denomination stamps from 1½d were mainly used on parcels and overseas mail, but also very often, either on their own or in combination, on Inland Parcel Post slips, which meant they received a cancellation in the form of a CDS. The Channel Island CDS was also used on Edward VII high values 2/6d – £1 as a receipt for payment of tobacco duty.

KING GEORGE V, EDWARD VIII, GEORGE VI

As machine cancellations were now well established, this, coupled with the introduction of slogan postmarks, had the result that almost all mail passing through Head Post Offices was cancelled with anything but a CDS.

The wide use of the Double Circle and Single Circle CDS at almost all other post offices meant that the majority of low value stamps, i.e. ½d to 2d are readily found in fine used condition, but above that value it is much more difficult. As with previous reigns a clear CDS on a high value stamp commands a premium.

It is possible to find George V stamps with Duplex cancellations and squared circles. These postmarks were not supposed to be used but were not withdrawn, and when found do add an element of interest to a collection.

QUEEN ELIZABETH II

An enormous number of different postmarks are now in use, CDS, double CDS, machine cancels, slogans, meter marks, registered and parcel cancels to name but a few.

Really fine single circle date stamps are just as difficult to find and equally as elusive on the high values. Stamps with parts of First Day of Issue postmarks are totally acceptable.

LONDON'S BIG YEAR – 1980
Kenneth F. Chapman – Editor: PHILATELIC MAGAZINE

Once every ten years each of the major, philatelically-important countries of the world act as host to an international philatelic exhibition. In 1980 it is Great Britain's turn and, as in 1950, 1960 and 1970, London will become the philatelic "capital" of the world for that year.

To be known as LONDON 1980, the exhibition will take place in the famous Earls Court exhibition building from Tuesday, May 6th (National Stamp Day) to Wednesday, May 14th, 1980. It will be the biggest stamp exhibition ever staged in Great Britain. Plans allow for over 4,000 frames of exhibits, both competitive and invited, and for about 250 trade stands. In the frames will be selections from many famous collections formed in all parts of the world while the stands will bring together under one roof the cream of the world's finest stocks of stamps and postal history.

There are some collectors who feel scared about visiting an international stamp exhibition. They fear that the exhibits will be above their heads technically; that all the very rare stamps on show, and which they cannot hope to acquire for themselves, may make them dissatisfied with their own collections and, finally, that as stamp collectors, rather than philatelists, they will not receive the welcome that more experienced philatelists can expect.

It will not be like that at all. Of course, there will be many valuable specialised exhibits in the frames but there will also be a wide range of more modest displays from collectors who have only just qualified to compete internationally and do so not expecting any high award, but for the privilege of taking part in the show.

One of the remarkable aspects of any international philatelic exhibition – and LONDON 1980 will be no exception – is the way the exhibitors vary their approach to single-country collecting. An hour or two studying the similarities and differences between exhibits based largely on the same stamps can provide the visitor with a great deal of food for thought concerning his own collection. It is not necessarily the great rarities (by force of circumstances few in number and quite often unattractive in design) that appeal to the keen philatelist.

LONDON 1980 will certainly include many of those gems of philately which will be gazed upon with awe by some visitors while others will enjoy studying thematic exhibits and the stories they tell.

For the first time at a London "international" there will be a competitive section for Postal History. This is an interesting development resulting from the setting-up of a Postal History Commission by the Fédération Internationale de Philatélie (F.I.P.) – under whose patronage the exhibition is being held – and publication of a scale of marking for exhibits in this class. Postal history is no longer confined to the pre-adhesive period and collections of covers, bearing stamps demonstrating postal rates for different services and periods can be both colourful and instructive.

Organisation
Organising an exhibition on the scale of LONDON 1980 is an immensely complicated exercise involving close contact with philatelic authorities all over the world. A company called International Philatelic Exhibitions Ltd, was set up under the sponsorship of the Royal Philatelic Society, London, the British Post Office, the British Philatelic Federation, the Philatelic Traders' Society, the Stamp Collecting Promotion Council of Great Britain, the National Philatelic Society and the Great Britain Philatelic Society.

An Executive Committee – on which each of the above bodies is represented – has provided a chairman for each of the many other committees responsible for separate aspects of the work involved and also has day-to-day control of affairs.

In broad terms, the breakdown of the duties of the Executive Committee covers: philatelic matters, the appointment of jurors and overseas commissioners, the allocation of frame space according to the importance of the exhibits offered; trade affairs involving the allocation of trade stands and the two-day dealers' bourse to be held during the exhibition; social functions such as organised outings, receptions and the all-important Palmares Banquet to be held on Tuesday, May 13th when the awards are announced; and publicity which includes production of the advance brochures, press releases, the catalogue and souvenirs.

Very wisely, hotel accommodation and travel arrangements have been entrusted to D.F. Long & Co (Travel) Ltd, of Travel House, Mornington Crescent Station, London NE1 2JD, England, who have extensive experience of catering for philatelic travellers and to whom all enquiries for hotel bookings should be directed.

Many British and overseas specialist societies are arranging meetings within Earls Court and elsewhere in London during LONDON 1980 and they will welcome visitors for whose collecting interests they cater. Details of these will be published nearer the event and will appear, also, in the Exhibition Catalogue.

An important part of the organisation will be the voluntary assistance given by individual collectors. This includes help during the mounting and dismounting of the exhibition, stewarding and manning the souvenir sales stands. In the weeks before the opening date, additional secretarial help will be essential in the exhibition office. All offers of such help should be notified at once to the Secretary, LONDON 1980, PO Box 300, 265 Strand, London WC2R 1AF.

The LONDON 1980 Club
Within Earls Court, and adjacent to the exhibition but with its own entrances, will be situated the LONDON 1980 Club, which will offer special refreshment facilities and a chance to meet friends in a more restful atmosphere than the exhibition itself. Membership, (if still available) costing £25 for the period of the event, will include all literature issued, the Official Catalogue, a season ticket and a special memento.

Outstanding Exhibits
This article has had to be prepared in advance of any news concerning the competitive exhibits but the nature of several of the invited exhibits can be anticipated. The Court of Honour will be dominated by pages from the collection of the Exhibition's Patron, HM Queen Elizabth II, and there is no doubt that the Keeper of the collection, John Marriott MVO, will advise Her Majesty on a selection which will do justice to the occasion. This will be supported by displays from famous collectors no longer able to compete because they have already won the F.I.P. Grand Prix d'Honneur elsewhere. Our own National Postal Museum will prepare an outstanding exhibit for the Official Class and Britain's expanding stamp printing industry will have the opportunity to demonstrate the skill of the designers and engravers with whom they co-operate in the production of stamps for use world-wide.

Exactly 140 years to the day after Britain's famous Penny Black became valid for use (that was on 6th May 1840), the doors of Earls Court will open to a philatelic display of world-wide variety and first class quality.

To Rowland Hill, "father" of the Penny Black, this outcome of his postal innovation would be astonishing. For you, the reader, there will be a rare opportunity to savour and enjoy the fruits of philatelic study from all quarters of the globe. Make the most of it!

FAKES AND REPAIRS – BE ON YOUR GUARD!

As stamps become more and more valuable the number of repairs and faked stamps grows at a much greater pace. It was felt that a few timely reminders on how to sort the wheat from the chaff would be of advantage to collectors in this 1980 edition.

Q.V. Line Engraved Issues
Beware of re-backed imperforate stamps, especially the 1840 black and blue, and the 3 embossed issues. Tests to check whether the stamp has been re-backed are as follows:-

1. **Immerse stamp in Ronsonol** – This will show any thickening of the paper as a line and, as a re-backed stamp has in effect an extra thickness, it will show up as a clear line in the liquid.

2. **Ultra-violet light** – If a modern glue has been used this will give a slight fluorescence which of course, will end where the new paper meets the old.

3. **A good quality magnifying glass** – To see where the design has been painted in, especially in the margins and on the corners, as it is quite normal for re-backed copies to start life as slightly cut down 3 margin examples!

A further warning on the line engraved issues – Take extra care when purchasing copies on cover as this is a very neat way of getting rid of a stamp which has a 'thin' or a tear. Unused copies should also be treated with great care as frequently they are found to be chemically cleaned and re-gummed. In the late 19th Century many people used to thread stamps on cotton to make decorations, and holes were caused by the needle piercing the stamp.

Finally, beware of faked coloured postmarks (e.g. Maltese Cross), and also faked postmarks on cover, especially the rarer ones.

Q.V. Surface Printed Issues
The following are points to watch when purchasing Surface Printed.

1. **Cleaned off postmarks and re-gummed** – These can easily be spotted with an ultra violet lamp.

2. **High Values with fiscal cancellations cleaned off** – Use ultra violet lamp.

3. **Repairs to used stamps by utilising portions of other stamps** – usually found on small piece or part of an envelope.

4. **Re-gumming** – To check use all the following methods:-

(a) High powered glass to check between perfs for gum on face.

(b) Place stamp face down in palm of hand and the edges should curl up; if they stay flat or curl the other way it is 90% certain that the stamp has been re-gummed.

(c) Lightly draw fingers across edge of perfs; if perfs appear sharp to the touch, this is again an indication of re-gumming.

5. **Re-perfing** – Normally found on cut down wing margin copies, but also this is a method of making a slightly split stamp appear acceptable by re-perfing it and making it smaller to cover up any tears etc.

6. **Colours changed by water immersion** – Many surface printed stamps are printed in fugitive inks and any moisture will affect the colour. A classic example is the 1883 Lilac and Green set.

7. **Fiscal cancellations covered by faked postmarks**, again usually found on small piece or part cover.

8. **Facsimiles** of the High Values cut out and used with faked postmarks.

9. **Altered plate numbers** by scratching out and/or bleaching.

10. **Blued paper** artificially created by soaking stamp in a solution of ink.

George V, VI and Q.E.II

Most of the foregoing problems also exist with these reigns and the special points to watch are painted in or scratched out varieties, i.e. the "Pencf" flaw, "Q" for "O" and "no cross on crown" on George V issues.

First Day Covers from the 1924 Wembley Exhibition up to the 1966 World Cup Winners issue are known with forged postmarks. Rare shades are created by chemical means, the Silver Jubilee prussian blue is an example and should be purchased only with a certificate.

Toned paper varieties again chemically created.

Cleaned and re-gummed High Values.

Missing colour varieties artificially produced by chemical or other means, e.g. Christmas 1966 issues – Queen's head removed with surgical spirit. These can be easily detected under U.V. light.

Graphite line varieties created with indian ink, and phosphor bands with nail varnish. Both of the latter are easily checked by the fact that the genuine graphite lines never get on the face or between the perfs and phosphor should react under an ultra violet lamp.

The foregoing warnings cover the most obvious areas to be watched, and the collector should always take great care to examine valuable stamps before acquisition and always be on his guard.

Commencing with the Penny Black and Twopence Blue issued on 6th May 1840, four values ½d, 1d, 1½d and 2d spanned a period of usage of just over forty years. They have presented a most complex study for collectors of British stamps.

In the following pages the main varieties are listed according to shades, watermarks, plate numbers, dies, alphabets and papers. The different plates, except where they are shown in the stamp design, can only be identified by minute detail differences.

Inverted watermark varieties for almost all of these stamps are known, but these are not separately listed and priced in this section. They invariably command a considerable premium on the prices for stamps with the normal upright watermarks.

The prices stated relate to stamps that comply with the following conditions:-

Imperforate Issues

Mounted Mint (M/M)   Stamps should have at least four clear margins and at least 75% original gum and be reasonably lightly hinged.
Stamps without gum should be purchased with caution as many line engraved issues were chemically cleaned to remove postmarks and pen cancels.

Fine Used (F/U)   Four clear margins.
Postmarks should be clear and distinct.

Average Used (A/U)   Four margins, but cut close and/or heavier postmark.

Stamps with large margins and/or margins with inscriptions are worth a considerable premium.

Perforate Issues

Mounted Mint (M/M)   Stamps should have at least 75% original gum and be reasonably centred.
Fine Used (F/U)   Reasonably centred with light clear cancel.
Average Used (A/U)   Heavier postmark but no defects and full perforations.

THE TWO DIES

DIE I

DIE II

Distinctive Features of Die II as compared with Die I

1 The stones are diamond-shaped and not round.

2 The shading is darker.

3 The eyelid shading is heavier and the lower lid consists of lines and not dots.

4 The nose is more aquiline.

5 The shading of the cheek is heavier.

6 The eyeball shading is heavier.

7 The nostril is larger and arched.

8 The mouth expression is firmer and the upper lip longer.

9 The lower lip is more pendulous.

10 The outline of the chin is redrawn.

11 The top edge of the band is clearer.

12 The lower edge of the band is one strong line.

13 The lowest curl is clearly in front of the one above.

14 The ear modelling is lighter.

15 The lobe seems to run straight into the cheek and does not curve upwards.

Reproduction by kind permission of The Great Britain Philatelic Society

THE ALPHABETS

Every serious student of our British Line-engraved stamps must sooner or later become conversant with the different types of check letters, which, for the sake of convenience, have long been classified under Alphabets I, II, III and IV.

Of these I, II and III show letters punched on the plates, whilst, in the cases of Alphabet IV, used on Plates 50 and 51, the letters were hand-engraved. Alphabets I and III, show a very wide range of variations both in type and size, though some of the letters remain relatively constant. Alphabet II exhibits small minor varieties and a few marked ones. Alphabet IV, being hand-engraved on to the plates, naturally displays many variations, both in size and form of letterings and yet possesses singular "character" in the main.

No. I might well be sub-divided into "I" and "I^a", for the later letterings are markedly smaller and, on the whole, inferior to the earlier ones. No. III has been conventionally subdivided into what we may call III, III^a and III^b. In this alphabet we cannot correctly and logically justify these subdivisions since some letters fail to exhibit three important variations, whilst others show considerably more, but the adopted classification must stand and will perhaps serve.

It has been the custom to issue nicely drawn letters, giving types side by side of one letter from each of the four alphabets. This practice would serve as an admirable guide to the beginner on the assumption that the letters of the several alphabets were constant in character and size. Variations from the conventional, however, exhibit so many types and sizes that the young collector may be puzzled in making a correct attribution, and in this connection we may instance the M's, L's and P's of No. III as examples.

The general difficulty begins perhaps between the G's of No. I and No. II and here we may remark that the most advanced specialists may still be thankful for the presence on occasion of a second letter placing the issue beyond doubt and more of us may be glad of a square footed J of the No. I, or of those "stocky" A's, B's and R's, which are so easily attributed to No. II.

The young collector may often find classification more difficult, owing to the malformation or retouching of letters. The punch, when new and sharp, yielded a thin and clear impression. Worn and blunted punches gave less satisfactory results and "over" or "under-inking" did not improve matters. The careless application of the punches in a number of instances, and retouches, often suggest haphazard effort. The depth of punchings on the plate complicated matters, for the punch, being slightly wedge-shaped, made a wider letter when more forcibly struck, or as its apex grew less acute through wear.

But the collector will quickly narrow down the problem with which he is confronted once he realises that there are variations from hidebound types and sizes, and as he learns which alphabets were given to certain stamps and only to those stamps. It is perhaps fortunate that certain poor letters of Alphabets I and III are automatically segregated owing to the fact that No. I was given only to certain early issues, and is never common to standard emissions bearing No. III. On the other hand Alphabets I and II, and again II and III, were, on occasion, common to stamps otherwise identical in appearance.

The later printings on Small Crown paper Perf. 14 may be found with the No. III Alphabet, but these stamps are from Die II. This is the only "clash" between No. I and No. III Alphabets. The former are so scarce that few collectors can hope for a specimen, and the fact that the Dies are different makes the distinction clear.

In collecting the "twin" letters we can notice those small deviations which punching, inking or re-touches account for. So we learn to discount the minor divergences we shall often meet. Now and then we shall happen on one of those occasions in which the workman, either casually, or of set purpose, perhaps owing to breakage of, or dissatisfaction with a tool, used two A or J punches say, on the same stamp – it has been postulated in connection with this peculiarity that the puncher may have put in the horizontal or vertical lines for the letters separately, and possibly picked up a different punch after completing one or other of the rows, or on ceasing work for a meal, etc.

Yet another method has been adopted by some collectors, viz., the gathering of the first stamp of each of the twenty rows, i.e. AA, BA, CA and so on to TA. As this system involves the acquisition of twenty-one A's and but one apiece of the remaining nineteen letters, it is to be deprecated. The A's are easily learnt and it is better to couple "pronounced" and "unpronounced" letters – as the individual finds these latter personally baulking. If, for instance, the No. II E is difficult to detect, it would be better to couple it AE, BE, RE and QE than to rely on EA alone.

And now comes the question of Alphabet study in its most simplified form for the beginner.

No.II – the buffer Alphabet between I and III – yields the readiest key and 999 out of every 1,000 copies of the 1d. "Red-brown" S.C. 16 on blued paper exhibit the No. II Alphabet.

Always remember that the No. II Alphabet is the key one! Mastering this is all important and well repays such study as is essential in the gaining of a ready conversancy with it.

Only a few collectors will endeavour to "plate" Reserve Plate 17, and we need not dwell on this mere variety of the No. III. But in the case of Reserve Plates 15 and 16 we have our old friend the No. II cropping up to emphasize its importance once more. Reserve Plate 15 has the letters placed low, whilst Reserve Plate 16 shows them punched in on the high side in the vast majority of instances and, by this peculiarity of placing, we can – generally speaking – separate the two Plates. Evidently the distinguishing feature was given of set purpose. A few specimens only form subject for debate owing to the appearance of a high and low letter on the same stamp.

The hand-engraved Plates 50 and 51 were experimental and form a fascinating study – the illustrations given will enable the collector to gain acquaintance with their type and every collector who masters this Alphabet will be well repaid for the trouble involved in study.

The study of No.IV presents difficulties – primarily owing to the scarcity of these stamps, and also owing to the varying sizes of the letters, together with some modification in their outlines. With experience diagnosis comes automatically for there is something in the drawing, something in the hand engraver's technique, or a trick in the fashioning of a serif, which over-rides all else.

So far we have rather stressed the importance of being able to determine between varieties bearing letterings of the different Alphabets, but there is a fund of interest in collecting the wide range of letter types, self-contained in single Alphabets, and subsequent illustrations will show the collector what a prolific field for study these afford.

Fortunately Alphabet III, the most easily found, is rich in varying forms of type and it would seem incredible that such departures from a standard as may be found in, shall we say the E's, F's, K's, L's, M's, and P's, should not have had specific catalogue mention on their own merits.

The variations in size and type of the L's, M's and P's, for instance, in our No. III are so wide that the stamps exhibiting the extremes stand out as marked varieties, and of infinitely more importance as such, than is the case with hundreds of other well-written-up and relatively minor varieties.

Bearing in mind the limited range of values in our line-engraved stamps it would almost seem that, as an act of compensation to philatelists, a kindly Providence stepped in to render all and sundry of these glorious stamps so rich as they are in collectable varieties.

Collectors should pay especial attention to all ot the "1857" type 1d. rose to rose carmine LC.14 specimens which are dated or on dated pieces from late 1861 to 1865. The majority of the rarities comprising stamps from the Reserve Plates and from 50 and 51 with hand-engraved letterings, when "dating" is practicable, show them to have been used between 1862 and 1865.

The above are extracts from the publication "The Alphabets of the British Line Engraved Stamps" 1937 second edition (out of print) re-produced by kind permission of R.C. Alcock Limited Cheltenham.

LINE ENGRAVED ISSUES 1840 – 1862

Alphabet I

Alphabet II

LINE ENGRAVED ISSUES 1840 – 1862

Alphabet III

Alphabet IV

LINE ENGRAVED ISSUES 1840 – 1862

Alphabet I

Alphabet II

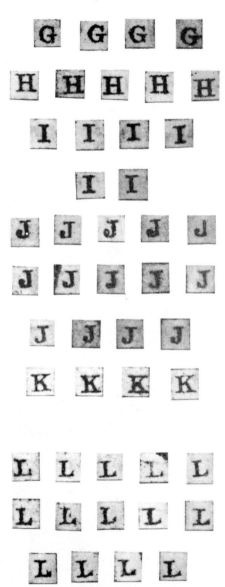

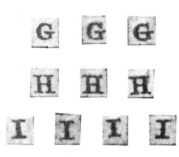

LINE ENGRAVED ISSUES 1840 – 1862

Alphabet III

Alphabet IV

LINE ENGRAVED ISSUES 1840 – 1862

Alphabet I	Alphabet II

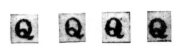

INVERTED

LINE ENGRAVED ISSUES 1840 – 1862

Alphabet III

Alphabet IV

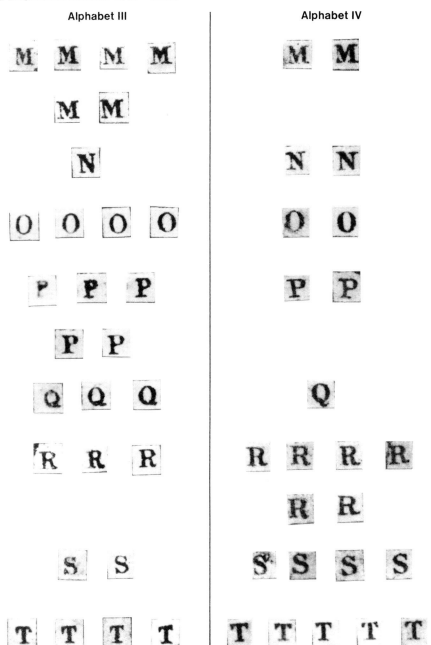

These Alphabets are reproduced by kind permission of R.C. Alcock Limited, Cheltenham.

LINE ENGRAVED IMPERFORATE ISSUES 1840 – 54
Letters in lower corners only – Plate numbers not in design

Printers: Perkins, Bacon & Co.　　*Watermark:* Small Crown　　*Die I*　　*Alphabet I* except where shown

No.	Issued	Type		Colour	Paper	Plate	M/M	F/U	A/U
V1	6/5/40	1	1d	**Greyish black**	White	1a	£1700	£325	£165
V2				Grey black	"	1a	£1800	£350	£180
V3				Intense black	"	1a	£1800	£350	£180
V4			1d	**Black**	"	1b	£1200	£200	£110
V5				Intense black	"	1b	£1300	£220	£125
V6			1d	**Black**	"	2	£1200	£200	£110
V7				Intense black	"	2	£1300	£220	£125
V8				Grey black	"	2	£1375	£240	£135
V9			1d	**Black**	"	3	£1375	£240	£135
V10				Grey black	"	3	£1375	£240	£135
V11			1d	**Black**	"	4	£1300	£220	£125
V12				Intense black	"	4	£1375	£240	£135
V13			1d	**Black**	"	5	£1200	£200	£110
V14				Intense black	"	5	£1300	£220	£125
V15			1d	**Black**	"	6	£1200	£220	£125
V16				Intense black	"	6	£1300	£220	£125
V17			1d	**Black**	"	7	£1300	£220	£125
V18				Greyish black	"	7	£1400	£250	£150
V19			1d	**Black**	"	8	£1600	£300	£170
V20			1d	**Black**	"	9	£1750	£350	£180
V21			1d	**Black**	"	10	£1800	£375	£190
V22				Grey black	"	10	£2000	£425	£225
V23			1d	**Black**	"	11	£2200	£1350	£650
V24				Grey black	"	11	£1800	£1250	£575
V25	10/2/41	1	1d	**Red brown** (shades)	Bluish	1b	£1600	£125	£65
V26			1d	**Red brown** (shades)	"	2	£1100	£65	£30
V27			1d	**Red brown** (shades)	"	5	£525	£45	£25
V28			1d	**Red brown** (shades)	"	8	£475	£40	£22
V29			1d	**Red brown** (shades)	"	9	£475	£40	£22
V30			1d	**Red brown** (shades)	"	10	£550	£50	£28
V31			1d	**Red brown** (shades)	"	11	£475	£40	£22
V32	10/2/41	1	1d	**Red brown**	"	12 –131	£90	4.00	75
V33				Deep red brown	"	12 – 131	£120	5.00	2.50
V34				Pale red brown	"	12 – 131	£150	6.00	2.50
V35				Lake red	"	12 – 131	£475	£75	£20
V36				Orange brown	"	12 – 131	£240	£40	£15
V37	6/2/52	1	1d	**Red brown** (Alph.II)	Bluish	132 – 175	£90	3.00	1.25
V37A				Red brown (Alph.II)	Lavender tinted	132 – 136	£625	£40	£18
V38				Lake red (Alph.II)	Bluish	132 – 175	£550	£55	£22
V39				Orange brown (Alph.II)	"	132 – 175	£250	£55	£25
V40	6/5/40	2	2d	**Blue**	White	1	£4000	£350	£150
V41				Deep blue	"	1	£4750	£400	£175
V42				Steel blue	"	1	£4750	£400	£175
V43				Pale blue	"	1	£5000	£425	£180
V44				Milky blue	"	1	£5000	£425	£180
V45				Violet blue	"	1	£6000	£500	£225
V46			2d	**Blue**	"	2	£4200	£385	£165
V47				Deep blue	"	2	£4750	£400	£175
V48				Pale blue	"	2	£5000	£425	£180
V49	13/3/41	3	2d	**Blue**	Bluish	3	£750	£30	£14
V50				Deep blue	"	3	£800	£32	£15
V51				Pale blue	"	3	£800	£32	£15
V52			2d	**Blue**	"	4	£750	£30	£14
V53				Deep blue	"	4	£800	£32	£15
V54				Pale blue	"	4	£800	£32	£15
V55				Violet blue	Lavender tinted	4	£4250	£400	£200

Type 1

Type 2

Type 3

Wmk. Small Crown (S C)

Wmk. Large Crown (L C)

LINE ENGRAVED PERFORATED ISSUES 1850 – 64
Letters in lower corners only – Plate numbers not in design

Printers: Perkins, Bacon & Co.

No.	Issued	Type		Colour	Paper	Wmk.	Perf.	Die	Alph.	Plate Nos.	M/M	F/U	A/U
V56	1850	1	**1d**	**Red brown**	Bluish	SC	16	I	I	Various	£375	£75	£40
				(*Archer experimental perfs.*)									
V57	–/2/54	1	**1d**	**Red brown**	Bluish	SC	16	I	II	155, 157; 160 – 204; R1 – R6	£70	1.50	75
V58				Yellow brown	,,	SC	16	I	II	,,	£90	3.50	1.75
V59				Brick red	,,	SC	16	I	II	,,	£90	3.50	1.75
V60				Orange red	,,	SC	16	I	II	,,	£250	£18	8.50
V61				Plum	,,	SC	16	I	II	,,	£225	£16	8.00
V62	–/1/55	1	**1d**	**Red brown**	Bluish	SC	14	I	II	192 – 204; R1 – R6	£150	7.50	3.50
V63				Yellow brown	,,	SC	14	I	II	,,	£150	7.50	3.50
V64				Brick red	,,	SC	14	I	II	,,	£250	£35	£15
V65				Orange red	,,	SC	14	I	II	,,	£300	£40	£18
V66				Plum	,,	SC	14	I	II	,,	£250	£35	£15
V67	28/2/55	1	**1d**	**Red brown**	Bluish	SC	14	II	II	1 –21	£150	7.50	3.50
V68				Deep red brown	,,	SC	14	II	II	,,	£160	9.50	4.50
V69				Orange brown	,,	SC	14	II	II	,,	£240	£45	£20
V70				Plum	,,	SC	14	II	II	,,	£250	£50	£22
V71	1/3/55	1	**1d**	**Red brown**	Bluish	SC	16	II	II	1 – 15	£140	7.00	3.25
V72				Yellow brown	,,	SC	16	II	II	,,	£150	8.00	3.75
V73				Brick red	,,	SC	16	II	II	,,	£150	8.00	3.75
V74				Plum	,,	SC	16	II	II	,,	£250	£30	£15
V75	15/5/55	1	**1d**	**Red brown**	Bluish	LC	16	II	II	1 – 16	£240	£15	7.00
V76				Deep red brown	,,	LC	16	II	II	,,	£295	£25	£11
V77	–/6/55	1	**1d**	**Red brown**	,,	LC	14	II	II	1 – 21	£140	7.00	3.00
V78				Yellow brown	,,	LC	14	II	II	,,	£185	£10	4.50
V79				Plum	,,	LC	14	II	II	,,	£240	£20	9.50
V80	18/8/55	1	**1d**	**Red brown**	Bluish	SC	14	II	III	22 – 27	£900	£175	£80
V81	–/8/55	1	**1d**	**Red brown**	Bluish	LC	14	II	III	22 - 38, 40, 42 – 49	£50	1.25	40
V82				Orange brown	,,	LC	14	II	III	,,	£160	£10	4.75
V83				Brick red	,,	LC	14	II	III	,,	£70	6.00	2.75
V84				Orange red	,,	LC	14	II	III	,,	£200	£14	6.75
V85				Plum	,,	LC	14	II	III	,,	£145	£12	5.50
V86				Brown rose	,,	LC	14	II	III	,,	£70	6.00	2.75
V87				Deep claret	Deep blue	LC	14	II	III	,,	£225	£25	£12
V88	1857	1	**1d**	**Red orange**	Cream toned	LC	14	II	III	Various 27 – 55	£140	£18	8.50
V89				Orange brown	,,	LC	14	II	III	,,	£170	£25	£12
V90				Pale red	,,	LC	14	II	III	,,	£190	£25	£12
V91				Pale rose	,,	LC	14	II	III	,,	£170	£25	£12
V92	1857	1	**1d**	**Rose red**	White	LC	14	II	III	Various 27 – 68; R17	£16	20	10
V93	1857			Deep rose red	,,	LC	14	II	III	,,	£16	20	10
V94	1857			Pale red	,,	LC	14	II	III	,,	£60	1.00	45
V95	1857			Pale rose	,,	LC	14	II	III	,,	£65	1.25	60
V96	1857			Bright rose red	,,	LC	14	II	III	,,	£80	5.00	2.25
V97	1863			Pale rose pink	,,	LC	14	II	III	,,	£65	95	40
V98	1856			Red brown	,,	LC	14	II	III	,,	£85	7.00	3.25
V99	29/12/57	1	**1d**	**Rose red**	White	LC	16	II	III	Various 27 – 60	£225	8.00	3.50
V100	1861	1	**1d**	**Rose red**	White	LC	14	II	IV	50 – 51	£80	3.50	1.75
V101				Pale rose red	,,	LC	14	II	IV	,,	£80	3.50	1.75
V102	1862	1	**1d**	**Rose red**	White	LC	14	II	II	R15 – R16	£80	3.50	1.75
V103				Pale rose red	,,	LC	14	II	II	,,	£80	3.50	1.75
V104				Pale red	,,	LC	14	II	II	R15	£200	£50	£20
V105	13/3/54	3	**2d**	**Deep blue**	Bluish	SC	16	I	I	4	£750	£20	£10
V106				Pale blue	,,	SC	16	I	I	4	£850	£25	£12
V107	4/3/55	3	**2d**	**Blue**	,,	SC	14	I	I	4	£1250	£60	£27
V108	5/7/55	3	**2d**	**Blue**	,,	SC	14	I	II	5	£1400	£45	£20
V109	20/7/55	3	**2d**	**Blue**	,,	LC	16	I	II	5	£2000	£100	£45
V110	20/7/55	3	**2d**	**Blue**	,,	LC	14	I	II	5	£750	£15	7.00
V111	28/8/55	3	**2d**	**Blue**	,,	SC	16	I	II	5	£1000	£110	£50
V112	2/7/57	3	**2d**	**Blue**	,,	LC	14	I	III	6	£750	£15	7.00
V113	1/12/58	3	**2d**	**Blue**	White	LC	16	I	III	6	£1850	£80	£38

LINE ENGRAVED PERFORATED ISSUES 1858 – 80
Letters in all four corners and plate numbers in the design

Printers: Perkins, Bacon & Co.   *Perf.:* 14   *Paper:* White   *Watermark:* Large Crown (except ½d value)

No.	Issued	Type	Colour	Plate No.	M/M	F/U	A/U
WITH THICK WHITE LINES							
V114	–/7/58	4	**2d Blue** (shades)	7	£300	£15	7.50
V115			**2d Blue** (shades)	8	£300	£15	7.50
V116			**2d Blue** (shades)	9	£90	3.00	1.50
V117			**2d Blue** (shades)	12	£350	£20	£10
WITH THIN WHITE LINES							
V118	–/7/69	4	**2d Blue** (shades)	13	£90	4.00	2.00
V119			**2d Blue** (shades)	14	£125	5.00	2.50
V120			**2d Blue** (shades)	15	£125	5.00	2.50

Type 4   *Type 5*

Showing position of plate no. ▷

Issued 1/4/64   Type 5   1d   Rose red (shades)

Large Crown (LC)

No.	Plate No.	M/M	F/U	A/U	No.	Plate No.	M/M	F/U	A/U	No.	Plate No.	M/M	F/U	A/U
V121	71	£20	50	30	V157	108	£25	90	50	V193	146	9.00	50	30
V122	72	£15	50	30	V158	109	£75	90	50	V194	147	9.50	50	30
V123	73	£16	50	30	V159	110	£14	50	30	V195	148	9.00	50	30
V124	74	£16	75	40	V160	111	£12	50	30	V196	149	£14	50	30
V125	76	£22	50	30	V161	112	£22	1.00	60	V197	150	9.00	50	30
V126	77	★	★	★	V162	113	£12	50	30	V198	151	£14	50	30
V127	78	£10	50	30	V163	114	£80	50	30	V199	152	£10	50	30
V128	79	£11	50	30	V164	115	£80	1.00	60	V200	153	£50	3.75	1.75
V129	80	£15	50	30	V165	116	£30	50	30	V201	154	£11	50	30
V130	81	£25	50	30	V166	117	£14	50	30	V202	155	£11	95	45
V131	82	£110	2.50	1.00	V167	118	9.00	50	30	V203	156	£12	50	30
V132	83	£140	6.00	3.00	V168	119	9.00	50	30	V204	157	£12	50	30
V133	84	£10	50	30	V169	120	9.00	50	30	V205	158	9.00	50	30
V134	85	£15	50	30	V170	121	9.00	50	30	V206	159	9.00	50	30
V135	86	£28	50	30	V171	122	9.00	50	30	V207	160	9.00	50	30
V136	87	£10	50	30	V172	123	9.00	1.00	60	V208	161	£30	1.75	90
V137	88	£125	7.50	3.75	V173	124	9.00	50	30	V209	162	£12	50	30
V138	89	£12	50	30	V174	125	£10	50	30	V210	163	£12	50	30
V139	90	£25	50	30	V175	127	£10	50	30	V211	164	£11	50	30
V140	91	9.00	50	30	V176	129	£10	50	30	V212	165	£10	50	30
V141	92	£14	50	30	V177	130	£10	50	30	V213	166	£12	50	30
V142	93	£14	90	45	V178	131	£12	50	30	V214	167	9.00	50	30
V143	94	£14	50	30	V179	132	£100	7.50	3.75	V215	168	9.00	50	30
V144	95	£12	50	30	V180	133	£90	6.00	3.00	V216	169	£12	1.50	80
V145	96	£25	80	45	V181	134	£10	70	40	V217	170	£12	50	30
V146	97	£12	50	30	V182	135	9.00	50	30	V218	171	9.00	50	30
V147	98	£12	50	30	V183	136	9.00	50	30	V219	172	9.50	50	30
V148	99	£14	50	30	V184	137	£12	50	30	V220	173	9.00	50	30
V149	100	£12	50	30	V185	138	9.00	50	30	V221	174	9.00	50	30
V150	101	£25	50	30	V186	139	£11	50	30	V222	175	9.00	50	30
V151	102	£14	50	30	V187	140	9.00	50	30	V223	176	£14	50	30
V152	103	£14	50	30	V188	141	£30	1.50	75	V224	177	9.00	50	30
V153	104	£25	2.00	1.00	V189	142	£12	50	30	V225	178	£12	1.25	65
V154	105	£50	4.25	2.00	V190	143	£18	50	30	V226	179	£12	1.25	65
V155	106	£12	80	45	V191	144	£25	50	30	V227	180	£15	1.25	65
V156	107	£25	50	30	V192	145	9.00	50	30	V228	181	£12	50	30

LINE ENGRAVED PERFORATED ISSUES 1858 – 80 (continued)

No.	Plate No.	M/M	F/U	A/U	No.	Plate No.	M/M	F/U	A/U	No.	Plate No.	M/M	F/U	A/U
V229	182	£12	2.00	95	V246	199	9.00	50	30	V263	216	9.00	95	45
V230	183	9.00	50	30	V247	200	9.50	50	30	V264	217	£12	3.00	1.50
V231	184	9.50	50	30	V248	201	9.00	50	30	V265	218	£10	2.75	1.40
V232	185	£12	1.25	65	V249	202	9.50	50	30	V266	219	£25	£20	9.00
V233	186	£12	1.25	65	V250	203	£10	50	30	V267	220	9.00	2.50	1.25
V234	187	£11	80	40	V251	204	£11	50	30	V268	221	£25	6.50	3.00
V235	188	£12	80	40	V252	205	£11	50	30	V269	222	£20	6.00	3.00
V236	189	£14	1.25	65	V253	206	£11	50	30	V270	223	£35	£12	5.00
V237	190	9.00	50	30	V254	207	9.00	50	30	V271	224	£55	£25	£10
V238	191	9.00	50	30	V255	208	9.50	50	30	V272	225	£1250	£300	£100
V239	192	9.00	50	30	V256	209	£12	50	30					
V240	193	9.00	50	30	V257	210	£14	75	40					
V241	194	£12	50	30	V258	211	£40	3.75	1.75					
V242	195	£12	50	30	V259	212	£12	75	40					
V243	196	9.00	50	30	V260	213	9.00	1.00	50					
V244	197	£12	50	30	V261	214	£12	90	45					
V245	198	9.00	50	30	V262	215	£12	90	45					

★ As stamps from **Plate No.77** are so extremely rare, it is not practical to price these.

Beware of stamps from **Plate No.177** with the figure '1' obscured or obliterated.

Large Crown (LC)

Type 6

Showing position ◁ of plate no.

No.	Issued	Type	Colour	Plate No.	M/M	F/U	A/U
V273	1/10/70	6	1½d **Rose red** (shades) Plate no. not in design	1	£250	£20	9.00
V274			1½d Rose red (printing error OP-PC)	1	£2000	£450	£200
V275	10/8/74		1½d **Rose red** (shades) Plate no. in design	3	£90	8.00	3.50

WATERMARK: *half penny*

V276	1/10/70	7	½d **Rose red** (shades)	1	£65	£15	6.50
V277			½d **Rose red** ,,	3	£40	3.50	1.50
V278			½d **Rose red** ,,	4	£30	3.00	1.35
V279			½d **Rose red** ,,	5	£30	3.00	1.35
V280			½d **Rose red** ,,	6	£30	3.00	1.35
V281			½d **Rose red** ,,	8	£60	£15	6.00
V282			½d **Rose red** ,,	9	£1000	£150	£90
V283			½d **Rose red** ,,	10	£30	3.00	1.35
V284			½d **Rose red** ,,	11	£30	3.00	1.35
V285			½d **Rose red** ,,	12	£30	3.00	1.35
V286			½d **Rosé red** ,,	13	£30	3.00	1.35
V287			½d **Rose red** ,,	14	£30	3.00	1.35
V288			½d **Rose red** ,,	15	£30	3.00	1.35
V289			½d **Rose red** ,,	19	£60	8.00	3.75
V290			½d **Rose red** ,,	20	£45	9.00	4.00

half penny

Watermark

Beware of stamps from **Plate No. 19** with the figure '1' obscured. In genuine Plate No. 9 the position of the figure '9' will be different.

Type 7

EMBOSSED ISSUES

The Embossed Issues, introduced in 1847 were unique in British stamp production. Produced at Somerset House on manual presses, each stamp was separately embossed, and consequently the spacing of the impressions was extremely variable from wide margins to overlapping in many instances. It is consequently difficult to find examples with four good margins. The quality of embossing varied from clear sharp impressions to blunted and blurred examples.

Later examples of the 6d value had green tinted gum.

The die numbers were sometimes inserted in the form of metal plugs in the base of the bust followed by the letters 'W.W.', (the initials of the master engraver, William Wyon). These die numbers on the stamps can be read under magnification, but are often missing.

Collectors are warned against cut-outs from Postal Stationery using the same design and "four margin" examples which have been re-backed. The silk threads go right through the paper, and as a consequence it is usually reasonably easy to spot re-backed 10d and 1/–d values. The 6d value is watermarked, whereas the Postal Stationery 6d is without watermark.

EMBOSSED ISSUES 1847 – 62

Printers: Somerset House *Imperforate* *Watermark: None except 6d value*
All embossed on Dickinson silk thread paper

No.	Issued	Type	Colour		Die	M/M	F/U	A/U
V291	11/9/47	8	**1/–d** **Green**		1 – 2	£2000	£175	£75
V292			Deep green		1 – 2	£2500	£275	£125
V293			Pale green		1 – 2	£2100	£190	£85
V294	6/11/48	9	**10d** **Brown**		1 – 4	£1500	£250	£120
V295			Deep brown		1 – 4	£1950	£290	£130
V296	1/3/54	10	**6d** **Mauve**	(Wmk. VR)	1	£1800	£175	£75
V297			Lilac	(Wmk. VR)	1	£1800	£175	£75
V298			Purple	(Wmk. VR)	1	£1800	£175	£75
V299			Violet	(Wmk. VR)	1	£2100	£300	£140

Watermark

Type 8

Type 9

Type 10

SURFACE PRINTED ISSUES 1855 – 1900

The Surface Printed issues form a very interesting section of British stamp production, with a wide variety of shades, watermarks and plate numbers. All these differences can be readily distinguished in contrast to the difficulties of the Line Engraved issues.

In order to clarify the listing of stamps for this period they are divided into logical groups as follows:

1. Early issues without corner letters.
2. With small white corner letters.
3. With large white corner letters.
4. With large coloured corner letters.
5. New design – low values.
6. Lilac and Green issues.
7. Jubilee issues.

With all the varieties for each value listed in sequence within each group.

The pricing basis for Surface Printed issues is as follows:–

Unmounted Mint (U/M) Full original gum, well centred, full perforations and good colour (Jubilee issue only).

Mounted Mint (M/M) At least 75% original gum, full perforations and clean unfaded shades.

Fine used (F/U) Reasonably centred, full perforations and light clear cancel.

Average used (A/U) Less well centred, one or two blunt perforations acceptable, and heavier postmark.

INVERTED WATERMARK VARIETIES

for almost all these stamps are known, but these are not separately listed and priced in this section, apart from 1880, 1883 and the Jubilee issues.

They invariably command a considerable premium on the prices for stamps with the normal upright watermarks, and especially for mint examples, which are generally very rare.

Small Garter (SG)

Medium Garter (MG)

Large Garter (LG)

Emblems (EMB)

Spray (SPR)

Small Anchor (A)

Orb

Imperial Crown (IC)

SURFACE PRINTED ISSUES 1855 – 62
No letters in corners

Printers: De La Rue & Co.   *Paper:* White except where stated   *Perf.:* 14   *Watermark:* As indicated.

No.	Issued	Type	Colour	Wmk.	M/M	F/U	A/U
V300	31/7/55	11	**4d** **Carmine** (shades) (paper glazed & blued)	SG	£1750	£100	£40
V301			**4d** **Carmine** (shades)	SG	£2500	£300	£175
V302	25/2/56		**4d** **Carmine** (shades) (paper glazed & blued)	MG	£2000	£100	£40
V303	–/9/56		**4d** **Pale carmine**	MG	£1350	£90	£30
V304	1/11/56		**4d** **Rose**	MG	£1600	£100	£40
V305			Deep rose	MG	£1700	£125	£55
V306	–/1/57		**4d** **Rose**	LG	£400	£12	6.00
V307			Rose carmine	LG	£450	£14	6.50
V308			**4d** **Rose carmine** (thick glazed paper)	LG	£1400	£60	£27
V309	21/10/56	12	**6d** **Lilac**	EMB	£350	£25	£12
V310			Pale lilac	EMB	£350	£25	£12
V311			Deep lilac	EMB	£400	£30	£14
V312	1/11/56	13	**1/–d** **Pale green**	EMB	£425	£35	£15
V313			Green	EMB	£440	£40	£18
V314			Deep green	EMB	£1250	£100	£45

Type 11

Type 12

Warning re wing margins
Collectors should be aware that the above issues are known
with re-perforated side after removal of wing margin

Type 13

SURFACE PRINTED ISSUES 1862 – 64
Small white letters in each corner – Bracketed plate numbers not in design

Printers: De La Rue & Co.   *Paper:* White   *Perf.:* 14   *Watermark:* As indicated.

No.	Issued	Type	Colour	Plate No.	Wmk.	M/M	F/U	A/U
V315	2/5/62	14	**3d** **Carmine rose**	(2)	EMB	£400	£50	£20
V316			Pale carmine rose	(2)	EMB	£400	£50	£20
V317			Deep carmine rose	(2)	EMB	£850	£100	£45
V318	15/1/62	15	**4d** **Pale red** (without hairlines)	(3)	LG	£300	£15	7.00
V319			Bright red „	(3)	LG	£425	£18	8.00
V320	16/10/63		**4d** **Pale red** (with hairlines)	(4)	LG	£300	£15	7.00
V321			Bright red „	(4)	LG	£375	£18	8.00
V322	1/12/62	17	**6d** **Lilac** (without hairlines)	(3)	EMB	£375	£15	7.00
V323			Deep lilac „	(3)	EMB	£400	£20	9.00
V324	20/4/64		**6d** **Lilac** (with hairlines)	(4)	EMB	£500	£30	£14
V325	15/1/62	19	**9d** **Bistre**	(2)	EMB	£675	£65	£30
V326			Straw	(2)	EMB	£675	£65	£30
V327	1/12/62	20	**1/–d** **Green**	(1)	EMB	£400	£30	£14
V328			Deep green	(1)	EMB	£425	£35	£16

Type 14

Type 15

Type 17

Type 19

Type 20

Hairlines across corners

SURFACE PRINTED ISSUES 1865 – 80
Large white letters in each corner

Printers: De La Rue & Co,   *Paper:* White   *Perf.:* 14   *Watermark:* As indicated.

No.	Issued	Type	Colour	Plate No.	Wmk.	M/M	F/U	A/U
V329	1/3/65	21	**3d** Rose	4	EMB	£325	£20	6.00
V330	–/7/67		**3d** Rose (shades)	4	SPR	£300	£25	£10
V331			**3d** Rose ,,	5	SPR	£175	£10	4.50
V332			**3d** Rose ,,	6	SPR	£185	£11	4.75
V333			**3d** Rose ,,	7	SPR	£225	£15	5.00
V334			**3d** Rose ,,	8	SPR	£225	£15	5.00
V335			**3d** Rose ,,	9	SPR	£225	£15	5.00
V336			**3d** Rose ,,	10	SPR	£275	£25	£10
V337	4/7/65	22	**4d** Vermilion (shades)	7	LG	£275	£20	8.00
V338			**4d** Vermilion ,,	8	LG	£185	£20	8.00
V339			**4d** Vermilion ,,	9	LG	£185	£15	6.00
V340			**4d** Vermilion ,,	10	LG (Inv.)	£275	£20	8.00
V341			**4d** Vermilion ,,	11	LG (Inv.)	£185	£15	6.00
V342			**4d** Vermilion ,,	12	LG	£165	£12	5.00
V343			**4d** Vermilion ,,	13	LG	£175	£15	6.00
V344			**4d** Vermilion ,,	14	LG	£300	£25	9.00
V345	1/4/65	23	**6d** Lilac (with hyphen)	5	EMB	£300	£20	8.00
V346			Deep lilac ,,	5	EMB	£350	£25	9.00
V347	22/11/66		**6d** Lilac ,,	6	EMB	£700	£45	£15
V348			Deep lilac ,,	6	EMB	£825	£60	£20
V349	21/6/67		**6d** Lilac ,,	6	SPR	£350	£15	6.00
V350			Deep lilac ,,	6	SPR	£400	£18	7.00
V351			Violet ,,	6	SPR	£400	£18	7.00
V352			Purple ,,	6	SPR	£425	£25	9.00
V353	13/3/69	24	**6d** Violet (without hyphen)	8	SPR	£235	£15	6.00
V354			Mauve ,,	8	SPR	£235	£15	6.00
V355			**6d** Mauve ,,	9	SPR	£235	£15	6.00
V356	12/4/72	25	**6d** Chestnut	11	SPR	£225	£12	4.50
V357			Deep chestnut	11	SPR	£295	£25	9.00
V358			Pale buff	11	SPR	£260	£20	8.00
V359	30/10/72		**6d** Pale buff	12	SPR	£500	£55	£18
V360	24/4/73		**6d** Grey	12	SPR	£375	£25	9.00
V361	1/12/65	26	**9d** Straw	4	EMB	£600	£120	£65
V362	3/10/67		**9d** Straw	4	SPR	£470	£40	£15
V363			Pale straw	4	SPR	£470	£40	£15
V364			Deep straw	4	SPR	£510	£45	£18
V365	1/7/67	27	**10d** Red brown	1	SPR	£700	£60	£25
V366			Pale red brown	1	SPR	£700	£60	£25
V367			Deep red brown	1	SPR	£825	£115	£45
V368	–/2/65	28	**1/–d** Green	4	EMB	£450	£20	6.00
V369	13/7/67		**1/–d** Pale green	4	SPR	£250	4.50	2.00
V370			Deep green	4	SPR	£300	5.00	2.25
V371			**1/–d** Pale green	5	SPR	£250	5.00	2.25
V372			**1/–d** Pale green	6	SPR	£375	7.00	3.00
V373			**1/–d** Pale green	7	SPR	£375	7.00	3.00
V374	1/7/67	29	**2/–d** Deep blue	1	SPR	£1250	£45	£20
V375			Dull blue	1	SPR	£1250	£45	£20
V376			Pale blue	1	SPR	£1250	£45	£20
V377			Milky blue	1	SPR	£2250	£175	£90
V378			Cobalt	1	SPR	£3600	£700	£300
V379	27/2/80		**2/–d** Brown	1	SPR	£4250	£900	£400

Type 21   *Type 22*

Type 23   *Type 24*

Type 25   *Type 26*

Type 27   *Type 28*

Type 29

Warning re wing margins
The 3d, 6d, 9d, 10d & 1/–d values with letters D, E, H or I in south east corner are known with re-perforated side. The 4d and 8d values with letters F or G in the same corner are also known in this condition.

SURFACE PRINTED ISSUES 1867 – 83
Large white letters in each corner
HIGH VALUES

Printers: De La Rue & Co.   *Watermarks:* Maltese Cross or Large Anchor as shown

No.	Issued	Type		Colour	Paper	Perf.	Plate No.	Watermark	M/M	F/U	A/U
V380	1/7/67	30	5/–d	Rose	White	15½ x 15	1	Maltese Cross	£2750	£230	£85
V381				Pale rose	,,	15½ x 15	1	Maltese Cross	£2750	£230	£85
V382			5/–d	Rose	,,	15½ x 15	2	Maltese Cross	£3500	£300	£125
V383	25/11/82		5/–d	Rose	,,	14	4	Large Anchor	£5750	£800	£300
V384			5/–d	Rose	Blued	14	4	Large Anchor	£6200	£875	£325
V385	26/9/68	31	10/–d	Grey green	White	15½ x 15	1	Maltese Cross	£14000	£1450	£500
V386	–/2/83		10/–d	Grey green	,,	14	1	Large Anchor	£13750	£1750	£650
V387			10/–d	Grey green	Blued	14	1	Large Anchor	£13750	£1750	£650
V388	26/9/68	32	£1	Brown lilac	White	15½ x 15	1	Maltese Cross	£15000	£1800	£750
V389	–/12/82		£1	Brown lilac	,,	14	1	Large Anchor	£18500	£2450	£975
V390			£1	Brown lilac	Blued	14	1	Large Anchor	£18500	£2600	£1100
V391	21/3/82	33	£5	Orange	White	14	1	Large Anchor	£5250	£2750	£975
V392			£5	Orange	Blued	14	1	Large Anchor	£12000	£3250	£1200

Type 30

Type 31

Type 32

Maltese Cross (MC)

Type 33

Large Anchor (LA)

SURFACE PRINTED ISSUES 1875 – 83
Large coloured letters in each corner

Printers: De La Rue & Co.   *Paper:* White except where stated   *Perf.:* 14   *Watermark:* Various as shown.

No.	Issued	Type	Colour	Plate No.	Wmk.	M/M	F/U	A/U
V393	1/7/75	34	**2½d Rose mauve**	1	A	£175	£12	3.00
V394			**2½d Rose mauve** (blued paper)	1	A	£250	£30	8.50
V395			**2½d Rose mauve**	2	A	£190	£12	3.00
V396			2½d Rose mauve (error LH-FL)	2	A	£6500	£450	£200
V397			**2½d Rose mauve** (blued paper)	2	A	£2000	£250	£100
V398			**2½d Rose mauve**	3	A	£250	£30	8.50
V399	16/5/76		**2½d Rose mauve**	3	ORB	£300	£30	£10
V400			**2½d** ,,	4	ORB	£175	9.00	3.00
V401			**2½d** ,,	5	ORB	£175	£12	4.00
V402			**2½d** ,,	6	ORB	£175	9.00	3.00
V403			**2½d** ,,	7	ORB	£175	9.00	3.00
V404			**2½d** ,,	8	ORB	£175	£10	3.50
V405			**2½d** ,,	9	ORB	£175	9.00	3.00
V406			**2½d** ,,	10	ORB	£200	£12	4.00
V407			**2½d** ,,	11	ORB	£175	9.00	3.00
V408			**2½d** ,,	12	ORB	£175	9.00	3.00
V409			**2½d** ,,	13	ORB	£175	9.00	3.00
V410			**2½d** ,,	14	ORB	£175	9.00	3.00
V411			**2½d** ,,	15	ORB	£175	9.00	3.00
V412			**2½d** ,,	16	ORB	£175	9.00	3.00
V413			**2½d** ,,	17	ORB	£400	£60	£20
V414	5/2/80		**2½d Blue**	17	ORB	£125	8.00	2.00
V415			**2½d Blue**	18	ORB	£175	£10	3.50
V416			**2½d Blue**	19	ORB	£125	8.00	2.00
V417			**2½d Blue**	20	ORB	£125	8.00	2.00
V418	23/3/81		**2½d Blue**	21	IC	£175	£10	1.50
V419			**2½d Blue**	22	IC	£120	3.00	1.00
V420			**2½d Blue**	23	IC	£120	3.00	1.00
V421	5/7/73	35	**3d Rose** (shades)	11	SPR	£150	9.00	3.00
V422			**3d** ,,	12	SPR	£175	£10	3.50
V423			**3d** ,,	14	SPR	£225	£12	4.00
V424			**3d** ,,	15	SPR	£150	9.00	3.00
V425			**3d** ,,	16	SPR	£150	9.00	3.00
V426			**3d** ,,	17	SPR	£175	£12	4.00
V427			**3d** ,,	18	SPR	£175	£12	4.00
V428			**3d** ,,	19	SPR	£150	9.50	3.25
V429			**3d** ,,	20	SPR	£175	£18	6.00
V430	–/2/81		**3d Rose**	20	IC	£150	£20	6.50
V431			**3d Rose**	21	IC	£120	7.00	2.50
V432	1/1/83	:36	**3d on 3d Lilac**	21	IC	£135	£30	£10
V433	1/3/76	37	**4d Vermilion** ★	15	LG	£400	£100	£25
V434	12/3/77		**4d Sage green** ★	15	LG	£225	£40	£10
V435			**4d Sage green** ★	16	LG	£200	£35	£10
V436	15/8/80		**4d Grey brown** ★	17	LG	£400	£60	£20
V437	9/12/80		**4d Grey brown**	17	IC	£125	6.50	2.25
V438			**4d Grey brown**	18	IC	£125	6.50	2.25
V439	31/3/74	38	**6d Grey** (shades)	13	SPR	£175	£12	3.50
V440			**6d Grey** ,,	14	SPR	£175	£12	3.50
V441			**6d Grey** ,,	15	SPR	£175	£12	3.50
V442			**6d Grey** ,,	16	SPR	£175	£12	3.50
V443			**6d Grey** ,,	17	SPR	£270	£25	6.00
V444	1/1/81		**6d Grey**	17	IC	£125	7.00	2.50
V445			**6d Grey**	18	IC	£125	7.00	2.50
V446	1/1/83	39	**6d on 6d Lilac**	18	IC	£135	£30	£10

★ **See warning at foot of page 29**

Type 34

Type 35

Type 36

Type 37

Type 38

Type 39

SURFACE PRINTED ISSUES 1875 – 83 (continued)

Printers: De La Rue & Co.   *Paper:* White except where stated   *Perf:* 14   *Watermark:* Various as shown.

No.	Issued	Type		Colour	Plate	Wmk.	M/M	F/U	A/U
V447	11/9/76	40	8d	Orange ★	1	LG	£400	£45	£20
V448	1/9/73	41	1/–d	Green (shades)	8	SPR	£250	£18	6.00
V449			1/–d	Green ,,	9	SPR	£250	£18	6.00
V450			1/–d	Green ,,	10	SPR	£235	£15	4.00
V451			1/–d	Green ,,	11	SPR	£235	£16	4.00
V452			1/–d	Green ,,	12	SPR	£175	£15	4.00
V453			1/–d	Green ,,	13	SPR	£175	£15	4.00
V454	14/10/80		1/–d	Orange brown	13	SPR	£800	£100	£30
V455	29/5/81		1/–d	Orange brown	13	IC	£200	£20	6.00
V456			1/–d	Orange brown	14	IC	£175	£18	5.00

★ See warning at foot of page 29

Type 40

Type 41

NEW DESIGN – LOW VALUES 1880 – 83

Printers: De La Rue & Co.   *Paper:* White   *Perf.:* 14   *Watermark:* Imperial Crown.

No.	Issued	Type		Colour	M/M	F/U	A/U
V457	14/10/80	42	½d	Deep green	7.50	1.75	90
V458				Pale green	£10	2.25	1.00
V459	1/1/80	43	1d	Venetian red	3.00	40	20
V460	14/10/80	44	1½d	Venetian red	£40	8.00	3.00
V461	8/12/80	45	2d	Rose	£60	£10	3.50
V462				Rose (Wmk. Inverted)	£100	£30	£16
V463				Deep rose	£60	£10	3.50
V464				Pale rose	£60	£10	3.50
V465	15/3/81	46	5d	Indigo	£400	£25	7.50

Type 42

PENNY LILAC ISSUE 1881 – 1900

V466	12/7/81	47	1d	Lilac (Die I)	£60	6.00	2.00
V467				Pale lilac (Die I)	£60	6.00	2.00
V468	12/12/81	48	1d	Lilac (Die II)	50	10	5
V469				Lilac (Die II) (Wmk. Inverted)	£10	5.00	3.75
V470				Lilac (Die II) (No watermark)	£175	£80	£40
V471				Deep purple (Die II)	75	20	10
V472				Mauve (Die II)	75	20	10
V473				Blue lilac (Die II)	£125	£25	8.00

Type 43

Type 45

Type 44

Type 46

Type 47

Die I – 14 dots

Type 48

Die II – 16 dots

SURFACE PRINTED ISSUES 1883 – 1900
HIGH VALUES

Printers: De La Rue & Co.　　　*Perf.:* 14　　　*Watermarks:* Anchor, 3 Imperial Crowns or 3 Orbs as shown.

No.	Issued	Type		Colour	Paper	Wmk.	M/M	F/U	A/U
V474	–/–/84	49	**2/6d**	**Lilac**	White	Anchor	£700	£35	£15
V475				Deep lilac	"	Anchor	£700	£35	£15
V476	2/7/83		**2/6d**	**Lilac**	Blued	Anchor	£1500	£350	£175
V477	–/–/84	50	**5/–d**	**Rose**	White	Anchor	£800	£75	£30
V478				Crimson	"	Anchor	£800	£75	£30
V479	1/4/84		**5/–d**	**Rose**	Blued	Anchor	£3250	£1000	£300
V480	–/–/84	51	**10/–d**	**Pale ultramarine**	White	Anchor	£1800	£300	£90
V481				Ultramarine	"	Anchor	£1800	£300	£90
V482				Cobalt	"	Anchor	£10000	£2500	£775
V483	1/4/84		**10/–d**	**Ultramarine**	Blued	Anchor	£8750	£1750	£550
V484				Cobalt	"	Anchor	£12000	£3000	£950
V485	1/4/84	52	**£1**	**Brown lilac**	White	3 Crowns	£8750	£1350	£350
V485A				Broken frame Var. JC or TA	"	3 Crowns	£10000	£1750	£500
V486	1/2/88		**£1**	**Brown/lilac**	"	3 Orbs	£14000	£2000	£575
V486A				Broken frame Var. JC or TA	"	3 Orbs	£17500	£2800	£700
V487	27/1/91		**£1**	**Green**	"	3 Crowns	£5000	£650	£275
V487A				Broken frame Var. JC or TA	"	3 Crowns	£6000	£800	£375

WATERMARK INVERTED

No.	Issued	Type		Colour	Paper	Wmk.	M/M	F/U	A/U
V487B		52	**£1**	**Green**	White	3 Crowns	–	£2500	£1500

Type 49

Type 50

Type 51

Type 52

SURFACE PRINTED ISSUES 1883 – 86
LILAC AND GREEN ISSUE

Printers: De La Rue & Co.   *Paper:* White   *Perf:* 14   *Watermark:* Imperial Crown

All prices stated are for those stamps in the correct colour.
Washed examples or colour changelings have no value.

No.	Issued	Type		Colour	M/M	F/U	A/U
V488	1/4/84	42	½d	Slate blue	5.00	75	40
V489		53	1½d	Lilac	£50	6.00	2.00
V490				Lilac (Wmk. Inverted)	–	£50	£30
V491		54	2d	Lilac			
				(Wmk. Sideways)	£75	£10	4.00
V492		55	2½d	Lilac			
				(Wmk. Sideways)	£35	3.50	1.00
V493		56	3d	Lilac	£100	£10	4.25
V494		57	4d	Dull green	£225	£50	£22
V495		58	5d	Dull green	£250	£80	£22
V496		59	6d	Dull green			
				(Wmk. Sideways)	£250	£80	£28
V497	1/8/83	60	9d	Dull green			
				(Wmk. Sideways)	£800	£175	£50
V498				Dull green (Wmk. Sideways & Inverted)	£900	£180	£60
V499		61	1/–d	Dull green	£650	£125	£35

Type 53

Type 54

Type 55

Type 56

Type 57

Type 58

Type 59

Type 60

Type 61

SURFACE PRINTED ISSUES 1887 – 1900
JUBILEE ISSUE

Printers: De La Rue & Co.   *Paper:* White except where stated   *Perf:* 14   *Watermark:* Imperial Crown

No.	Issued	Type		Colour	U/M	M/M	F/U
WATERMARK UPRIGHT							
V500	1/1/87	62	½d	**Vermilion**	1.00	70	15
V501				Pale vermilion	1.00	70	15
V502				Orange vermilion	1.00	70	15
V503				Deep vermilion	1.50	1.00	50
V504	17/4/00		½d	**Dull blue green**	75	40	15
V505				Bright blue green	75	40	15
V506	1/1/87	63	1½d	**Pl. dl. pur./pl. green**	£18	6.00	45
V507				Dl. purple/pl. green	£18	6.00	45
V508				Dp. pur./pl. green	£18	6.00	45
V509	1/1/87	64	2d	**Grey grn./carmine**	£32	£15	1.50
V510				Yellow grn./carmine	£32	£15	1.50
V511				Dp. grey green/car.	£45	£20	2.00
V512				Green/vermilion	£250	£150	£65
V513	1/1/87	65	2½d	**Purple** (blue paper)	£20	7.00	25
V514				Pl. pur. (blue paper)	£20	7.00	25
V515				Dp. pur. (blue paper)	£28	7.50	40
V516	1/1/87	66	3d	**Purple** (yellow paper)	£30	£10	75
V517				Dp. pur. (yel. paper)	£30	£12	75
V518				Pur. (orange paper)	£600	£400	£75
V519	1/1/87	67	4d	**Green/deep brown**	£40	£16	3.00
V520				Green/purple brown	£40	£16	3.00
V521				Green/dp. choc. brn.	£60	£25	3.50
V522	15/9/92	68	4½d	**Green/carmine**	4.00	2.75	6.00
V523				Dp. green/carmine	6.00	3.00	8.00
V524				Green/dull scarlet	£12	8.00	£15
V525				Green/dp. brt. car.	£175	£85	£75
V526	1/1/87	69	5d	**Dull purple/blue** (Duty Pl. I)	£275	£200	£20
V527			5d	**Dull purple/blue** (Duty Pl. II)	£48	£16	1.75
V528				Dl. purple/brt. blue (Duty Pl. II)	£48	£16	1.75
V529	1/1/87	70	6d	**Pur.** (rose red paper)	£40	£15	1.50
V530				Dp. purple ,,	£40	£15	1.50
V531				Sl. purple ,,	£40	£15	1.50
V532	1/1/87	71	9d	**Dull purple/blue**	£135	£45	9.00
V533				Slate purple/blue	£140	£50	9.50
V534				Dl. purple/brt. blue	£140	£50	9.50
V535	24/2/90	72	10d	**Dull purple/carmine**	£140	£50	9.50
V536				Dl. purple/dl. scarlet	£140	£50	9.50
V537				Dl. pur./dp. brt. car.	£285	£200	£40
V538	1/1/87	73	1/–d	**Dull green**	£500	£190	£18
V539				Grey green	£550	£200	£19
V540	11/7/90		1/–d	**Green/carmine**	£130	£40	£25
Set of 14 (1 of each value incl. colour changes)					£1000	£350	£65
WATERMARK: INVERTED							
V541		62	½d	Vermilion	£20	£15	£10
V542		62	½d	Blue green	£20	£15	£10
V543		63	1½d	Purple/green	£230	£155	£90
V544		64	2d	Green/carmine	£300	£200	£100
V545		65	2½d	Purple (blue paper)	£300	£200	£100
V546		67	4d	Green/brown	£380	£225	£130
V547		69	5d	Purple/blue (Duty Pl. II)	£400	£275	£130
V548		70	6d	Pur. (rose red paper)	£450	£300	£175
V549		71	9d	Purple/blue	£450	£300	£175
V550		72	10d	Purple/carmine	£500	£375	£200
V551		73	1/–d	Green	£700	£450	£250
V552		73	1/–d	Green/carmine	£350	£225	£150

WARNING

Many of the colours are highly fugitive, especially the 1½d, 2d, 4d, 4½d, 9d and both 1/–d values. Any contact with water seriously affects these colours.

Type 62

Type 63

Type 64

Type 65

Type 66

Type 67

Duty Plate I

Duty Plate II

Type 68

Type 69

Type 70

Type 71

Type 72

Type 73

OFFICIAL OVERPRINTS 1882 – 1900

Collectors should be warned that examples of all the overprinted stamps are known to have been forged, and therefore great care should be taken in purchasing the scarcer and higher priced values.

Some guidance in checking the authenticity of the overprints is given below:–

(a) Exact comparison with a known genuine overprint.
The commoner and cheapest varieties are far more likely to be genuine.

(b) The impressions should be easily read from the backs of the stamps, as the overprinting was heavily impressed

(c) The postmark should obviously be on top of the overprint, but many forged examples are known with the overprint on top.

(d) When in any doubt, obtain an expert opinion, with certificate.

I.R. **I. R.** **O.W.**

OFFICIAL **OFFICIAL** **OFFICIAL**

GOVT. PARCELS

ARMY **ARMY** **BOARD OF EDUCATION**

OFFICIAL **OFFICIAL**

OVERPRINTED: "I.R. OFFICIAL"

No.	Issued	Type		Colour	M/M	F/U	A/U
V553	28/10/82	42	½d	Deep green	6.00	2.00	1.00
V554	28/10/82	42	½d	Pale green	7.50	2.25	1.25
V555	8/5/85	42	½d	Slate blue	8.00	2.00	1.00
V556	27/9/82	48	1d	Lilac (Die II)	1.00	60	30
V557	12/3/85	55	2½d	Lilac	£40	£15	7.00
V558	30/10/82	38	6d	Grey	£55	£15	7.00
V559	12/3/85	61	1/–d	Dull green	£1650	£375	£175
V560	12/3/85	50	5/–d	Rose on w.p.	£950	£300	£145
V561	12/3/85	50	5/–d	Rose on b.p.	£2500	£500	£200
V562	12/3/85	51	10/–d	Ultramarine on w.p.	£2000	£400	£185
V563	12/3/85	51	10/–d	Ultramarine on b.p.	£4500	£1500	£650
V564	12/3/85	51	10/–d	Cobalt on w.p.	£4250	£1000	£400
V565	12/3/85	52	£1	Brown lilac (wmk. Crowns)	£9500	£2750	£1250
V566	–/–/90	52	£1	Brown lilac (Wmk. Orbs)	£9250	£2650	£1200
V567	13/4/92	52	£1	Green	£2250	£400	£195
V568	21/1/88	62	½d	Vermilion	1.50	75	35
V569	–/4/01	62	½d	Blue green	2.50	1.00	50
V570	20/10/89	65	2½d	Purple	£40	4.00	1.85
V571	14/6/01	70	6d	Purple	£90	£15	7.00
V572	15/3/89	73	1/–d	Green	£125	£30	£12
V573	–/12/01	73	1/–d	Green/carmine	£400	£85	£30

No.	Issued	Type		Colour	M/M	F/U	A/U
OVERPRINTED: "GOVT. PARCELS"							
V574	30/4/86	53	1½d	Lilac	£70	£12	5.50
V575	30/4/86	59	6d	Dull green	£275	£55	£25
V576	1/8/83	60	9d	Dull green	£500	£125	£40
V577	1/7/83	41	1/–d	Orange brown Pl. 13	£300	£50	£20
V578	1/7/83	41	1/–d	Orange brown Pl. 14	£425	£70	£30
V579	–/6/97	48	1d	Lilac (Die II)	3.50	70	30
V580	20/10/87	63	1½d	Dl. purple/green	£12	1.50	70
V581	24/10/91	64	2d	Green/carmine	£45	6.00	2.50
V582	–/9/92	68	4½d	Green/carmine	£50	£75	£25
V583	19/12/87	70	6d	Purple	£25	7.00	3.00
V584	21/8/88	71	9d	Dull purple/blue	£50	£12	4.00
V585	25/3/90	73	1/–d	Green	£125	£60	£25
V586	–/11/00	73	1/–d	Green/carmine	£175	£50	£18
OVERPRINTED: "O.W. OFFICIAL"							
V587	24/3/96	62	½d	Vermilion	£35	6.50	2.50
V588	5/11/01	62	½d	Blue green	£45	£15	5.00
V589	24/3/96	48	1d	Lilac (Die II)	£35	6.50	2.50
V590	29/4/02	69	5d	Purple/blue (D. Pl.II)	£400	£100	£35
V591	28/5/02	72	10d	Dull purple/carmine	£800	£200	£90
OVERPRINTED: "ARMY OFFICIAL"							
V592	1/9/96	62	½d	Vermilion	1.00	35	15
V593	–/4/00	62	½d	Blue green	1.50	35	15
V594	1/9/96	48	1d	Lilac (Die II)	1.00	35	15
V595	1/9/96	65	2½d	Purple	3.50	1.25	50
V596	7/11/01	70	6d	Purple	£12	8.00	2.75
OVERPRINTED: "BOARD OF EDUCATION"							
V597	19/2/02	69	5d	Purple/blue (D. Pl. II)	£375	£110	£30
V598	19/2/02	73	1/–d	Green/carmine	£725	£325	£150

A GUIDE TO ASSIST IN DISTINGUISHING THE DIFFERENT PRINTERS

It is recommended that identification is best carried out by a series of eliminations and the chart following provides a degree of guidance.

Certain printings can be positively distinguished by perforation size (i.e. Harrison 15 x 14) or the chalky paper test – lightly rub the surface of the margin of the stamp with a small piece of silver and the chalky surface paper will react with a black mark like a pencil stroke. This can be removed with a light rubber. All chalky papers, with the exception of the 6d, are De La Rue.

The exercise then proceeds with the clues listed. Quality of printing, gum, centring, perforations, date of cancel (when available) plus the illustrated differences shown below, and finally a comparison of the various shades of colour.

USED
Beware colour changes being produced by water immersion on the following values ½d, 1½d, 2d, 3d, 4d green/ brown, 5d, 6d, 9d, 10d, 1/–d, as many of the colours were highly fugitive, especially the greens and purples.

A	**DE LA RUE**	Shading lines around crown are light and gradually darken towards frame sides.
B	**HARRISON** (SOMERSET HOUSE 6d)	Shading lines virtually same depth from frame to edge of crown giving 'halo' effect.
X	**DE LA RUE**	Top 'frame' line on right of value tablet extending upwards, always very thin and/or indistinct.
Y	**SOMERSET HOUSE**	The same 'frame' line, distinct and thick.

PRINTERS	DE LA RUE		HARRISON		SOMERSET HOUSE	
Perf. size	14	14	14	15 x 14	14	14
Paper type	Ordinary, smooth and coated	Chalky	Ordinary, less smooth		Ordinary, less smooth. Plate glazed, appears chalky but does not react to silver test	Chalky
Quality of printing	Fine		Coarser		Coarser	
Gum	Yellowish		Colourless (see Note II)		Colourless	
Centring	Good		Poor		Less poor	
Perforations	Generally clean		Often ragged		Often ragged	
Date of cancel	From 1902 Seldom after 1910		From 1911		From 1911	
½d	See illustration A		See illustration B	★		
1d	See illustration A		See illustration B some shades also fluoresce gold	★		
1½d	See illustration X Dull purple Slate purple	C			See illustration Y Reddish purple Slate purple (fluoresces gold)	
2d	Green is yellowish or bluish	C			Green is dull to deep greyish	
2½d	Straight blues See illustration A	C	Duller blues See illustration B	★		
3d	Paper appears chalky when not so	C	Purple appears as shades of brown on lemon paper	★		
4d Bi-colour	Only D.L.R.	C				
4d Orange	Finer impression, brownish, pale to deep orange		White specks in solid background. Coarser impression. Bright orange shades	★		
5d	Purple and slate purple	C			Reddish tinge to purple	
6d	See illustration A dull and slate purple (does not fluoresce)	C see A			See illustration B reddish purples some fluoresce (see Note I)	C
7d	No olive tinge to grey black				Grey is tinged with olive	
9d	Purple is dull or slate	C			Purple is reddish	
10d	Purple is dull or slate	C			Purple is reddish	
1/–d	Pale bluish green shades	C			Pale to dark green	
2/6d	Lilac and dull purple (does not fluoresce)	C			Reddish to deep black purple. Dull greyish purple (fluoresces gold)	
5/–d	Carmine (shows on reverse)				Carmine-red	
10/–d	Pale to deep ultramarine				Coarser printing; dull pale to deep ultramarine	
£1	Bluish green				Less bluish but deeper green	

NOTES

(I) **6d** Dickinson Paper. Somerset House experimental printing.
A coated paper which does not react to the silver test. Shades are dull to deep rose purple with white gum.

(II) There is an exception to the colourless gum on the printing of the Harrison Penny value, a small printing was made with a double gum – very yellowish, as a result of complaints from the public that the stamps did not appear to be gummed at all. The last issue of the 6d Somerset House also had yellowish gum, but the shades of deep purple were quite different from De La Rue.

C Denotes chalky paper variety exists.   ★ Variety exists (Perf. 15 x 14)

LOW VALUE SURFACE PRINTED ISSUES 1902 – 13

Type 1

Type 2

Type 3

Type 4

Type 5

Type 6

Type 7

Type 8

Type 9

Type 10

Type 11

Type 12

Type 13

Imperial
Crown

LOW VALUE SURFACE PRINTED ISSUES 1902 – 13

Watermark: Imperial Crown Upright (except where shown)   *Paper:* Ordinary except where marked (C) = chalky

PRINTED BY DE LA RUE & CO.

PERF. 14

No.	Issued	Type		Colour	U/M	M/M	F/U
E1	1/1/02	1	½d	Blue green	1.00	50	15
E2				Dull blue green	1.00	50	15
E3				Deep blue green	2.25	75	25
E4	26/11/04	1	½d	Yellow green	1.00	50	15
E5				Pale yellow green	1.00	50	15
E6	1/1/02	2	1d	Scarlet	85	30	15
E7				Bright scarlet	85	30	15
E8				Deep bright scarlet	2.00	75	25
E9				Rose carmine	£15	£10	2.00
E10	21/3/02	3	1½d	Dull purple/green	£35	£20	1.25
E11				Slate purple/green	£35	£20	1.25
E12	6/9/05	3	1½d	Pl. dull pur./grn. (C)	£35	£20	1.25
E13				Slate purple/ bluish green (C)	£40	£22	1.75
E14				Deep slate purple/ bluish green (C)	£45	£25	4.00
E15	25/3/02	4	2d	Yellowish grn./car.	£30	£18	1.75
E16				Grey green/carmine	£30	£18	1.75
E17				Yellowish green/ver.	£150	£100	7.50
E18	6/9/05	4	2d	Grey green/car. (C)	£45	£30	3.50
E19				Deep grey green/ scarlet (C)	£45	£30	3.50
E20				Grey green/scar. (C)	£45	£30	3.50
E21				Pale blue green/ carmine (C)	£90	£60	6.00
E22	1/1/02	5	2½d	Ultramarine	£10	4.00	45
E23				Pale ultramarine	£12	5.00	55
E24				Deep ultramarine	£18	£12	1.50
E25	20/3/02	6	3d	Dull purple/yellow (back: orange yellow)	£30	£15	1.00
E26				Deep purple/yellow (back: orange yellow)	£35	£20	1.50
E27	31/3/06	6	3d	Purple/lemon (C) (back: lemon)	£30	£15	90
E28				Pl. purple/lemon (C) (back: lemon)	£30	£15	90
E29				Dl. red pur./yel. (C) (back: lemon)	£120	£75	3.50
E30				Pl. red pur./or. yel (C) (back: orange yellow)	£120	£75	3.50
E31				Dull pur./or. yel. (C) (back: orange yellow)	£250	£150	8.50
E32	27/3/02	7	4d	Green/brown	£45	£25	4.00
E33				Green/grey brown	£45	£25	4.00
E34				Green/choc. brown	£55	£30	4.75
E35	19/1/06	7	4d	Grn./choc. brn. (C)	£45	£25	4.00
E36				Deep green/ Choc. brown (C)	£45	£25	4.00
E37	1/11/09	7	4d	Pale orange	£15	6.50	2.50
E38				Red orange	£15	6.50	2.50
E39				Brown orange	£150	£75	£30
E40	14/5/02	8	5d	Dull purple/ultra.	£40	£20	2.75
E41				Slate purple/ultra.	£45	£22	3.00
E42	19/5/06	8	5d	Dull pur./ultra. (C)	£50	£25	3.50
E43				Slate pur./ultra. (C)	£50	£25	3.50

No.	Issued	Type		Colour	U/M	M/M	F/U
E44	1/1/02	9	6d	Slate purple	£35	£12	1.75
E45				Pale dull purple	£35	£12	1.75
E46	1/10/05	9	6d	Dull purple (C)	£40	£15	2.25
E47				Slate purple (C)	£40	£15	2.25
E48				Pale dull purple (C)	£45	£16	2.25
E49	4/5/10	10	7d	Grey black	2.50	1.50	1.50
E50				Deep grey black	£90	£60	£18
E51	7/4/02	11	9d	Dull purple/ultra.	£120	£40	8.50
E52				Slate purple/ultra.	£120	£40	8.50
E53				Sl. purple/dp. ultra.	£145	£60	£10
E54	29/6/05	11	9d	Dull pur./ultra. (C)	£120	£40	£15
E55				Sl. purple/ultra. (C)	£120	£40	£15
E56				Sl. pur./pl. ultra. (C)	£120	£40	£15
E57				Sl. pur./dp. ultra. (C)	£140	£50	£18
E58	3/7/02	12	10d	Dull purple/carmine	£120	£40	£12
E58A			Var.	(No cross on crown)	£350	£135	£55
E59				Slate purple/car.	£120	£40	£12
E60				Sl. purple/car. pink	£175	£60	£15
E61	6/9/05	12	10d	Dull purple/car. (C)	£130	£40	£10
E62				Slate purple/car. (C)	£130	£40	£10
E62A			Var.	(No cross on crown)	£300	£125	£50
E63				Dull purple/scar. (C)	£160	£55	£14
E63A			Var.	(No cross on crown)	£300	£130	£45
E64				Slate pur./scar. (C)	£160	£55	£14
E65				Sl. pur./dp. car. (C)	£300	£130	£45
E66	24/3/02	13	1/–d	Dull green/carmine	£120	£45	8.00
E67				Dull green/bt. car.	£120	£45	8.00
E68	6/9/05	13	1/–d	Dull green/car.(C)	£130	£48	£10
E69				Dull green/scar. (C)	£130	£48	£10
E70				Dp. dl. grn./scar. (C)	£145	£50	£12
E71				Dl. green/pl. car.(C)	£185	£65	£15

WATERMARK INVERTED

No.	Issued	Type		Colour	U/M	M/M	F/U
E72		1	½d	Yellow green	5.00	3.50	1.50
E73		2	1d	Scarlet	2.00	1.25	25
E73A		4	2d	Green/carmine (C)	£800	£650	–
E74		8	5d	Purple/ultra. (C)	£500	£350	£300

PRINTED BY HARRISON & SONS

PERF. 14

No.	Issued	Type		Colour	U/M	M/M	F/U
E75	3/5/11	1	½d	Dull yellow green	1.00	75	25
E76				Dull green	1.25	85	25
E77				Deep dull green	6.00	4.00	2.00
E78				Pale bluish green	£30	£20	6.00
E79				Dp. dl. yellow green (patchy)	£100	£70	8.50
E80				Deep bright green	£225	£130	£50
E81				Bright green	£275	£175	£60
E82	3/5/11	2	1d	Rose red	2.50	1.50	35
E83				Deep rose red	5.00	3.00	50
E84				Pale rose carmine	£45	£30	5.00
E85				Rose carmine	£50	£35	5.50
E86				Deep rose carmine	£80	£55	£12
E87				Aniline rose	£175	£110	£40
E88				Aniline pink	£750	£500	£75
E89				Intense rose red	£750	£500	£75
E90	10/7/11	5	2½d	Bright blue	£35	£20	4.00
E91				Dull blue	£35	£20	4.00
E92				Deep bright blue	£55	£30	5.00

LOW VALUE SURFACE PRINTED ISSUES 1902 – 13 (continued)

Watermark: Imperial Crown Upright (except where shown)　　　*Paper:* Ordinary except where marked (C) = chalky

No.	Issued	Type		Colour	U/M	M/M	F/U
E93	12/9/11	6	**3d**	**Purple/lemon**	£50	£25	£60
E94				Grey/lemon	£3500	£2250	★
E95	13/7/11	7	**4d**	**Bright orange**	£40	£25	£12
E96				Deep bright orange	£50	£25	£12

WATERMARK INVERTED

No.	Issued	Type		Colour	U/M	M/M	F/U
E97		1	**½d**	Yellow green	£15	£10	5.00
E98		2	**1d**	Rose red	£15	£10	5.00
E99		2	**1d**	Pale rose carmine	£100	£75	£25
E100		2	**1d**	Rose carmine	£120	£80	£35
E101		2	**1d**	Aniline rose	£300	£175	£85
E102		5	**2½d**	Blue	£350	£275	£225

NO WATERMARK

No.	Issued	Type		Colour	U/M	M/M	F/U
E103		2	**1d**	Rose red	£135	£100	£100

PRINTED BY HARRISON & SONS

PERF. 15 x 14

No.	Issued	Type		Colour	U/M	M/M	F/U
E104	30/10/11	1	**½d**	**Dull green**	£15	8.00	4.50
E105				Blue green	£18	£10	5.00
E106				Deep dull green	£22	£15	7.00
E107				Dp. dl. green (patchy)	£175	£125	£60
E108	5/10/11	2	**1d**	**Rose carmine**	8.00	4.00	2.00
E109				Pale rose carmine	8.00	4.00	2.00
E110				Deep rose carmine	£12	8.00	6.00
E111				Rose red	£25	£15	£10
E112				Deep rose red	£40	£30	£20
E113	14/10/11	5	**2½d**	**Bright blue**	£25	£12	2.25
E114				Dull blue	£30	£15	2.25
E115				Deep bright blue	£40	£17	6.50
E116	22/9/11	6	**3d**	**Purple/lemon**	£30	£20	75
E117				Grey purple/lemon	£30	£20	75
E118				Grey/lemon	£3500	£2250	★
E119	22/11/11	7	**4d**	**Bright orange**	£15	£10	2.00
E120				Deep bright orange	£15	£10	2.00
E121				Very deep orange	£40	£25	8.00

WATERMARK INVERTED

No.	Issued	Type		Colour	U/M	M/M	F/U
E114A		5	**2½d**	Dull blue	U	U	£250

PRINTED BY SOMERSET HOUSE

PERF: 14

No.	Issued	Type		Colour	U/M	M/M	F/U
E122	13/7/11	3	**1½d**	**Dull purple/green**	£15	8.00	2.50
E123				Dull redd. pur./green	£15	8.00	2.50
E124				Dull redd. purple/ bright green	£30	£15	3.50
E125				Slate purple/green	£30	£15	3.50
E126				Dp. plum/dp. green	£40	£20	4.50
E127				Redd. pur./bt. green	£50	£22	8.00
E128				Redd. pur./yell. grn.	£50	£22	8.00
E129	8/8/11	4	**2d**	**Dp. dull green/red**	£15	8.00	3.50
E130				Grey green/bt. car.	£22	£12	4.50
E131				Dp. dull green/car.	£22	£12	4.50
E132				Dp. dl. green/bt. car.	£30	£15	5.50
E133	7/8/11	8	**5d**	**Dull redd. purple/ cobalt blue**	£15	8.00	3.00
E134				Dp.dl.redd.purple/ bt.blue	£15	8.00	3.00

No.	Issued	Type		Colour	U/M	M/M	F/U
E135				Dp. redd. pur./bt. bl.	£25	£15	3.75
E136				Dp. plum/cobalt blue	£25	£15	3.75
E137	31/10/11	9	**6d**	**Dull purple**	£20	£10	2.50
E138				Pale dull purple	£20	£10	2.50
E139				Reddish purple	£22	£11	3.00
E139A				Redd.pur.(shades)	£135	£80	£70
E140			Var.	(No cross on crown) Pale reddish purple	£22	£11	3.00
E141				Dark purple	£20	£10	3.00
E142				Royal purple	£45	£25	£20
E143				Very dp.redd. purple	£50	£30	5.50
E144	31/10/11	9	**6d**	**Deep plum** (C)	£35	£20	5.00
E144A			Var.	(No cross on crown)	£175	£110	£90
E145				Bright magenta (C)	£2750	£2000	★
E146	–/3/13	9	**6d**	**Dull purple** (Dickinson coated paper)	£200	£125	£35
E147				Dull redd. purple (Dickinson coated paper)	£225	£130	£40
E148	1/8/12	10	**7d**	**Slate grey**	5.00	2.00	3.50
E149				Pale grey	£15	8.00	4.75
E150				Deep slate grey	£75	£30	£18
E151	24/7/11	11	**9d**	**Dull redd. pur./blue**	£110	£40	£15
E152				Dp. dl. redd. pur. /bl.	£110	£40	£15
E153				Redd. purple/lt. blue	£130	£60	£18
E154				Slate pur./cobalt bl.	£150	£75	£20
E155				Dp. dl. redd. purple/ deep bright blue	£150	£75	£20
E156	9/10/11	12	**10d**	**Dull redd. pur.**	£120	£45	£15
E157				Dull purple/scarlet	£120	£45	£15
E158				Dp. dl. purple/car.	£120	£45	£15
E158A			Var.	(No cross on crown)	£500	£325	£100
E159				Dp.dl.purple/scarlet	£130	£50	£20
E160				Dl. redd. pur./scarlet	£130	£50	£20
E161				Dl. redd. purple/ scarlet (FL)	£145	£55	£25
E162				Dk. plum/carmine	£145	£55	£25
E163				Dl. purple/dp. scarlet	£250	£120	£55
E164				Dl. redd. purple/ aniline pink	£500	£250	£75
E165	17/7/11	13	**1/-d**	**Green/carmine**	£70	£25	5.00
E166				Green/scarlet	£85	£30	6.00
E167				Dp. green/scarlet	£100	£45	8.00
E168				Green/bt. scarlet	£100	£45	8.00
E169				Dk. green/scarlet	£110	£50	£10

WATERMARK INVERTED

No.	Issued	Type		Colour	U/M	M/M	F/U
E170		13	**1/-d**	Green/scarlet	£100	£70	£70

NO WATERMARK

No.	Issued	Type		Colour	U/M	M/M	F/U
E171		13	**1/-d**	Green/scarlet	£400	£275	£275

N.B. (FL) – E161: fluoresces under ultra violet lamp

★ Denotes impossible to identify in used condition.

U = Unrecorded Mint

HIGH VALUE SURFACE PRINTED ISSUES 1902 – 13

Watermark: Anchor or Three Crowns (£1 only)   *Perf:* 14   *Paper:* Ordinary except where marked (C) = chalky

No.	Issued	Type	Colour	U/M	M/M	F/U

PRINTED BY DE LA RUE & CO.

No.	Issued	Type		Colour	U/M	M/M	F/U
E172	5/4/02	14	**2/6d**	**Lilac**	£750	£650	£35
E173				Slate purple	£750	£650	£35
E174	7/10/05	14	**2/6d**	**Dull purple** (C)	£750	£650	£40
E175				Pale dull purple (C)	£750	£650	£40
E176				Slate purple (C)	£750	£650	£40
E177	5/4/02	15	**5/–d**	**Bright carmine**	£1100	£850	£60
E178				Dp. bright carmine	£1200	£875	£65
E179	5/4/02	16	**10/–d**	**Ultramarine**	£2000	£1600	£300
E180				Deep ultramarine	£2100	£1650	£310
E181	16/7/02	17	**£1**	**Dull blue green**	£4000	£3000	£700

WATERMARK INVERTED

No.	Issued	Type		Colour	U/M	M/M	F/U
E182		14	**2/6d**	**Lilac**	£1500	£1200	£450
E183				Purple (C)	£1600	£1250	£500

Large Anchor

PRINTED BY SOMERSET HOUSE

No.	Issued	Type		Colour	U/M	M/M	F/U
E184	27/9/11	14	**2/6d**	**Dark purple**	£800	£675	£50
E185				Dull redd. purple	£800	£675	£50
E186				Pl. dull redd. purple	£800	£675	£50
E187				Dull greyish pur.(FL)	£1400	£1100	£200
E188	29/2/12	15	**5/–d**	**Carmine**	£1100	£850	£60
E189				Carmine red	£1200	£875	£65
E190	14/1/12	16	**10/–d**	**Blue**	£2000	£1600	£300
E191				Bright blue	£2100	£1650	£310
E192				Deep blue	£2250	£1750	£350
E193	3/9/11	17	**£1**	**Deep green**	£4000	£3000	£650

N.B. (FL) – E187: fluoresces gold under ultra violet lamp

Imperial Crown

Type 14

Type 15

Type 16

Type 17

OFFICIAL OVERPRINTS 1902 – 04

All Overprints were on original De La Rue printings.

No.	Issued	Type		Colour	U/M	M/M	F/U

OVERPRINTED: "I.R. OFFICIAL"

No.	Issued	Type		Colour	U/M	M/M	F/U
E194	4/2/02	1	½d	Blue green	5.00	4.00	1.00
E195	4/2/02	2	1d	Scarlet	3.00	2.00	40
E196	19/2/02	5	2½d	Ultramarine	£400	£300	£50
E197	14/3/04	9	6d	Dull purple	£42000	£30000	£22000
E198	29/4/02	13	1/–d	Green/carmine	£400	£300	£55
E199	29/4/02	15	5/–d	Carmine	£3500	£2750	£1250
E200	29/4/02	16	10/–d	Ultramarine	£15000	£10000	£7500
E201	29/4/02	17	£1	Dull blue green	£10000	£8000	£3000

OVERPRINTED: "GOVT. PARCELS"

No.	Issued	Type		Colour	U/M	M/M	F/U
E202	30/10/02	2	1d	Scarlet	9.00	6.00	4.50
E203	29/4/02	4	2d	Green/carmine	£60	£45	£10
E204	19/2/02	9	6d	Dull purple	£120	£80	£10
E205	28/8/02	11	9d	Purple/ultramarine	£250	£175	£35
E206	17/12/02	13	1/–d	Green/carmine	£450	£300	£75

OVERPRINTED: "O.W.OFFICIAL"

No.	Issued	Type		Colour	U/M	M/M	F/U
E207	11/2/02	1	½d	Blue green	£90	£60	£25
E208	11/2/02	2	1d	Scarlet	£90	£60	£25
E209	29/3/02	4	2d	Green/carmine	£200	£150	£50
E210	20/3/02	5	2½d	Ultramarine	£475	£350	£30
E211	28/5/03	12	10d	Purple/carmine	£2000	£1500	£700

OVERPRINTED: "ARMY OFFICIAL"

No.	Issued	Type		Colour	U/M	M/M	F/U
E212	11/2/02	1	½d	Blue green (Style A)	2.00	1.50	50
E213	11/2/02	2	1d	Scarlet (Style A)	1.25	85	30
E214	23/8/02	9	6d	Dull purple (Style A)	£70	£50	£18
E215	–/9/03	9	6d	Dull purple (Style B)	£850	£650	£350

OVERPRINTED: "BOARD OF EDUCATION"

No.	Issued	Type		Colour	U/M	M/M	F/U
E216	19/2/02	1	½d	Blue green	£18	£14	2.50
E217	19/2/02	2	1d	Scarlet	£18	£14	2.50
E218	19/2/02	5	2½d	Ultramarine	£300	£225	£55
E219	6/2/04	8	5d	Purple/blue	£800	£600	£325
E220	23/12/02	13	1/–d	Green/carmine	£17000	£14000	£11500

OVERPRINTED: "R.H.OFFICIAL"

No.	Issued	Type		Colour	U/M	M/M	F/U
E221	29/4/02	1	½d	Blue green	£150	£100	£80
E222	19/2/02	2	1d	Scarlet	£135	£90	£50

OVERPRINTED: "ADMIRALTY OFFICIAL" – STYLE A

No.	Issued	Type		Colour	U/M	M/M	F/U
E223	3/3/03	1	½d	Blue green	6.00	4.00	2.50
E224	3/3/03	2	1d	Scarlet	5.00	3.75	2.00
E225	3/3/03	3	1½d	Purple/green	£65	£45	£25
E226	3/3/03	4	2d	Green/carmine	£80	£60	£35
E227	3/3/03	5	2½d	Ultramarine	£60	£40	£25
E228	3/3/03	6	3d	Purple/yellow	£85	£65	£30

OVERPRINTED: "ADMIRALTY OFFICIAL" – STYLE B

No.	Issued	Type		Colour	U/M	M/M	F/U
E229	–/9/03	1	½d	Blue green	9.00	6.00	3.00
E230	–/11/03	2	1d	Scarlet	7.00	5.00	2.75
E231	–/2/04	3	1½d	Purple/green	£125	£90	£50
E232	–/3/04	4	2d	Green/carmine	£300	£200	£100
E233	–/3/04	5	2½d	Ultramarine	£600	£400	£275
E234	–/2/04	6	3d	Purple/yellow	£300	£200	£90

I.R.
OFFICIAL

GOVT
PARCELS

O.W.
OFFICIAL

ARMY
OFFICIAL
(Style A)

ARMY
OFFICIAL
(Style B)

BOARD
OF
EDUCATION

R.H.
OFFICIAL

ADMIRALTY
OFFICIAL
(Style A)

ADMIRALTY
OFFICIAL
(Style B)

Please see warning re forgeries on page 36

COLLECTING DOWNEY HEAD ISSUES

Mike Jackson – Editor: PHILATELIC REVIEW

Winner of the 'Albert H. Harris Memorial Award' for research – B.P.E. 1978 and the 'N.P.S. Queen Elizabeth Silver Jubilee Trophy' for presentation – STAMPEX 1979.

Introduction

The early Georgian issues of 1911 and 1912 represent a particularly important period in the philately of Great Britain, being born as they were out of the relative inexperience and experimentation of both the plate makers (the Royal Mint) and the printers (Harrison and Sons), neither of whom had undertaken this sort of work before. The uncertainties and frustrations which seem to have characterised the development of the stamps are reflected in the issued ½d and 1d stamps themselves. The printing on the first issues (Dies 1A and 1B) was blotchy and uneven, and although the redrawn die (Die 2) was a great improvement, the decision was taken to replace the three-quarter face Downey Head with the profile Coinage or Medal Head. This decision cut short any plans to issue more values with the Downey Head, as was originally intended, and so the series to the 1/– value was completed with the profile head. There is enormous scope for specialists in these issues, but space permits only an introduction to some aspects of these stamps.

Separating the Dies

Sorting out the different dies shouldn't present too many problems, especially if a strong glass is used on the ½d Dies 1A and 1B, when the different appearance of the centre jewel of the crown becomes readily apparent. I have always found a certain amount of inconsistency in the printing of the scales on the dolphin, especially on Die 1A, where uneven printing often breaks up the top scale on the right hand dolphin. I have also seen an example of Die 1B which had an almost complete top scale, which caused its original owner to wrongly identify it as Die 1A. As this example was a control copy of control A 11 (close), which is extremely scarce on Die 1A, this confusion was quite serious. However, the 'centre jewel' test is consistent, and should be used whenever possible.

Separating the 1d Dies 1A and 1B is quite straightforward, even without a glass, as the line of shading on the ribbon is a relatively strong line. The ½d and 1d Die 2 stamps are substantially different in overall appearance from their Die 1A and 1B counterparts and these can be identified at first glance.

| ½d Die 1A | ½d Die 1B | 1d Die 1A | 1d Die 1B |

Shades

Perhaps the most popular pastime amongst collectors of Georgian Great Britain stamps is the study of shades, and although they do not have the variety of the 1912–22 series (what stamps do?) the Downey Head issues do provide for an impressive array, a complete set of specialised shades as listed requiring some sixty-three stamps.

It is worth repeating here that the best way to approach the collecting of shades is to first amass a range of different shades before sorting them out and attempting to classify them. It then becomes clear that there are not, say, four discrete shades of a particular issue, but four 'shade bands'. For example, although a stamp may have shades listed as 'Pale Green' and 'Green', it may be possible to put together a series of examples which begin 'Pale' and get progressively darker until 'Green' is reached. There are exceptions to this but these are usually the more outstanding, and often rarer, shades (e.g. the 1d Die 2, watermark Crown, Very Deep Bright Scarlet – G70). But generally speaking, the more 'ordinary' shades do occur in shade groups, and for the collector who **doesn't** want to demonstrate this fact in his album, it is nevertheless a good idea to remember it so that good, average representatives of each group can be selected.

It is also a good idea to collect control copies of shades, as these are worth a premium and very often shades are related to certain controls. An example of this is to be found in the Somerset House printings of the 1d Die 1A. These were preliminary printings, the plates being subsequently handed over to Harrisons, and can be recognised by the full stop after the letter of the control, thus: A. 11. These Somerset House printings are in shades of carmine, while most of the 1d Die 1A Harrison printings are in shades of carmine-red. This could be demonstrated by a series of shades, all showing the control, and arranged by printers. Some stamps were only issued in booklets, and do not therefore have controls (e.g. the 1d Die 1B scarlet stamps). These issues are best collected either in whole booklet panes of six or as singles showing the booklet selvedge, thus demonstrating their origin at a glance.

Watermarks
There were three different papers used on these issues, each with a different watermark. This can occur variously as upright, inverted, reversed, inverted and reversed, sideways, as well as no watermark at all and watermark 'POSTAGE', the latter due to misplaced paper on the printing press. The problem with collecting watermark varieties is displaying them. The best way to collect them is in marginal pieces which, especially if mounted on black paper, show the watermark clearly in the margin. In the case of the Crown watermark paper being inverted, the most desirable pieces are from the bottom of the sheet, which usually shows the tops of the inverted crowns in the margin. This is due to the layout of the watermark on the sheet, which after all was designed to be the correct way up. However, compared to the 'cypher' watermarks, the Crown watermark was quite easy to 'read' by the printer, and so sheets with inverted watermarks are very rare.

A point to remember is that 50% of the stamps issued in booklets have inverted watermarks due to the arrangement of the printing plates, so it is important to know whether a stamp with inverted watermark is from a sheet or from a booklet. For instance, the 1d Die 1B Carmine with inverted watermark (G 37) is relatively common from booklets, and is priced accordingly. However, a specimen from a **sheet** printing (if it exists!) would be worth more, and would be comparable to the 1d Die 1A inverted (G 15), which was not issued in booklet form.

Perforation
The normal perforation on the Downey Head issues is gauge 15 x 14. This gauge was adopted by Harrison and Sons soon after the start of their contract, the first of their Edwardian provisional printings gauging 14 all round. This change is assumed to have taken place to equalise the tearing force required to separate the stamps. With 14 gauge, the nature of the paper was such that the sheet of stamps separated more easily down the vertical gutters. The addition of one hole per stamp along the horizontal gutters (to give gauge 15 x 14) balanced the situation. The fact that rolls of stamps for vending and stamp-affixing machines were being thought of at this time may also have influenced the change of gauge. When the first Post Office issue of rolls of stamps appeared in September 1912, they were reeled vertically, and so easier separation of single stamps from the roll may have been desired by the manufacturers of the machines in which they were to be used.

The ½d and 1d Die 1A 'perf 14' varieties are not errors, as is usually thought, but were brought about by pressure of work necessitating the temporary use of one of the old machines which had been used for some of the Edwardian issues. At least three unused ½d and four unused 1d stamps are known perforated 14 all round, one of the ½d examples being a control copy. No used examples of the 1d are known but the ½d used, often on postcards, is frequently met with.

The ½d and 1d Die 2 watermark Multiple Cypher **imperforate** stamps are something of a mystery. They are possibly trials of some sort, although apart from the lack of holes, they are identical to the normal issue.

This important section of British Philately provides much opportunity for specialisation, with the great variety of shades and watermarks that exist.

Whilst the watermark varieties are reasonably simple to identify with the latest types of watermark detectors, the shades are difficult except by comparison. As the collector builds up his range of different shades it becomes much easier to identify the specific shade descriptions of the individual stamps.

The basis of pricing for stamps of this reign is as follows:-

Unmounted Mint (U/M)   Full original gum, full perforations and good colour.

Mounted Mint (M/M)   Lightly hinged, full perforations and clear colour without toning.

Fine Used (F/U)   Clear and light cancel on a reasonably well centred stamp, with full perforations.

DOWNEY HEAD ISSUES 1911 – 12

½d   **DIE 1A**   Centre jewel of cross in middle of crown is suggested by a comma; top scale on right hand dolphin ends with a triangle.

  DIE 1B   Centre jewel in crown is suggested by a crescent; top scale on right hand dolphin has only two sides.

  DIE 2   One thick line in ornament above 'FP' of 'Halfpenny' compared with two thinner lines on Dies 1A and 1B. Beard has also been lightened and is better defined.

1d   **DIE 1A**   The second line of shading is complete on the ribbon at the right of the crown; on the large leaf which overlaps the right hand side ribbons, there is a line of shading to the left of the central line.

  DIE 1B   The second line of shading on the ribbon is broken; on the leaf the line of shading is much smaller.

  DIE 2   The lion is shaded and the beard is more defined; the ends of the ribbons above the figures '1' have been removed.

Type 1
Die 1A or 1B

Type 2
Die 2

Type 3
Die 1A or 1B

Type 4
Die 2

TYPOGRAPHIC DEFINITIVE ISSUES 1911 – 12

Printers: Harrison & Sons and Somerset House   *Perf:* 15 x 14   *Watermark:* As indicated, all upright except where marked

★Used marked with an asterisk should only be purchased with a certificate.

No.	Issued	Type	Colour	U/M	M/M	F/U

Imperial Crown

Royal Cypher

DIE 1A. WATERMARK: IMPERIAL CROWN

No.	Issued	Type		Colour	U/M	M/M	F/U
G1	22/6/11	1	½d	**Green**	1.50	1.00	30
G2				Pale green	3.00	2.25	50
G3				Deep green	4.00	3.00	75
G4				Bluish green	£250	£190	★
G5				Green (Perf. 14)	£4250	£3750	£350
G6	22/6/11	3	1d	**Carmine red**	1.75	1.25	30
G7				Carmine red			
				(chalky paper)	£275	£210	£175
G8				Pale carmine red	1.75	1.25	30
G9				Pale carmine red			
				(no cross on crown)	£225	£175	£100
G10				Pale carmine	4.50	3.00	1.00
G11				Carmine	6.00	4.50	1.50
G12				Deep carmine red	£12	9.00	3.00
G13				Rose pink	£35	£27	£10
G14				Deep carmine			
				(varnish ink)	£900	£700	★
G15				Carmine red			
				(watermark inverted)	£400	£325	£175
G16				Carmine red			
				(without watermark)	£450	£375	£200

DIE 1B. WATERMARK: IMPERIAL CROWN

No.	Issued	Type		Colour	U/M	M/M	F/U
G17	–/–/11	1	½d	**Bright green**	4.00	3.00	50
G18				Green	4.00	3.00	50
G19				Yellow green	7.00	5.00	65
G20				Pale bright green	6.00	4.00	65
G21				Deep green	£10	8.00	5.00
G22				Bright yellow green	£15	£10	7.00
G23				Bluish green	£130	£110	£55
G24				Very deep green	£225	£195	£90
G25				Deep green			
				(varnish ink)	£900	£700	★
G26				Bright green			
				(watermark inverted)	5.00	4.00	2.50
G27	–/–/11	3	1d	**Carmine**	2.00	1.50	30
G28				Pale carmine	2.00	1.50	30
G29				Pale carmine			
				(no cross on crown)	£200	£175	£95
G30				Deep carmine	4.00	3.00	50
G31				Bright carmine	4.00	3.00	50
G32				Carmine red	4.00	3.00	50
G33				Pale carmine red	5.00	4.00	75
G34				Deep bright carmine	£20	£15	3.50
G35				Rose pink	£40	£30	£10
G36				Carmine			
				(varnish ink)	£1000	£800	★
G37				Carmine			
				(watermark inverted)	5.00	4.00	1.50
G38	–/6/12	3	1d	**Scarlet**	£15	£10	3.00
G39				Bright scarlet	£15	£10	3.00
G40				Pale scarlet	£20	£15	4.50
G41				Aniline scarlet	£145	£120	£70
G42				Scarlet			
				(watermark inverted)	£15	£10	3.00

DIE 1B. WATERMARK: ROYAL CYPHER

No.	Issued	Type		Colour	U/M	M/M	F/U
G43	–/8/12	1	½d	**Green**	£15	£10	4.00
G44				Pale green	£15	£10	4.00
G45				Deep green	£30	£20	8.00
G46				Deep green			
				(varnish ink)	£1000	£750	★
G47				Green			
				(watermark inverted)	£15	£10	4.00
G48				Green			
				(wmk. reversed)	£300	£225	£100
G49				Green			
				(watermark inverted & reversed)	£375	£275	£125
G50	–/8/12	3	1d	**Scarlet**	8.00	6.00	3.50
G51				Bright scarlet	8.00	6.00	3.50
G52				Pale scarlet	£15	£10	5.00
G53				Deep bright scarlet	£20	£15	9.00
G54				Bright scarlet			
				(varnish ink)	£1000	£750	★
G55				Scarlet			
				(watermark inverted)	8.00	6.00	3.50
G56				Scarlet			
				(wmk. reversed)	£375	£225	£110
G56A				Scarlet			
				(watermark inverted & reversed)	£700	£575	£175

TYPOGRAPHIC DEFINITIVE ISSUES 1912

Printers: Harrison & Sons and Somerset House   *Perf:* 15 x 14   *Watermark:* As indicated, all upright except where marked

★Used marked with an asterisk should only be purchased with a certificate.

Multiple Royal Cypher

No.	Issued	Type		Colour	U/M	M/M	F/U
DIE 2. WATERMARK: IMPERIAL CROWN							
G57	1/1/12	2	½d	**Green**	1.50	1.00	20
G58				Green			
				(no cross on crown)	£60	£40	£10
G59				Yellow green	1.50	1.00	20
G60				Pale green	2.00	1.50	40
G61				Deep green	9.00	6.50	90
G62				Bright yellow green	£15	£10	1.00
G63				Myrtle green	£50	£40	8.00
G64				Bluish green	£60	£45	£15
G65				Green			
				(watermark inverted)	£250	£200	£100
G66	1/1/12	4	**1d**	**Scarlet**	65	45	10
G67				Scarlet			
				(no cross on crown)	£40	£30	£18
G68				Bright scarlet	65	45	10
G69				Deep bright scarlet	2.50	1.75	45
G70				Very deep bright scarlet	£100	£80	£25
G71				Aniline scarlet	£130	£100	£65
G72				Aniline scarlet			
				(no cross on crown)	£575	£450	£225
G73				Scarlet			
				(watermark inverted)	£100	£85	£50
G74				Bright scarlet			
				(no cross on crown, watermark inverted)	£150	£120	£60
DIE 2. WATERMARK: ROYAL CYPHER							
G75	–/8/12	2	½d	**Green**	75	50	25
G76				Green			
				(no cross on crown)	£90	£60	£40
G77				Pale green	1.25	1.00	35
G78				Deep green	2.50	1.95	60
G79				Yellow green	5.00	4.00	1.25
G80				Green (watermark inverted)	£45	£35	£15
G81				Green (wmk. reversed)	£30	£25	£15
G82				Green (watermark inverted & reversed)	5.00	4.00	1.50
G83				Green (without watermark)	£175	£150	£100
G84	–/8/12	4	**1d**	**Scarlet**	60	45	20
G85				Scarlet (no cross on crown)	£60	£45	£18
G86				Bright scarlet	75	50	25
G87				Deep bright scarlet	£15	£12	1.25
G88				Scarlet (watermark inverted)	£12	9.00	5.00
G89				Scarlet (wmk. reversed)	£20	£15	6.00
G90				Scarlet (watermark inverted & reversed)	£10	8.00	5.00
G91				Scarlet (without watermark)	£200	£175	£125

No.	Issued	Type		Colour	U/M	M/M	F/U
DIE 2. WATERMARK: MULTIPLE ROYAL CYPHER							
G92	–/10/12	2	½d	**Green**	1.25	95	35
G93				Green (imperforate)	£100	£75	£50
G94				Pale green	2.50	1.95	45
G95				Deep green	8.00	6.00	65
G96				Yellow green	5.00	4.00	65
G97				Green (watermark inverted)	5.00	4.00	1.50
G98				Green (wmk. reversed)	6.00	4.50	2.50
G99				Green (watermark inverted & reversed)	£30	£20	7.50
G100	–/10/12	4	**1d**	**Scarlet**	4.00	3.00	1.25
G101				Scarlet (no cross on crown)	£60	£45	£30
G102				Scarlet (imperforate)	£100	£75	£50
G103				Bright scarlet	6.00	4.00	2.00
G104				Deep bright scarlet	£25	£18	5.00
G105				Scarlet (watermark inverted)	8.00	6.50	4.50
G106				Scarlet (wmk. reversed)	8.00	6.50	4.50
G107				Scarlet (watermark inverted & reversed)	£450	£375	£100
G108				Scarlet (wmk. sideways)	£150	£125	£125

TYPOGRAPHIC DEFINITIVE ISSUES 1912 – 23

Printers: Harrison & Sons and Somerset House   *Perf:* 15 x 14   *Paper:* Ordinary except where marked (C) = chalky

★Used marked with an asterisk should only be purchased with a certificate.

No.	Issued	Type		Colour	U/M	M/M	F/U

Type 5	Type 6	Type 7	Type 8/9	Type 10	Type 11

WATERMARK: ROYAL CYPHER UPRIGHT

No.	Issued	Type		Colour	U/M	M/M	F/U
G109	–/–/13	5	½d	**Green**	15	10	10
G110				Bright green	15	10	10
G111				Deep green	3.00	2.00	1.50
G112				Pale green	3.00	2.00	1.50
G113				Deep bright green	3.00	2.00	1.50
G114				Yellow green	4.50	3.00	1.25
G115				Cobalt green	9.00	6.00	2.00
G116				Apple green	£10	7.50	3.50
G117				Blue green	£14	£11	5.00
G118				Pale olive green	£35	£27	£12
G119				Olive green	£35	£27	£12
G120				Bright yellow green	£40	£30	★
G121				Very pale green	£125	£100	★
G122				Deep cobalt green	£135	£110	★
G123				Very deep green	£125	£100	★
G124				Myrtle green	£150	£120	★
G125				Deep myrtle green	£350	£275	★
G126				Very yellow green	£3000	£2500	★
G127	–/10/12	6	1d	**Scarlet**	15	10	10
G128				Bright scarlet	15	10	10
G129				Bright scarlet			
				'Q' for 'O' var.	£225	£150	£75
G130				Vermilion	1.50	1.00	40
G131				Deep scarlet	3.00	2.00	55
G132				Pale red	7.50	6.00	£10
G133				Brick red	2.50	1.75	65
G134				Carmine red	3.75	2.25	1.00
G135				Deep bright scarlet	£10	7.50	2.00
G136				Pale rose red	6.00	4.00	1.50
G137				Bright carmine red	£10	7.50	2.50
G138				Deep brick red	£25	£17	3.00
G139				Deep carmine red	£75	£50	5.00
G140				Scarlet vermilion	£75	£50	5.00
G141				Orange vermilion	£125	£100	£30
G142				Pink	£200	£160	★
G143				Dp. or. vermilion	£220	£185	£75
G144	–/10/12	7	1½d	**Red brown**	50	35	10
G144A				Red/brown			
				"PENCF" Var.	£250	£175	£175
G145				Deep red brown	1.75	1.35	40
G146				Chestnut	1.25	85	35
G147				Chest. "PENCF" var.	£125	£100	£100
G148				Chocolate brown	1.50	1.00	40
G149				Orange brown	2.00	1.50	50
G150				Pale red brown	3.00	2.00	70
G151				Yellow brown	£10	7.50	50
G152				Bright yellow brown	£15	£10	3.50
G153				Bright chestnut	£40	£28	7.50
G154				Deep choc. brown	£20	£15	6.00
G155				Deep yellow brown	£25	£18	£12
G156				Bright orange brown	£35	£25	£15
G157				Chocolate	£150	£125	£40
G158				Very dp. red brown	£150	£125	£40
G159				Pale brown	£225	£175	★
G160				Brown	£325	£250	★
G161	–/8/12	8	2d	**Orange (Die I)**	50	35	20
G162				Bright orange	1.25	90	40
G163				Reddish orange	1.25	90	40
G164				Pale orange	1.50	1.10	55
G165				Deep bright orange	5.00	4.00	1.25
G166				Orange yellow	4.00	3.00	1.00
G167				Brown orange	£15	£10	2.50
G168				Dp. reddish orange	£50	£40	£15
G169				Intense bt. orange	£1450	£1100	★
G170	–/9/21	9	2d	**Orange (Die II)**	2.50	1.75	35
G171				Pale orange	3.00	2.00	75
G172				Deep orange	5.00	4.00	1.25
G173				Bright orange	3.00	2.00	1.00
G174	–/10/12	10	2½d	**Bright blue**	5.00	4.00	90
G175				French blue	£10	7.50	90
G176				Blue	5.00	4.00	90
G177				Cobalt blue	7.00	5.00	90
G178				Ultramarine	£10	7.50	1.50
G179				Deep blue	8.00	5.00	1.00
G180				Pale blue	8.00	5.00	1.00
G181				Dull blue	8.00	5.00	1.00
G182				Powder blue	9.00	6.00	1.25
G183				Milky blue	£20	£15	5.00
G184				Violet blue	£20	£15	5.00
G185				Cobalt violet blue	£20	£15	5.00
G186				Pale milky blue	£1350	£1000	★
G187				Deep bright blue	£225	£175	★
G188				Royal blue	£225	£175	★
G189				Indigo blue	£575	£485	★
G190				Dull prussian blue	£550	£475	★
G191	–/10/12	11	3d	**Violet**	2.50	1.75	45
G192				Bluish violet	3.50	2.25	60
G193				Pale violet	4.00	3.00	90
G194				Bright violet	4.00	3.00	90
G195				Dull violet	5.00	4.00	1.00
G196				Lavender violet	6.00	4.50	1.00
G197				Dull reddish violet	7.50	6.00	1.00
G198				Heliotrope	9.00	7.00	2.00
G199				Brownish violet	12.00	9.50	2.50
G200				Reddish violet	£10	7.50	2.00
G201				Very pale violet	£150	£120	★
G202				Very deep violet	£70	£50	6.00

TYPOGRAPHIC DEFINITIVES 1912 – 23 (continued)

Printers: Harrison & Sons and Somerset House   *Perf:* 15 x 14   *Paper:* Ordinary except where marked (C) = chalky

★Used marked with an asterisk should only be purchased with a certificate.

Type 12

Type 13

Type 14

Type 15

Type 16

Type 17

Type 18

Type 19

No.	Issued	Type		Colour	U/M	M/M	F/U
G203	–/1/13	12	**4d**	**Slate green**	3.00	2.00	45
G204				Grey green	3.00	2.00	45
G205				Pale grey green	6.00	4.00	55
G206				Pale slate green	6.00	4.00	55
G207				Deep grey green	£16	£12	3.00
G208				Deep slate green	£20	£15	3.50
G209				Bluish grey green	£18	£14	3.50
G210	–/6/13	13	**5d**	**Brown**	6.00	4.00	75
G211				Reddish brown	6.00	4.00	75
G212				Yellow brown	6.00	4.00	75
G213				Ginger brown	£15	£10	2.00
G214				Ochre brown	£35	£27	3.00
G215				Bistre brown	£90	£60	6.00
G216	–/8/13	14	**6d**	**Reddish purple** (C)	6.00	4.00	40
G217				Pl. redd. purple (C)	8.00	6.00	50
G218				Rosy mauve (C)	8.00	6.00	50
G219				Purple (C)	9.00	7.00	60
G220				Dp. redd. purple (C)	£10	7.50	75
G221				Plum (C)	£10	7.50	75
G222				Dull purple (C)	£12	8.00	1.50
G223				Slate purple (C)	£75	£50	8.00
G224	–/–/21	14	**6d**	**Reddish purple** (C)			
				Perf. 14	£90	£60	£25
G225	–/8/13	15	**7d**	**Olive**	£12	9.00	2.00
G226				Olive grey	£12	9.00	2.00
G227				Sage green	£30	£24	4.00
G228				Bronze green	£45	£30	6.00
G229	–/8/13	16	**8d**	**Black/yellow**	£50	£35	6.00
G230				Black/yellow buff			
				(granite paper)	£50	£35	6.00
G231	–/6/13	17	**9d**	**Agate**	£10	7.00	1.75
G232				Deep agate	£10	7.00	1.75
G233				Pale agate	£12	8.00	2.25
G234				Very deep agate	£250	£175	★
G235	–/9/22	17	**9d**	**Olive green**	£140	£110	8.50
G236				Pale olive green	£140	£110	8.50
G237				Deep olive green	£165	£115	£10
G238	–/8/13	18	**10d**	**Turquoise blue**	£20	£15	2.00
G239				Bright turquoise bl.	£22	£16	2.00
G240				Greenish blue	£20	£15	2.00
G241				Pale greenish blue	£20	£15	3.00
G242				Deep turquoise blue	£35	£28	4.00
G243	–/8/13	19	**1/–d**	**Bistre brown**	£15	£10	75
G244				Pale bistre brown	£20	£15	85
G245				Deep bistre brown	£20	£15	90
G246				Olive bistre	£25	£18	1.25
G247				Buff brown	£20	£15	1.25
G248				Pale olive bistre	£20	£15	1.25
G249				Olive brown	£20	£15	1.25
G250				Pale buff brown	£20	£15	1.25
G251				Fawn brown	£30	£20	2.50
G252				Deep bronze brown	£550	£425	★
				Set (One each of			
				14 values)	£125	£85	£15

TYPOGRAPHIC DEFINITIVES 1912 – 23 (continued)

Printers: Harrison & Sons and Somerset House Perf: 15 x 14 Paper: Ordinary except where marked (C) = chalky

*Used marked with an asterisk should only be purchased with a certificate.

No.	Type		Colour	U/M	M/M	F/U
WATERMARK: ROYAL CYPHER INVERTED						
N253	5	½d	Green	75	50	25
N254	6	1d	Scarlet	75	50	25
N255	7	1½d	Red brown	1.50	1.25	1.00
N256	8	2d	Orange (Die I)	8.00	6.00	4.00
N257	9	2d	Orange (Die II)	£14	9.50	6.50
N258	10	2½d	Blue	£20	£15	£12
N259	11	3d	Bluish violet	£25	£20	£15
N260	12	4d	Grey brown	£15	£10	£10
N261	13	5d	Brown	£175	£150	£150
N262	14	6d	Reddish purple (C)	£15	£10	£10
N263	15	7d	Olive	£25	£18	£18
N264	16	8d	Black/yellow	£75	£60	£60
N265	17	9d	Agate	£40	£30	£30
N266	17	9d	Olive green	£500	£400	£300
N267	18	10d	Turquoise blue	£175	£150	£150
N268	19	1/–d	Bistre brown	£50	£35	£35
WATERMARK: ROYAL CYPHER REVERSED						
N269	5	½d	Green	£12	9.00	5.00
N270	6	1d	Scarlet	£12	9.00	6.00
N271	7	1½d	Red brown	9.00	6.00	3.50
N272	8	2d	Orange (Die I)	£14	£10	6.00
N273	10	2½d	Blue	£15	£11	£10
N274	11	3d	Bluish violet	£40	£30	£25
N275	12	4d	Grey green	£25	£18	£15
N276	14	6d	Reddish purple (C)	£700	£600	£250
N277	16	8d	Black/yellow	£75	£50	£50
WATERMARK: ROYAL CYPHER INVERTED AND REVERSED						
N278	5	½d	Green	1.75	1.25	75
N279	6	1d	Scarlet	1.75	1.25	75
N280	7	1½d	Red brown	6.00	4.00	1.50
N281	8	2d	Orange (Die I)	8.00	6.00	2.00
N282	9	2d	Orange (Die II)	£20	£15	£10
N283	10	2½d	Blue	£15	£10	7.50
N284	11	3d	Bluish violet	£15	£10	£10
N285	12	4d	Grey green	£15	£10	£10
N286	13	5d	Brown	£100	£75	£75
N287	14	6d	Reddish purple (C)	£25	£18	£18
N288	16	8d	Black/yellow	£700	£575	£575
N289	17	9d	Agate	£40	£30	£30
N290	17	9d	Olive green	£500	£400	£400
N291	18	10d	Turquoise blue	£100	£80	£80
N292	19	1/–d	Bistre brown	£40	£30	£30

No.	Issued	Type		Colour	U/M	M/M	F/U
WITHOUT WATERMARK							
G293		5	½d	Green	£25	£20	£15
G294		6	1d	Scarlet	£28	£22	£18
G295		7	1½d	Chocolate brown	£100	£75	£35
G296		8	2d	Orange (Die I)	£50	£40	£30
G297		9	2d	Orange (Die II)	£200	£175	£90
G298		10	2½d	Blue	£300	£200	£100
G299		11	3d	Bluish violet	£135	£85	£80
G300		12	4d	Grey green	£125	£80	£75
G301		13	5d	Yellow brown	£400	£275	£275
G302		14	6d	Reddish purple (C)	£375	£285	£285
G303		15	7d	Olive	£200	£175	£135
G304		16	8d	Black/yellow	£650	£550	£550
G305		17	9d	Agate	£220	£180	£180
G306		19	1/–d	Bistre brown	£350	£285	£285
WATERMARK: MULTIPLE ROYAL CYPHER UPRIGHT							
G307	–/8/13	5	½d	**Green**	£170	£135	£75
G308				Bright green	£170	£135	£75
G309	–/8/13	6	1d	**Scarlet**	£335	£255	£150
G310				Dull scarlet	£335	£255	£150
				Set of 2 values	£475	£375	£200
WATERMARK: MULTIPLE ROYAL CYPHER INVERTED							
G311		5	½d	Green	£550	£400	£300
G312		6	1d	Scarlet	£550	£400	£300

Type 8 Die I
4 lines of shading between top of head and oval frame
Inner frame line not central

Type 9 Die II
Only 3 lines of shading
Inner frame line central

TYPOGRAPHIC DEFINITIVE ISSUES 1924 – 33

Printers: Harrison & Sons, Waterlow & Sons and Somerset House (6d value)   *Perf:* 15 x 14   *Paper:* Ordinary except where marked (C) = chalk

Multiple Block Cypher

WATERMARK: MULTIPLE BLOCK CYPHER UPRIGHT

No.	Issued	Type	Colour	U/M	M/M	F/U
G313	–/4/24	5	**½d** **Green**	20	15	5
G314			Pale green	60	40	15
G315			Bright green	20	15	5
G316			Deep green	1.00	75	20
G317			Deep bright green	3.00	2.00	25
G318			Yellow green	£15	£10	2.00
G319	–/4/24	6	**1d** **Scarlet**	20	15	5
G320			Pale scarlet	50	30	10
G321			Scarlet vermilion	50	30	15
G322			Deep scar. vermilion	5.00	4.00	1.50
G323			Scarlet (Experimental paper)	£25	£20	£12
G324			Scarlet (Inverted 'Q' for 'O' var.)	£275	£195	£125
G325	–/4/24	7	**1½d** **Red Brown**	40	30	5
G326			Yellow brown	50	35	10
G327			Deep red brown	1.00	75	15
G328			Orange brown	1.50	1.00	25
G329			Chestnut	1.50	1.00	25
G330			Bright chestnut	2.00	1.50	35
G331			Chocolate brown	3.25	2.75	40
G332			Deep yellow brown	2.25	1.75	40
G333			Bright yellow brown	2.50	1.85	55
G334			Pale red brown	£12	8.00	2.50
G335			Red brown (Experimental paper)	£80	£60	£50
G336			Red brown Tête-bêche pair	£300	£250	£190
G337			Red brown Tête-bêche pair w/gutter	£325	£275	£200
G338	–/4/24	9	**2d** **Orange** (Die II)	1.50	1.00	20
G339			Yellow orange	1.50	1.00	20
G340			Deep orange	3.00	2.00	40
G341			Pale yellow orange	4.00	3.00	55
G342			Deep yellow orange	7.00	5.00	75
G343	–/4/24	10	**2½d** **Blue**	5.00	3.50	35
G344			Pale blue	5.00	3.50	45
G345			Bright blue	£10	7.50	45
G346			Ultramarine	6.00	4.00	65
G347	–/4/24	11	**3d** **Violet**	6.00	4.00	35
G348			Pale violet	6.00	4.00	40
G349			Bright violet	9.00	6.00	40
G350			Deep violet	9.00	6.00	85
G351			Pale reddish violet	£12	8.00	1.00
G352			Deep brownish violet	£15	£10	2.00

No.	Issued	Type	Colour	U/M	M/M	F/U
G353	–/4/24	12	**4d** **Grey green**	£15	£10	40
G354			Deep grey green	£15	£10	40
G355			Very dp. grey green	£20	£15	2.50
G356	–/4/24	13	**5d** **Brown**	£18	£12	50
G357			Deep brown	£18	£12	50
G358			Reddish brown	£18	£14	75
G359			Bright ochre brown	£20	£15	85
G360			Deep ochre brown	£25	£18	1.00
G361	–/4/24	14	**6d** **Rosy mauve** (C)	£15	£10	60
G362			Plum (C)	£18	£12	75
G363	–/–/36		**6d** **Reddish purple** (C)	£15	£10	60
G364			Dp. redd. purple (C)	£18	£12	75
G365	–/–/26		**6d** **Rosy mauve**	5.00	3.50	20
G366			Reddish purple	5.00	3.50	20
G367			Pale rosy mauve	5.00	3.50	20
G368	–/–/34		**6d** **Purple**	5.00	3.50	20
G369			Deep reddish purple	6.00	4.00	30
G370			Deep purple	6.00	4.00	30
G371	–/4/24	17	**9d** **Olive green**	£15	£10	1.00
G372			Deep olive green	£16	£11	1.00
G373			Pale olive green	£18	£12	1.00
G374			Olive yellow green	£25	£18	1.50
G375	–/4/24	18	**10d** **Turquoise blue**	£55	£35	5.00
G376			Dl. greenish blue	£55	£35	5.50
G377			Dp. greenish blue	£60	£40	6.00
G378			Dp. dl. greenish blue	£60	£40	6.50
G379	–/4/24	19	**1/–d** **Bistre brown**	£35	£20	30
G380			Buff brown	£35	£20	30
G381			Fawn brown	£35	£20	30
G382			Pale buff brown	£35	£20	45
G383			Deep fawn brown	£55	£35	75
			Set (One each of 12 values)	£150	£100	7.50

WATERMARK: MULTIPLE BLOCK CYPHER INVERTED

No.	Type		Colour	U/M	M/M	F/U
G384	5	**½d**	Green	1.50	1.10	30
G385	6	**1d**	Scarlet	1.50	1.10	30
G386	7	**1½d**	Red brown	1.25	1.00	25
G387	9	**2d**	Orange (Die II)	£20	£15	8.00
G388	10	**2½d**	Blue	£25	£18	£18
G389	11	**3d**	Violet	£20	£15	£15
G390	12	**4d**	Grey green	£25	£18	£18
G391	13	**5d**	Brown	£30	£20	£20
G392	14	**6d**	Purple (C)	£20	£15	£15
G393	14	**6d**	Purple	£35	£25	£25
G394	17	**9d**	Olive green	£35	£25	£25
G395	18	**10d**	Turquoise blue	£1000	£750	£750
G396	19	**1/–d**	Bistre brown	£250	£175	£120

WATERMARK: MULTIPLE BLOCK CYPHER INVERTED & REVERSED

No.	Type		Colour	U/M	M/M	F/U
G397	14	**6d**	Purple (C)	£35	£25	£25

WATERMARK: MULTIPLE BLOCK CYPHER SIDEWAYS

No.	Type		Colour	U/M	M/M	F/U
G398	5	**½d**	Green	£14	8.50	2.50
G399	6	**1d**	Scarlet	£40	£25	6.00
G400	7	**1½d**	Red brown	£14	8.50	2.50
G401	9	**2d**	Orange (Die II)	£330	£185	£60
			Set of 4	£360	£200	£65

WITHOUT WATERMARK

No.	Type		Colour	U/M	M/M	F/U
G402	9	**2d**	Orange (Die II)	£300	£225	£225
G403	10	**2½d**	Blue	£350	£275	£275

PHOTOGRAVURE DEFINITIVE ISSUES 1934 – 36

Printers: Harrison & Sons Ltd.   *Perf:* 15 x 14   *Watermark:* Multiple Block Cypher

Type 20

Type 21

Type 22

Type 23

Type 24

Type 25

Type 26

Type 27

Type 28

Type 29   *Type 30*

No.	Issued	Type		Colour	U/M	M/M	F/U
LARGE FORMAT (18.6 x 22.5 mm) – WATERMARK UPRIGHT							
G404	24/9/34	21	**1d**	**Scarlet**	75	50	15
G405				Bright scarlet	75	50	15
G406	20/8/34	22	**1½d**	**Red brown**	65	45	10
G407				Bright red brown	65	45	10
LARGE FORMAT – WATERMARK INVERTED							
G408		21	**1d**	Scarlet	£75	£50	£25
G409		22	**1½d**	Red brown	£145	£95	£35
INTERMEDIATE FORMAT (18.3 x 22.2 mm) – WATERMARK UPRIGHT							
G410	19/11/34	20	**½d**	**Green**	35	25	5
G411				Bluish green	35	25	5
G412	–/–/34	21	**1d**	**Scarlet**	6.00	4.00	75
G413				Bright scarlet	6.00	4.00	75
G414				Pale scarlet	6.00	4.00	75
G415	–/–/34	22	**1½d**	**Red brown**	6.00	4.00	55
G416	21/1/35	23	**2d**	**Orange**	2.75	2.25	45
G417				Bright orange	2.75	2.25	45
INTERMEDIATE FORMAT – WATERMARK INVERT							
G418		20	**½d**	Green	£25	£18	6.00
G419		21	**1d**	Scarlet	£25	£18	6.00
G420		22	**1½d**	Red brown	£10	8.00	2.50
SMALL FORMAT (18.0 x 21.7 mm) – WATERMARK UPRIGHT							
G421	–/–/35	20	**½d**	**Green**	15	10	5
G422				Bluish green	15	10	5
G423	–/–/35	21	**1d**	**Scarlet**	15	10	5
G424				Bright scarlet	15	10	5
G425	–/–/35	22	**1½d**	Red brown	15	10	5
G426				Bright red brown	15	10	5
G427	–/–/35	23	**2d**	Orange	45	30	10
G428				Bright orange	45	30	10
G429	18/3/35	24	**2½d**	**Bright blue**	2.50	1.75	30
G430				Ultramarine	2.50	1.75	30
G431	18/3/35	25	**3d**	**Violet**	2.00	1.50	30
G432				Reddish violet	2.00	1.50	30
G433	2/12/35	26	**4d**	**Deep grey green**	2.00	1.50	30
G434				Blackish green	6.00	4.00	1.00
G435	17/2/36	27	**5d**	**Yellow brown**	8.00	6.00	50
G436				Deep yellow brown	8.00	6.00	50
G437	2/12/35	28	**9d**	**Deep olive green**	£20	£14	60
G438	24/2/36	29	**10d**	**Turquoise blue**	£38	£25	3.50
G439	24/2/36	30	**1/–d**	**Bistre brown**	£32	£20	50
				Set (One each of 11 values)	£100	£65	5.50
SMALL FORMAT – WATERMARK INVERTED							
G440		20	**½d**	Green	£10	7.50	1.25
G441		21	**1d**	Scarlet	£10	7.50	1.25
G442		22	**1½d**	Red brown	2.00	1.50	50
				Set of 3	£20	£15	2.65
SMALL FORMAT – WATERMARK SIDEWAYS							
G443		20	**½d**	Green	£30	£20	4.00
G444		21	**1d**	Scarlet	£40	£25	6.50
G445		22	**1½d**	Red brown	£10	7.50	3.50
G446		23	**2d**	Orange	£400	£275	£75
				Set of 4	£450	£300	£80

HIGH VALUE ENGRAVED ISSUES 1913 – 36

Printers: Various (as indicated) *Perf:* 11 x 12 *Watermark:* Royal Cypher Upright, except where shown

★Used marked with an asterisk should only be purchased with a certificate.

Type 31

Type 32

Type 33

Type 34

PRINTED BY WATERLOW BROS. & LAYTON

No.	Issued	Type		Colour	U/M	M/M	F/U
G447	–/7/13	31	**2/6d**	**Sepia brown**	£600	£400	£70
G448				Deep sepia brown	£650	£425	£80
G449	–/7/13	32	**5/–d**	**Carmine red**	£975	£775	£125
G450				Rose carmine	£975	£775	£125
G451				Pale rose carmine	£975	£775	£125
G452	–/7/13	33	**10/–d**	**Indigo blue**	£2000	£1500	£350
G453				Indigo	£2150	£1600	£360
G454	–/7/13	34	**£1**	**Dull blue green**	£5750	£4250	£1200
G455				Green	£5750	£4250	£1200
G456				Deep green	£6500	£5000	£1350

PRINTED BY DE LA RUE & CO.

No.	Issued	Type		Colour	U/M	M/M	F/U
G457	–/12/15	31	**2/6d**	**Pale brown**	£725	£500	£75
G458				Pl. brn. (worn plate)	£725	£500	£75
G459				Seal brown	£725	£500	£75
G460				Grey brown	£725	£500	£75
G461				Yellow brown	£775	£525	£80
G462				Pale yellow brown	£775	£525	£80
G463				Deep yellow brown	£775	£525	£80
G464				Bright yellow brown	£850	£600	£125
G465				Very deep brown	£2000	£1500	£600
G466				Blackish brown	£2000	£1500	£600
G467				Cinnamon brown	£2500	£1750	£700
G468	–/12/15	32	**5/–d**	**Bright carmine**	£1350	£850	£150
G469				Pl. car. (worn plate)	£1350	£850	£150
G470				Carmine	£1350	£850	£150
G471	–/12/15	33	**10/–d**	**Blue**	£5750	£4250	£325
G472				Pale blue	£5750	£4250	£325
G473				Deep blue	£6000	£4500	£325
G474				Dp. blue (worn plate)	£6250	£4750	£1400
G475				Deep bright blue	£7000	£5000	£1500
G476				Bt. Cambridge blue	£7500	£5200	£1600

DE LA RUE & CO – WATERMARK INVERTED

No.		Type		Colour	U/M	M/M	F/U
G477		31	**2/6d**	Pl. brn. (worn plate)	£1800	£1350	£750
G478				Yellow brown	£1750	£1250	£725
G479				Deep yellow brown	£1750	£1250	£725
G480				Seal brown	£1800	£1350	£750
G481				Very dp. brown	£3500	£2500	£1500
G482		32	**5/–d**	Carmine	£2700	£2000	£1250

DE LA RUE & CO – WATERMARK REVERSED

No.		Type		Colour	U/M	M/M	F/U
G483		31	**2/6d**	Yellow brown	£1500	£1200	£600
G484				Pl. brn. (worn plate)	£1600	£1300	£675
G485				Seal brown	£1600	£1300	£675
G486		32	**5/–d**	Carmine	£2600	£2000	£1200

DE LA RUE & CO – WATERMARK INVERTED & REVERSED

No.		Type		Colour	U/M	M/M	F/U
G487		32	**5/–d**	Carmine	£3500	£2750	£1500

DE LA RUE & CO – WITHOUT WATERMARK

No.		Type		Colour	U/M	M/M	F/U
G488		32	**5/–d**	Carmine	£2750	£2000	£1400

PRINTED BY BRADBURY WILKINSON & CO.

No.	Issued	Type		Colour	U/M	M/M	F/U
G489	–/12/18	31	**2/6d**	Olive brown	£450	£300	£15
G490				Chocolate brown	£450	£300	£15
G491				Pale brown	£450	£300	£15
G492				Reddish brown	£450	£300	£15
G493	–/12/18	32	**5/–d**	Rose red	£650	£475	£30
G494				Rose carmine	£650	£475	£30
G495	–/–/18	33	**10/–d**	Dull blue	£1500	£975	£110
G496				Dull grey blue	£1500	£975	£110
				Set of 3 values	£2500	£1600	£135

RE-ENGRAVED – PRINTED BY WATERLOW & SONS

No.	Issued	Type		Colour	U/M	M/M	F/U
G497	–/10/34	31	**2/6d**	Chocolate brown	£375	£275	7.50
G498				Reddish brown	£400	£300	7.50
G499	–/10/34	32	**5/–d**	Bright rose red	£600	£400	£25
G500	–/10/34	33	**10/–d**	Indigo	£1250	£850	£25
				Set of 3 values	£2000	£1200	£60

"SEAHORSES" – GUIDE NOTES TO ASSIST IDENTIFICATION

Four printings were used during the issue and major problems only arise when trying to differentiate between the first Waterlow printings and the De La Rue issue.

Bradbury Wilkinson printings were of a different size to any of the others. The stamps being 22.5 to 23mm in height as against the 22mm of the other two printers. On many occasions they also printed a small coloured guide dot centred between the top frame line and the top of the stamp.

The second Waterlow printing was re-engraved, the most obvious difference being the crossed lines behind the head.

When sorting Seahorses we suggest the following steps be taken:-

1st Step.   Check for crossed line behind head, all those with this printing are re-engraved Waterlow.

2nd Step.   Measure the height of the remaining stamps, all those which measure between 22.5 and 23mm are Bradbury Wilkinson.

This then leaves us with either Waterlow or De La Rue.

The chart below should help collectors in sorting out the first Waterlow and De La Rue printings.

	WATERLOW	**DE LA RUE**
Paper		
All Values	Usually toned	White
Gum	White or Pale Yellowish **evenly** applied	Streaky & Yellowish
Perfs	Teeth evenly spaced	Upper teeth both sides are wider than the rest. Holes are always smaller and undulating.
Colours		
Values 2/6	Sepia to Deep Sepia	Yellow brown shades *Pale to Dark Brown Cinnamon Grey Brown
5/–	Rose Carmine shades Colours do not show through	*Pale Carmine to Deep. Colour invariably shows through.
10/–	Indigo Blue shades	Pale Blue to Deep Blue Intense Blue "Cambridge" Blue
£1	Green to Deep Green Bluish Green	–

*The pale shades were caused mainly by plate wear and are quite distinct.

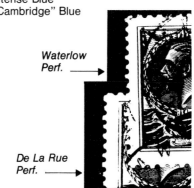

Waterlow Perf. ⟶

De La Rue Perf. ⟶

COMMEMORATIVE ISSUES 1924 – 35

Printers: Various (as indicated)   *Perf:* 15 x 14   *Watermark: Multiple Block Cypher Upright (except where shown)*

No.	Type	Colour	U/M	M/M	F/U	No.	Type	Colour	U/M	M/M	F/U

Type 38   Type 39

Type 40   Type 41

BRITISH EMPIRE EXHIBITION Issued 23/4/24
Recess printed by Waterlow & Sons
PERF. 14

No.		Type	Colour	U/M	M/M	F/U
G501	38	**1d**	Scarlet	£15	8.00	7.00
G502	39	**1½d**	Brown	£23	£14	£11
			Set of 2	£35	£20	£17
			First Day Cover			£200

Issued 9/5/25

G503	40	**1d**	Scarlet	£35	£20	£18
G504	41	**1½d**	Brown	£130	£90	£80
			Set of 2	£155	£100	£90
			First Day Cover			£450

Type 42

Type 43

Type 44

Type 45

Type 46

POSTAL UNION CONGRESS Issued 10/5/29
Typograph printed by Waterlow & Sons

G505	42	**½d**	Green	4.75	3.25	25
G506	43	**1d**	Scarlet	4.25	3.00	75
G507	44	**1½d**	Purple brown	2.00	1.50	25
G508	45	**2½d**	Blue	£33	£20	5.50
G509	45		Pale blue	£36	£22	6.50
			Set of 4	£40	£25	6.00
			First Day Cover			£225

Watermark Large Royal Cypher
Recess printed by Bradbury, Wilkinson & Co.
Perf. 12

G510	46	**£1**	Black	£2500	£1500	£1000
			First Day Cover			£3000

Watermark Inverted

G511	42	**½d**	Green	£10	7.50	7.50
G512	43	**1d**	Scarlet	£20	£15	£15
G513	44	**1½d**	Purple brown	8.00	6.00	6.00
G514	45	**2½d**	Blue	£650	£500	£350
G515	45		Pale blue	£750	£550	£375
			Set of 3 – (G511/2/3)	£35	£25	£25

Watermark Sideways

G516	42	**½d**	Green	£90	£60	£30
G517	43	**1d**	Scarlet	£160	£115	£55
G518	44	**1½d**	Purple brown	£75	£45	£25
			Set of 3	£300	£200	£100

COMMEMORATIVE ISSUES 1925 – 35 (cont.)

Watermark: Multiple Block Cypher

DEFINITIVE ISSUE 1936 – 37

Printers: Harrison & Sons   *Perf:* 15 x 14   *Watermark:* E8R Upright

Type 47

Type 48

Type 1

Type 49

Type 50

Type 3

Type 2

No.	Type		Colour	U/M	M/M	F/U
SILVER JUBILEE Issued 7/5/35						
Printed by Harrison & Sons in Photogravure						
G519	47	½d	Green (I)	10	8	5
G520			Green (III)	2.75	2.00	1.50
G521	48	1d	Scarlet (I)	85	60	40
G522			Scarlet (III)	4.00	3.00	2.00
G523	49	1½d	Red brown (I)	65	40	10
G524			Red brown (III)	2.25	1.75	1.25
G525	50	2½d	Blue	8.00	5.50	4.75
G526		2½d	Prussian blue	£5750	£3750	£3000
			Set of 4	9.00	6.00	5.00
			First Day Cover			£125

Watermark Inverted

No.	Type		Colour	U/M	M/M	F/U
G527	47	½d	Green (II)	4.00	3.00	1.75
G528	48	1d	Scarlet (II)	5.00	4.00	3.25
G529	49	1½d	Red brown (II)	2.00	1.50	1.00
			Set of 3	£10	7.75	5.50

SILVER JUBILEE ISSUE

There are three types of the ½d, 1d and 1½d values. The first type is from the sheet printing and the other two from booklets.

Type I	Ex sheets	Upright watermark.
Type II	Ex booklet	All with inverted watermark.
Type III	Ex booklet	Upright watermark.

½d Type I – the 'FPE' of "halfpenny" is shaded throughout whereas in Type III it is shaded at the bottom and solid at the top; the two lines underneath "halfpenny" are also noticeably thinner on the booklet printing.

1d Type I & Type III – are the most difficult to differentiate and although the shading within the crown on the right is deeper in Type III, the easiest method of distinguishing Type III is to check the perforations to see if they have been cut straight on either the top or bottom, proving that they are from booklets.

1½d Type I – the two lines above "Silver Jubilee" are evenly printed whereas in Type III there is a definite thickening of the frame line above "JU".

Type 4

No. | Issued | Type | Colour | U/M | F/U

No.	Issued	Type		Colour	U/M	F/U
ED1	1/9/36	1	½d	Green	5	5
ED2	14/9/36	2	1d	Scarlet	10	5
ED3	1/9/36	3	1½d	Red brown	5	5
ED4	1/9/36	4	2½d	Bright blue	45	40
				Set of 4	60	50

WATERMARK: INVERTED

No.		Type		Colour	U/M	F/U
ED5		1	½d	Green	4.25	75
ED6		2	1d	Scarlet	6.00	3.00
ED7		3	1½d	Red brown	3.25	1.00
				Set of 3	£13	4.25

LOW VALUE DEFINITIVE ISSUES 1937 – 52

Printers: Harrison & Sons in Photogravure　　　*Perf:* 15 x 14　　　*Watermark: Multiple GvıR and Crown*

Type 1

Type 2

Type 3

Type 4

Type 5

Type 6

Type 7

Type 8

Type 9

Type 10

Type 11

Type 12

Type 13

Type 14

Type 15

LOW VALUE DEFINITIVE ISSUES 1937 – 52

Printers: Harrison & Sons in Photogravure   *Perf:* 15 x 14   *Watermark: GᵥᵢR and Crown*

The basis for the prices quoted in this period are as follows:–

Unmounted Mint (U/M)   Full original gum, full perforations plus good centring and colour.
Mounted Mint (M/M)   Lightly hinged and otherwise as above.
Fine Used (F/U)   Clean and light cancel, with full perforations plus good centring and colour.

ORIGINAL COLOURS

No.	Issued	Type		Colour	U/M	M/M	F/U
WATERMARK UPRIGHT							
B1	10/5/37	1	½d	Green	10	5	5
B2	10/5/37	2	1d	Scarlet	10	5	5
B3	30/7/37	3	1½d	Red brown	10	5	5
B4	31/1/38	4	2d	Orange	75	40	10
B5	10/5/37	5	2½d	Ultramarine	45	25	5
B6	31/1/38	6	3d	Violet	2.50	1.50	25
B7	21/11/38	7	4d	Grey green	75	40	20
B8	21/11/38	8	5d	Brown	3.50	2.00	40
B9	30/1/39	9	6d	Purple	2.00	1.25	15
B10	27/2/39	10	7d	Emerald green	4.50	2.75	35
B11	27/2/39	11	8d	Carmine	7.50	4.25	45
B12	1/5/39	12	9d	Olive green	5.00	2.75	20
B13	1/5/39	13	10d	Turquoise blue	6.00	3.50	45
B14	29/12/47	14	11d	Plum	5.50	3.00	75
B15	1/5/39	15	1/–d	Bistre brown	6.50	4.00	15
				Set of 15	£40	£25	3.25
WATERMARK INVERTED							
B16		1	½d	Green	2.00	1.00	50
B17		2	1d	Scarlet	£55	£28	5.50
B18		3	1½d	Red brown	2.50	1.50	50
B19		4	2d	Orange	£75	£38	7.00
B20		5	2½d	Ultramarine	£50	£25	5.00
				Set of 5	£165	£85	£16
WATERMARK SIDEWAYS							
B21		1	½d	Green	55	25	50
B22		2	1d	Scarlet	5.50	3.50	3.00
B23		3	1½d	Red brown	1.10	65	50
B24		4	2d	Orange	£40	£25	£18
B25		5	2½d	Ultramarine	£62	£38	£25
				Set of 5	£100	£60	£45

NEW PALE SHADES

No.	Issued	Type		Colour	U/M	M/M	F/U
WATERMARK UPRIGHT							
B26	1/9/41	1	½d	Pale green	10	5	5
B27	11/8/41	2	1d	Pale scarlet	25	15	10
B28	28/9/42	3	1½d	Pale red brown	75	50	25
B29	6/10/41	4	2d	Pale orange	75	50	25
B30	21/7/41	5	2½d	Light ultramarine	50	30	15
B31	3/11/41	6	3d	Pale violet	2.00	1.25	30
				Set of 6	4.00	2.50	1.00
WATERMARK INVERTED							
B32		1	½d	Pale green	3.00	1.75	75
B33		4	2d	Pale orange	6.00	3.50	1.75
B34		5	2½d	Light ultramarine	4.00	2.45	1.25
				Set of 3	£12	7.00	3.50
WATERMARK SIDEWAYS							
B35		2	1d	Pale scarlet	6.00	3.25	2.00
B36		4	2d	Pale orange	£15	8.00	6.00
B37		5	2½d	Light ultramarine	£12	6.25	4.00
				Set of 3	£30	£16	£11

NEW COLOURS

No.	Issued	Type		Colour	U/M	M/M	F/U
WATERMARK UPRIGHT							
B38	3/5/51	1	½d	Pale orange	15	10	5
B39	3/5/51	2	1d	Light ultramarine	15	10	5
B40	3/5/51	3	1½d	Pale green	75	45	25
B41	3/5/51	4	2d	Pale red brown	1.25	70	25
B42				Bright red brown	1.50	85	35
B43	3/5/51	5	2½d	Scarlet	50	30	10
B44	2/10/50	7	4d	Light ultramarine	2.00	1.25	35
				Set of 6			
				(excluding B42)	4.00	2.50	1.00
WATERMARK INVERTED							
B45		1	½d	Pale orange	20	15	10
B46		2	1d	Light ultramarine	2.75	1.65	1.00
B47		3	1½d	Pale green	2.50	1.50	75
B48		4	2d	Red brown	6.50	3.50	2.00
B49		5	2½d	Scarlet	1.25	75	50
				Set of 5	£12	7.00	4.00
WATERMARK SIDEWAYS							
B50		2	1d	Light ultramarine	20	15	10
B51		3	1½d	Pale green	2.00	1.20	1.00
B52		4	2d	Red brown	1.00	60	50
B53		5	2½d	Scarlet	1.20	75	60
				Set of 4	4.00	2.50	2.00

ɘGᵥᵢRɛ
ıR⏥Gı
ɘGᵥᵢRɛ

Watermark

HIGH VALUE DEFINITIVE ISSUES 1939 – 52

Recess Printed: Waterlow & Sons   *Watermark:* Multiple GviR and Crown

No.	Issued	Type	Colour	U/M	M/M	F/U

Type 16

Type 17

Type 18

Type 19

PERF. 14

No.	Issued	Type	Value	Colour	U/M	M/M	F/U
B54	4/9/39	16	**2/6d**	Brown	£110	£75	7.00
B55	9/3/42	16	**2/6d**	Yellow green	£12	8.00	35
B56	21/8/39	17	**5/–d**	Red	£25	£15	65
B57	30/10/39	18	**10/–d**	Dark blue	£210	£135	£18
B58				Steel blue	£235	£145	£20
B59	30/11/42	18	**10/–d**	Ultramarine	£35	£25	2.00
B60	1/10/48	19	**£1**	Brown	£50	£35	£20
				Set of 6			
				(excluding B58)	£400	£250	£42

Watermark

No.		Type	Colour	U/M	M/M	F/U

Type 20

Type 21

Type 22

Type 23

WATERMARK UPRIGHT

NEW DESIGNS AND FORMAT Issued 3/5/51
PERF. 11 x 12

No.	Type	Value	Colour	U/M	M/M	F/U
B61	20	**2/6d**	Yellow green	£10	5.00	25
B62	21	**5/–d**	Red	£45	£25	75
B63	22	**10/–d**	Ultramarine	£20	£10	5.00
B64	23	**£1**	Brown	£90	£45	£15
			Set of 4	£150	£75	£20

COMMEMORATIVE ISSUES 1937 – 52

Printers: Harrison & Sons in Photogravure   *Perf:* 15 x 14 (except where shown)   *Watermark:* Multiple GvIR and Crown

No.	Type		Colour	U/M	M/M	F/U

Type 24

Type 31

CORONATION Issued 13/5/37

No.	Type		Colour	U/M	M/M	F/U
B65	24	**1½d**	Maroon	12	8	5
			First Day Cover			3.75

Type 32

Type 25

VICTORY Issued 11/6/46

No.	Type		Colour	U/M	M/M	F/U
B72	31	**2½d**	Ultramarine	10	8	5
B73	32	**3d**	Violet	10	8	5
			Set of 2	20	15	10
			First Day Cover			2.50

Type 25

Type 26

Type 27

Type 28

Type 33

Type 25, Type 26, Type 27, Type 28, Type 29, Type 30

Type 29   *Type 30*

Type 34

CENTENARY OF FIRST ADHESIVE POSTAGE STAMPS
PERF. 14½ x 14 Issued 6/5/40

No.	Type		Colour	U/M	M/M	F/U
B66	25	**½d**	Green	20	12	5
B67	26	**1d**	Scarlet	30	20	10
B68	27	**1½d**	Red brown	50	35	15
B69	28	**2d**	Orange	30	20	10
B70	29	**2½d**	Ultramarine	70	45	25
B71	30	**3d**	Violet	5.25	4.00	3.75
			Set of 6	6.50	4.50	4.00
			First Day Cover			£10

SILVER WEDDING Issued 26/4/48

No.	Type		Colour	U/M	M/M	F/U
B74	33	**2½d**	Ultramarine	10	8	5
B75	34	**£1**	Blue (Perf. 14 x 15)	£80	£55	£55
			First Day Cover			£200

COMMEMORATIVE ISSUES 1937 – 52 (continued)

Printers: Harrison & Sons in Photogravure   *Perf:* 15 x 14 (except where shown)   *Watermark:* Multiple GvıR and Crown

No.	Type		Colour	U/M	M/M	F/U

Type 35

Type 41

Type 42

Type 36

Type 43

Type 44

CHANNEL ISLANDS LIBERATION Issued 10/5/48

No.	Type		Colour	U/M	M/M	F/U
B76	35	**1d**	Scarlet	25	15	10
B77	36	**2½d**	Ultramarine	30	25	25
			Set of 2	50	35	30
			First Day Cover			
			(Channel Islands Postmark)			5.00

UNIVERSAL POSTAL UNION Issued 10/10/49

No.	Type		Colour	U/M	M/M	F/U
B82	41	**2½d**	Ultramarine	20	10	10
B83	42	**3d**	Violet	50	30	30
B84	43	**6d**	Bright purple	70	50	50
B85	44	**1/–d**	Brown	1.90	1.40	1.40
			Set of 4	3.00	2.00	2.00
			First Day Cover			8.50

Type 37

Type 38

Type 39

Type 40

Type 45

Type 46

OLYMPIC GAMES Issued 29/7/48

No.	Type		Colour	U/M	M/M	F/U
B78	37	**2½d**	Ultramarine	20	15	10
B79	38	**3d**	Violet	50	30	30
B80	39	**6d**	Bright purple	70	50	50
B81	40	**1/–d**	Brown	1.30	1.00	1.00
			Set of 4	2.50	1.75	1.70
			First Day Cover			6.75

FESTIVAL OF BRITAIN Issued 3/5/51

No.	Type		Colour	U/M	M/M	F/U
B86	45	**2½d**	Scarlet	15	10	10
B87	46	**4d**	Ultramarine	25	15	15
			Set of 2	35	25	25
			First Day Cover			2.75

WILDING LOW VALUE DEFINITIVES 1952 – 67

Printers: Harrison & Sons in Photogravure   *Perf:* 15 x 14

Type 1   Type 2   Type 3   Type 4

Type 5   Type 6   Type 7   Type 8

Type 9   Type 10   Type 11

Type 12   Type 13   Type 14   Type 15

Type 16   Type 17   Type 18

Many G.B. collectors, and particularly the younger ones have restricted their collections to this modern period, and the scope for specialisation is enormous and still growing.

Both the Wilding and the Machin definitives have provided a very rich field for all these enthusiasts. The combination of watermarks, graphite lines and phosphor bands in the Wilding, and now the increasing complexity of papers, gums, and phosphor bands in the Machin issues, gives great scope to the specialist. Particularly in the Machin listings, this catalogue has separated the different paper/gum combinations, and the collector will require a good ultra-violet lamp to be sure of the differences between OCP and FCP. The missing phosphor varieties are not listed as these are all "errors".

Prices have been based on the following conditions:—

Unmounted Mint (U/M)   Full original gum, full perforations, plus good centring.

Mounted Mint (M/M)   Lightly hinged and otherwise as above.

Fine Used (F/U)   Very light and clean cancel, full perforations, good centring and colour.

WILDING LOW VALUE DEFINITIVES 1952 – 57

Printers: Harrison & Sons in Photogravure
Perf: 15 x 14

Tudor Crown

St. Edward's Crown

TUDOR ISSUE

No.	Issued	Type	Colour	U/M	M/M	F/U
WATERMARK: TUDOR CROWN UPRIGHT						
W1	31/8/53	1	½d Orange red	10	5	5
W2	31/8/53	2	1d Dp. ultramarine	10	5	5
W3	5/12/52	3	1½d Green	10	5	5
W4			Deep green	2.00	65	1.00
W5	31/8/53	4	2d Red brown	45	15	10
W6	5/12/52	5	2½d Carmine red (Type I)	15	5	5
W7	–/5/53	5	2½d Carmine red (Type II)	50	20	20
W8	18/1/54	6	3d Deep violet	60	20	10
W9	2/11/53	7	4d Ultramarine	1.00	35	30
W10	6/7/53	9	5d Brown	1.00	35	75
W11	18/1/54	10	6d Red purple	2.00	60	30
W12	18/1/54	11	7d Pastel green	3.30	1.10	2.00
W13	6/7/53	12	8d Cerise	1.20	40	60
W14	8/2/54	13	9d Greyish green	£22	7.50	60
W15	8/2/54	14	10d Deep blue	£12	4.00	1.00
W16	8/2/54	15	11d Yellowish brown	£32	£11	5.00
W17	6/7/53	16	1/–d Bistre brown	1.50	50	20
W18	2/11/53	17	1/3d Deep green	2.70	90	30
W19	2/11/53	18	1/6d Grey blue	£26	8.50	60
			Set of 17 values	£95	£33	£10
WATERMARK: TUDOR CROWN INVERTED						
W20	–/3/54	1	½d Orange red	20	10	25
W21	–/3/54	2	1d Dp. ultramarine	2.75	1.00	1.00
W22	–/5/53	3	1½d Green	25	10	25
W23	–/3/54	4	2d Red brown	£24	8.50	£10
W24	–/5/53	5	2½d Carmine red (Type II)	30	10	25
			Set of 5	£25	9.50	£11
WATERMARK: TUDOR CROWN SIDEWAYS						
W25	15/10/54	3	1½d Green	25	15	30
W26	8/10/54	4	2d Red brown	50	35	35
W27	15/11/54	5	2½d Carmine red (Type I)	3.00	2.00	1.80
			Set of 3	3.50	2.25	2.25

EDWARD ISSUE

No.	Issued	Type	Colour	U/M	M/M	F/U
WATERMARK: ST. EDWARD'S CROWN UPRIGHT						
W28	–/9/55	1	½d Orange red	10	5	5
W29	19/9/55	2	1d Dp. ultramarine	10	5	5
W30	–/9/55	3	1½d Green	10	5	5
W31			Deep green	35	15	10
W32	6/9/55	4	2d Red brown	30	10	10
W33	17/10/56	4	2d Light red brown	20	10	5
W34	28/9/55	5	2½d Carmine red (Type I)	15	10	5
W35	–/9/55	5	2½d Carmine red (Type II)	25	15	20
W36	17/7/56	6	3d Deep violet	15	10	5
W37	14/11/55	7	4d Ultramarine	1.45	50	20
W38	21/9/55	9	5d Brown	2.50	1.00	1.50
W39	20/12/55	10	6d Red purple	3.00	1.00	30
W40	8/5/58	10	6d Claret	1.80	60	40
W41	23/4/56	11	7d Pastel green	£48	£16	3.00
W42	21/12/55	12	8d Cerise	5.50	2.00	50
W43	15/12/55	13	9d Greyish green	£20	7.00	50
W44	22/9/55	14	10d Deep blue	£15	5.00	75
W45	28/10/55	15	11d Yellowish brown	75	25	1.00
W46	3/11/55	16	1/–d Bistre brown	8.50	3.00	25
W47	27/3/56	17	1/3d Deep green	£36	£12	30
W48	27/3/56	18	1/6d Grey blue	£36	£12	45
			Set of 17 values	£160	£55	8.50
WATERMARK: ST. EDWARD'S CROWN INVERTED						
W49	–/9/55	1	½d Orange red	35	20	30
W50	–/9/55	2	1d Dp. ultramarine	85	50	75
W51	–/9/55	3	1½d Green	45	25	40
W52	–/9/55	4	2d Red brown	9.00	5.00	3.75
W53	–/1/57	4	2d Light red brown	2.00	1.15	1.00
W54	–/9/55	5	2½d Carmine red (Type II)	40	25	35
W55	1/10/57	6	3d Deep violet	1.75	1.00	75
			Set of 7	£13	7.75	6.75
WATERMARK: ST. EDWARD'S CROWN SIDEWAYS						
W56	7/3/56	3	1½d Green	30	15	20
W57	31/7/56	4	2d Red brown	60	30	35
W58	5/3/57	4	2d Light red brown	1.25	70	1.10
W59	23/3/56	5	2½d Carmine red (Type I)	1.20	65	75
W60	9/12/57	6	3d Deep violet	£11	6.00	6.00
			Set of 5	12.50	7.00	7.50

WILDING LOW VALUE DEFINITIVES 1957 – 65

Printers: Harrison & Sons in Photogravure   *Perf:* 15 x 14   (C) = chalky paper

No.	Issued	Type	Colour	U/M	M/M	F/U

GRAPHITE LINED ISSUE

Two vertical graphite lines on back under gum, except 2d value with one line only.
This experimental issue was introduced in the Southampton postal area in connection with an automatic letter facing machine.

WATERMARK: ST. EDWARD'S CROWN UPRIGHT

No.	Issued	Type		Colour	U/M	M/M	F/U
W61	19/11/57	1	½d	Orange red	25	10	20
W62		2	1d	Dp. ultramarine	30	15	25
W63		3	1½d	Green	75	35	65
W64		4	2d	Light red brown	2.00	65	65
W65		5	2½d	Carmine red (Type II)	8.00	4.00	4.50
W66		6	3d	Deep Violet	1.75	75	30
				Set of 6	£12	5.50	6.00

2½d Type I
Frame of centre cross is weak

2½d Type II
Frame is strengthened

Multiple Crowns

CROWNS ISSUE

WATERMARK: MULTIPLE CROWNS UPRIGHT

No.	Issued	Type		Colour	U/M	M/M	F/U
W67	25/11/58	1	½d	Orange red	5	5	5
W68	15/7/63	1	½d	Orange red (C)	1.75	1.15	1.75
W69	–/11/58	2	1d	Dp. ultramarine	5	5	5
W70	–/12/58	3	1½d	Green	5	5	5
W71				Deep green	20	15	10
W72	4/12/58	4	2d	Light red brown	5	5	5
W73	11/9/59	5	2½d	Carmine red (Type I)	30	20	5
W74	4/10/61	5	2½d	Carmine red (Type II)	10	5	10
W75	15/7/63	5	2½d	Carmine red (C) (Type II)	25	15	25
W76	8/12/58	6	3d	Deep violet	15	10	5
W77	29/10/58	7	4d	Ultramarine	45	30	15
W78	28/4/65	7	4d	Dp. ultramarine	20	15	5
W79	9/2/59	8	4½d	Chestnut red	10	5	10
W80	10/11/58	9	5d	Brown	40	25	20
W81	23/12/58	10	6d	Claret	40	25	5
W82	26/11/58	11	7d	Pastel green	75	50	10
W83	24/2/60	12	8d	Cerise	40	25	10
W84	24/3/59	13	9d	Greyish green	60	40	10
W85	18/11/58	14	10d	Deep blue	60	40	15
W86	30/10/58	16	1/–d	Bistre brown	45	30	5
W87	17/6/59	17	1/3d	Deep green	1.00	65	10
W88	16/12/58	18	1/6d	Grey blue	3.50	2.35	10
				Set of 17 values	8.00	5.30	1.25

WATERMARK: MULTIPLE CROWNS INVERTED

No.	Issued	Type		Colour	U/M	M/M	F/U
W89	–/11/58	1	½d	Orange red	25	15	10
W90	15/7/63	1	½d	Orange red (C)	1.75	1.15	1.25
W91	–/11/58	2	1d	Dp. ultramarine	40	25	15
W92	–/12/58	3	1½d	Green	75	50	30
W93	10/4/61	4	2d	Light red brown	£55	£30	£27
W94	–/11/58	5	2½d	Carmine red (Type I)	1.50	1.00	75
W95	15/7/63	5	2½d	Carmine red (C) (Type II)	25	15	20
W96	–/11/58	6	3d	Deep violet	20	15	15
W97	21/6/65	7	4d	Dp. ultramarine	30	20	15
				Set of 9	£57	£32	£28

WATERMARK: MULTIPLE CROWNS SIDEWAYS

No.	Issued	Type		Colour	U/M	M/M	F/U
W98	26/5/61	1	½d	Orange red	15	10	15
W99	26/5/61	2	1d	Dp. ultramarine	40	25	25
W100	26/5/61	3	1½d	Green	5.50	3.80	3.50
W101	3/4/59	4	2d	Light red brown	35	25	25
W102	10/11/60	5	2½d	Carmine red (Type I)	15	10	20
W103	1/7/64	5	2½d	Carmine red (Type II)	50	35	35
W104	24/10/58	6	3d	Deep violet	20	15	15
W105	31/5/65	7	4d	Dp. ultramarine	25	15	15
				Set of 8	6.75	4.50	4.50

Presentation Pack

	1960		18 stamps – includes 11d (W45)	£45		

(C) These chalky paper varieties originate from booklets only.

WILDING LOW VALUE DEFINITIVES 1958 – 67

Printers: Harrison & Sons in Photogravure *Perf:* 15 x 14 (C) = chalky paper

No.	Issued	Type	Colour	U/M	M/M	F/U

GRAPHITE LINED ISSUE

Two vertical graphite lines on back under gum, except 2d value with one line only.

WATERMARK: MULTIPLE CROWNS UPRIGHT

No.	Issued	Type	Colour	U/M	M/M	F/U
W106	16/6/59	1	½d	Orange red	2.25	1.30	1.30
W107	18/12/58	2	1d	Dp. ultramarine	1.10	65	65
W108	4/8/59★	3	1½d	Green	£85	£50	£50
W109	24/11/58	4	2d	Light red brown	4.50	2.75	2.00
W110	9/6/59	5	2½d	Carmine red (Type !!)	9.00	5.75	5.75
W111	24/11/58	6	3d	Deep violet	55	35	35
W112	29/4/59	7	4d	Ultramarine	3.75	2.25	2.75
W113	3/6/59	8	4½d	Chestnut red	3.75	2.25	2.75
				Set of 8	£100	£60	£60

WATERMARK: MULTIPLE CROWNS INVERTED

No.	Issued	Type	Colour	U/M	M/M	F/U
W114	4/8/59	1	½d	Orange red	2.00	80	1.25
W115		2	1d	Dp. ultramarine	85	35	65
W116	★	3	1½d	Green	£31	£13	£13
W117		5	2½d	Carmine red (Type II)	£55	£25	£25
W118		6	3d	Deep violet	40	20	35
				Set of 5	£85	£35	£35

★These stamps are from booklets only and the price quoted is for good perforations all round. Clipped perforations can be purchased at a considerable discount.

PHOSPHOR – GRAPHITE ISSUE

Two phosphor bands on face and two graphite lines on back, except 2d value with 1 band and 1 line.

This further experimental issue was also introduced in the Southampton postal area, the phosphor bands serving the same purpose as the graphite lines to facilitate automatic letter facing.

WATERMARK: ST. EDWARD'S CROWN UPRIGHT

No.	Issued	Type	Colour	U/M	M/M	F/U
W119	18/11/59	1	½d	Orange red	2.00	1.35	1.65
W120		2	1d	Deep ultramarine	2.50	1.70	1.80
W121		3	1½d	Green	2.00	1.35	2.00
W122		4	2d	Light red brown	£325	£165	£150

WATERMARK: MULTIPLE CROWNS UPRIGHT

No.	Issued	Type	Colour	U/M	M/M	F/U
W123	18/11/59	4	2d	Light red brown	3.00	2.00	2.25
W124		5	2½d	Carmine red (Type II)	£11	7.50	8.00
W125		6	3d	Deep violet	£15	£10	2.50
W126		7	4d	Ultramarine	5.00	3.50	5.00
W127		8	4½d	Chestnut red	£60	£40	£20
				Set of 8	£95	£62	£38
				(excludes W122)			

Presentation Pack

1960			16 stamps includes 2	£200		
			each Nos. W119–121			
			and Nos. W123–127.			

PHOSPHOR ISSUE

WATERMARK: MULTIPLE CROWNS UPRIGHT

Two phosphor bands on face, except where otherwise stated.

No.	Issued	Type	Colour	U/M	M/M	F/U
W128	22/6/60	1	½d	Orange red	10	5	10
W129	22/6/60	2	1d	Dp. ultramarine	10	5	5
W130	22/6/60	3	1½d	Green	5	5	10
W131	22/6/60	4	2d	Lt. red brown SB	£18	£12	8.50
W132	4/10/61	4	2d	Lt. red brown	5	5	5
W133	22/6/60	5	2½d	Carmine red (Type II)	15	10	15
W134	4/10/61	5	2½d	Car. red (Type II) SB	75	50	35
W135	7/11/61	5	2½d	Car. red (Type I) SB	£28	£20	£16
W136	22/6/60	6	3d	Deep violet	40	25	15
W137	29/4/65	6	3d	Deep violet SB (L)	30	20	20
W138	29/4/65	6	3d	Deep violet SB (R)	30	20	20
W139	8/12/66	6	3d	Deep violet CB	25	15	15
W140	22/6/60	7	4d	Ultramarine	4.50	3.00	3.25
W141	15/4/65	7	4d	Dp. ultramarine	20	15	5
W142	13/9/61	8	4½d	Chestnut red	15	10	20
W143	9/6/67	9	5d	Brown	20	15	10
W144	27/6/60	10	6d	Claret	20	15	15
W145	15/2/67	11	7d	Pastel green	35	25	15
W146	28/6/67	12	8d	Cerise	35	25	20
W147	29/12/66	13	9d	Greyish green	35	25	20
W148	30/12/66	14	10d	Deep blue	40	25	20
W149	28/6/67	16	1/–d	Yellowish brown	40	25	10
W150	22/6/60	17	1/3d	Deep green	1.75	1.15	50
W151	12/12/66	18	1/6d	Greyish blue	2.25	1.45	40
				Set of 17 values	6.50	4.25	2.50

WATERMARK: MULTIPLE CROWNS INVERTED

No.	Issued	Type	Colour	U/M	M/M	F/U
W152	14/8/60	1	½d	Orange red	35	20	30
W153	14/8/60	2	1d	Dp. ultramarine	30	15	15
W154	14/8/60	3	1½d	Green	3.75	2.15	1.25
W155	14/8/60	5	2½d	Carmine red (Type II)	£125	£50	£40
W156	–/3/62	5	2½d	Car. red (Type II) SB	£18	9.00	8.00
W157	14/8/60	6	3d	Deep violet	70	40	35
W158	8/12/66	6	3d	Deep violet CB	1.10	65	50
W159	–/2/67	6	3d	Deep violet SB (L)	5.00	3.00	2.50
W160	–/2/67	6	3d	Deep violet SB (R)	1.10	65	50
W161	21/6/65	7	4d	Dp. ultramarine	20	15	15
				Set of 10	£150	£65	£48

WATERMARK: MULTIPLE CROWNS SIDEWAYS

No.	Issued	Type	Colour	U/M	M/M	F/U
W162	26/5/61	1	½d	Orange red	8.00	5.25	5.25
W163	14/7/61	2	1d	Dp. ultramarine	20	15	15
W164	14/7/61	3	1½d	Green	8.00	5.25	4.00
W165	6/4/67	4	2d	Lt. red brown	20	15	20
W166	14/7/61	6	3d	Deep violet	65	45	45
W167	16/8/65	6	3d	Deep violet SB (L)	3.00	2.00	1.00
W168	16/8/65	6	3d	Deep violet SB (R)	3.00	2.00	1.00
W169	19/6/67	6	3d	Deep violet (CB)	25	15	35
W170	16/8/65	7	4d	Dp. ultramarine	15	10	15
				Set of 9	£21	£14	£11

WILDING HIGH VALUE DEFINITIVES 1955 – 68

Printers: Various. Recess Printed   *Perf:* 11 x 12   *Watermark:* As indicated. (C) = chalky paper

Type 19

Type 20

Type 21

Type 22

No.	Issued	Type		Colour	U/M	M/M	F/U

PRINTED BY WATERLOW & SONS
WATERMARK: ST. EDWARD'S CROWN UPRIGHT

No.	Issued	Type		Colour	U/M	M/M	F/U
W171	23/9/55	19	**2/6d**	Blackish brown	9.00	3.00	50
W172	23/9/55	20	**5/–d**	Rose carmine	£50	£16	2.00
W173	1/9/55	21	**10/–d**	Ultramarine	£100	£33	6.50
W174	1/9/55	22	**£1**	Black	£225	£75	8.00
				Set of 4	£350	£115	£15

PRINTED BY DE LA RUE & CO.
WATERMARK: ST. EDWARD'S CROWN UPRIGHT

No.	Issued	Type		Colour	U/M	M/M	F/U
W175	17/7/57	19	**2/6d**	Blackish brown	£35	£12	1.00
W176	30/4/58	20	**5/–d**	Rose carmine	£100	£33	3.50
W177	25/4/58	21	**10/–d**	Dull blue	£400	£125	8.00
W178	28/4/58	22	**£1**	Black	£1200	£375	£15
				Set of 4	£1650	£490	£25

PRINTED BY DE LA RUE & CO.
WATERMARK: MULTIPLE CROWNS UPRIGHT

No.	Issued	Type		Colour	U/M	M/M	F/U
W179	22/7/59	19	**2/6d**	Blackish brown	£15	5.00	50
W180	15/6/59	20	**5/–d**	Red	£75	£25	80
W181	21/7/59	21	**10/–d**	Blue	£75	£25	2.50
W182	23/6/59	22	**£1**	Black	£180	£60	4.50
				Set of 4	£325	£105	7.50

Presentation Pack

	1960			4 stamps	£350		
				Nos W179–182			

PRINTED BY BRADBURY WILKINSON & CO.
WATERMARK: MULTIPLE CROWNS UPRIGHT

No.	Issued	Type		Colour	U/M	M/M	F/U
W183	1/7/63	19	**2/6d**	Blackish brown	40	20	10
W184	30/5/68	19	**2/6d**	Blackish brown (C)	60	30	50
W185	3/9/63	20	**5/–d**	Red	3.25	1.25	25
W186				Light brownish red	4.50	1.50	50
W187	16/10/63	21	**10/–d**	Ultramarine	8.00	4.00	75
W188	14/11/63	22	**£1**	Black	£22	£15	1.50
				Set of 4 values	£30	£20	2.25

PRINTED BY BRADBURY WILKINSON & CO.
WATERMARK: MULTIPLE CROWNS INVERTED

No.	Issued	Type		Colour	U/M	M/M	F/U
W189		19	**2/6d**	Blackish brown	£125	£55	£25
W190		20	**5/–d**	Red	£140	£60	£30

PRINTED BY BRADBURY WILKINSON & CO.
WITHOUT WATERMARK

No.	Issued	Type		Colour	U/M	M/M	F/U
W191	1/7/68	19	**2/6d**	Blackish brown	30	15	20
W192	10/4/68	20	**5/–d**	Brownish red	1.50	75	30
W193	10/4/68	21	**10/–d**	Ultramarine	£18	9.00	1.25
W194	4/12/67	22	**£1**	Black	5.00	2.50	2.50
				Set of 4	£22	£11	3.75

THE "CASTLE" HIGH VALUES – IDENTIFICATION GUIDE

To make the distinctions between the three printers as clear as possible it has been decided that this year's edition will use the chart/comparison guide, which will enable collectors to detect the difference between the printers more easily. Where shades are mentioned we have endeavoured to describe the shades as closely as possible as per the catalogue list. However, where there is a small but distinctive difference this has been noted on the chart as a further aid in distinguishing the printers.

The basic steps are as follows:-

1.   Sort by watermarks. All those with St. Edward's Crown (1st) are either Waterlow or De La Rue, and those with Multiple Crowns Watermarks (2nd) are either the second De La Rue or Bradbury Wilkinson. Those without watermark are Bradbury.

2.   Check the Waterlow and De La Rue first watermark against the list below.

3.   It is relatively easy to sort the De La Rue from the Bradbury in the Multiple Crowns watermark series by the way the paper curls when the face is breathed upon. This is due to the method of printing in relation to the paper web. On De La Rue printings the paper curls vertically, i.e. top and bottom pull together, whereas on the Bradbury it will curl horizontally, i.e. left and right sides pull together.

If difficulties are still found the list below should readily solve them.

		Waterlow	De La Rue	Bradbury Wilkinson
Paper Type		Cream/lightish cream	Light cream/white	White/chalky
Paper Characteristics		Curls vertically	Curls vertically	Curls horizontally
Watermarks	1st	St. Edward's Crown	St. Edward's Crown	–
	2nd	–	Multiple Crown	Multiple Crown
	Without	–	–	None
Perforations	Wmk.1st	Thick tooth top right	Thin tooth top right	–
	Wmk.2nd	–	Vert. perf. 11.8	Vert. perf. 11.9 to 12
Shades				
2/6 value	Wmk.1st	Blackish brown	Blackish brown (less blackish tinge)	–
	Wmk.2nd	–	Blackish brown	Dp.blk. brown
	Without	–	–	Dp.blk.brown
5/– value	Wmk.1st	Rose carmine	Rose carmine (noticeably less carmine)	–
	Wmk.2nd	_	Red	Brownish red
	Without	–	–	Brownish red
10/– value	Wmk.1st	Ultramarine	Dull blue	–
	Wmk.2nd	–	Dull blue	Bt.ultramarine
	Without	–	–	Bt.ultramarine
£1 value	Wmk.1st	Black	Dp.greyish black	–
	Wmk.2nd	–	Greyish black	Intense black
	Without	–	–	Intense black

Notes

Some plates of the De La Rue 2nd Watermark had either 1 or 2 coloured plate dots in the bottom margin, row 10, stamp No. 1. These marginal pieces are worth 150% premium.

Waterlow and **De La Rue** both used guide marks.

Waterlow – small guide lines 2-3mm. at top and bottom, centre and centre left and right of each sheet.

De La Rue – only on the side margins between rows 5 and 6, usually in the form of a 'T' or a cross, which marked a guide "pinhole".

Bradbury Wilkinson also used guide holes, row 6, left and right.

THE MACHIN PORTRAIT VARIATIONS

Dr. A. S. Law – Triple "POST OFFICE TROPHY" Winner – STAMPEX 1973–75

". . . the Postmaster-General hopes shortly to settle the terms of an invitation which he will be sending to a number of artists inviting them to submit designs for a new definitive series of postage stamps." *Hansard, June 1965.*

Doubtless the recent acceptance of Arnold Machin's profile portrait for the decimal coinage determined his inclusion in this invitation. His early work revolved around adaptations of his coinage head. Later he submitted a new sculptured plaque. A second one was provisionally accepted in January 1967, but it was a third which, with full corsage, won final acceptance. It was revealed to the public as the 4d value in March.

Arnold Machin personally supervised the photography of his plaque and was at pains to ensure the correct lighting. He persisted until the result he desired was achieved and would not permit retouching of the negatives. Type I (dark background) used a dark grey surround; Type II was left white. Two further differences can be noted:

(a) Two dark curves near the crown – I   (b) missing small pearl in necklace – I
    single dark curve – II   complete necklace – II

The first is probably due to the different lighting, the second is a flaw in the plaster plaque.

With the successful production of the early stamps completed, the artist's work was considered concluded. This in the event, was unfortunate. The production of cylinders to his meticulous standards was no easy task. In Type I difficulty was found in preserving the outline of the portrait. Retouching of the master negative removed much of the shading and thereby strengthened the outline. Unhappily some of the reflected shadow was incorporated in the portrait – see nose, chin and base. This amended form (IB) appeared on the later cylinders of the £sd series and continued into the early decimal ones.

About the time the Jumelle press was becoming operative new values were being considered. The artist's advice was sought on the choice of new colours and also on the possibility of a variant of Type II. The presses, then in use were tending to diffuse the outline. On his suggestion the graded shading was removed and the outline strengthened (IIB). It was intended to replace the Type II values with this variant. In practice it was used as a third variant as the series was running out of suitable colours, with more and more values striving to keep up with inflation.

It was at this time that the Type I portrait (IAr) was "restored". All the new Jumelle cylinders showed the facial features of the original Machin head although faint traces of the rounded base remained. More recently, from 1977, a larger head has appeared. It continues the restored form, but lacks the master negative flaws of the original.

For the High Values, the same simple design was eventually agreed upon and the portrait was adapted for recess printing using a dark background. (Variations exist both in background and head but are beyond the scope of this work). In 1977, the values became higher and photogravure. Now as £5, £2 and £1 they appear as Type IA head enlarged to fit the Jumelle special issue layout.

In the regional (or Country) decimal series a design incorporating the local symbol in the top left hand corner with a reduced size head to the right was accepted. The early values used the IB head, the later the IA whereas those with graded background employed IIA.

Although beyond the scope of this catalogue the Type I portrait has been used on airletters and cards. On envelopes a modified embossed form has now been superseded by a flat silhouette with yet another variation in portrait outline.

When the new definitive series was envisaged it was intended that the new portrait would be suitable for the special issues. In fact Arnold Machin produced a separate portrait – more apt for diminutive use. It was first employed on the "Bridges" issue, April 1968, and almost invariably since. Most usually in silhouette form, the corsage has been reduced in some instances and omitted in others. In one issue, General Anniversaries – 1972, both the old coinage head and Arnold Machin's were used – on different values!

THE MACHIN PORTRAIT VARIATIONS

I

II

IA

IB

THE MACHIN PORTRAIT VARIATIONS

IIA IIB

IA r IB

MACHIN STERLING LOW VALUE DEFINITIVES 1967 – 70

Printers: Harrison & Sons in Photogravure   *Perf:* 15 x 14   *No Watermark*

All Type **23** except 7d, 8d and 9d values – Type **24**
All with two phosphor bands except where stated

2d Type I

2d Type II

Type 23

Type 24

Coil abbreviations: V = vertical delivery
                      H = horizontal delivery
                      MV = multi-value coil

SOURCE

No.	Issued		Colour	Head Type	U/M	F/U	No.	Sheet Cylinder Nos.	Booklet Panes Nos.	Coils
PVA Gum										
M1	5/2/68	½d	Brownish orange	A	5	10	M1	2,3	–	–
M2	5/2/68	1d	Olive	A	25	15	M2	2	–	–
M3		1d	Yellow Olive	B	20	5	M3	4	BP141,142,144,145,146	V
M4			Olive green	B	15	5	M4	6	–	–
M5	16/9/68	1d	Olive CB	B	50	35	M5	–	BP143	–
M6	5/2/68	2d	Reddish brown (Type I)	A	20	5	M6	1	–	–
M7	4/4/68	2d	Reddish brown (Type II)	B	15	10	M7	5,6	–	V,H
M8	12/3/68	3d	Violet CB	A	15	5	M8	1,3,4	–	–
M9			Bluish violet CB	A	5.00	1.25	M9	–	–	H
M10		3d	Violet CB	B	1.00	10	M10	–	BP147	–
M11	6/4/68	3d	Violet	A	45	25	M11	3,4	–	V
M12		3d	Violet	B	60	25	M12	–	BP145,146	V
M13	22/1/68	4d	Olive brown	A	15	5	M13	4,10,12,13	BP150	–
M14			Olive sepia	A	15	5	M14	–	BP150	–
M15		4d	Olive brown	B	15	5	M15	14,15	BP151	–
M16			Olive sepia	B	15	5	M16	14,15	BP151	–
M17	16/9/68	4d	Olive brown CB	A	20	5	M17	4,12,13	BP152	V,H
M18		4d	Olive sepia CB	B	50	20	M18	14,15	–	–
M19		4d	Olive brown CB	B	50	20	M19	14,15	BP143,153,154	–
M20	6/1/69	4d	Vermilion CB	A	15	5	M20	4,10,13	BP155	V,H
M21		4d	Vermilion CB	B	15	5	M21	15,16,17	BP157,158,159,160,161	H
M22	6/1/69	4d	Vermilion SB (L)	B	1.25	1.00	M22	–	BP142,144	–
M23	1/12/69	4d	Vermilion SB (R)	B	4.00	2.00	M23	–	BP142	–
M24	1/7/68	5d	Royal blue (shades)	A	20	5	M24	1	–	–
M25		5d	Royal blue (shades)	B	20	5	M25	7,10,11,13,15	BP142,162,163	V,H
M26	5/2/68	6d	Reddish purple	A	40	5	M26	2,3,4,5	–	–
M27			Bright magenta	A	2.00	1.00	M27	3	–	–
M28			Claret	A	1.00	20	M28	5	–	–
M29		6d	Reddish purple	B	7.00	3.00	M29	–	–	V
M29A			Claret	B	£20	8.00	M29A	–	–	V
M30	1/7/68	7d	Emerald green	B	50	15	M30	3,4	–	–
M31	1/7/68	8d	Vermilion	A	20	20	M31	2	–	–
M32	6/1/69	8d	Turquoise blue	B	1.00	35	M32	3	–	–
M33	29/11/68	9d	Myrtle green	A	80	10	M33	2	–	–
M34	1/7/68	10d	Drab	A	1.00	25	M34	1	–	–
M35	26/4/68	1/–d	Pale violet blue	A	50	10	M35	11	–	–
M36	28/8/68	1/6d	Pr. blue/dp. blue	A	90	10	M36	3A–1B	–	–
M37			Light blue/deep blue	A	90	10	M37	3A–2B	–	–
M38	10/12/69	1/6d	Pr. blue/dp.blue AOP	A	4.00	1.50	M38	5A–2B	–	–
M39	16/11/70	1/9d	Orange/black	A	2.00	20	M39	1A–1B	–	–

MACHIN STERLING LOW VALUE DEFINITIVES 1967 – 70

Printers: Harrison & Sons in Photogravure   *Perf:* 15 x 14   *No Watermark*

No.	Issued		Colour	Head Type	U/M	F/U
Gum Arabic						
M40	27/8/69	**1d**	Olive CB	B	60	–
M41	27/8/69	**2d**	Reddish brown CB (Type II)	B	50	50
M42	8/8/67	**3d**	Violet CB	A	20	–
M43			Deep violet CB	A	20	5
M44		**3d**	Violet CB	B	35	–
M45	5/6/67	**4d**	Olive brown	A	15	–
M46			Olive sepia	A	20	–
M47		**4d**	Olive brown	B	£225	–
M48	20/2/69	**4d**	Vermilion CB	A	£15	–
M49	27/8/69	**4d**	Vermilion CB	B	35	–
M50	8/8/67	**9d**	Myrtle green	A	75	–
M51	5/6/67	**1/-d**	Light violet blue	A	50	–
M52			Pale violet blue	A	60	–
M53	8/8/67	**1/6d**	Green blue/dp. blue	A	90	–
M54			Light blue/deep blue	A	1.50	–
M55		**1/6d**	Pr. blue/indigo (phosphor omitted)	A	4.50	1.25
M56	5/6/67	**1/9d**	Dull orange/black	A	1.00	–
M57			Bright orange/black	A	1.50	–
MV1	27/8/69	**1/-d**	**Multi-value coil strip** 5 stamps se-tenant (2d+2d+3d+1d+4d) all CB	B	2.00	2.00
	5/3/69		**Presentation Pack** 14 stamps (½d–1/9d)		6.00	
			Presentation Pack with German Text 14 stamps (½d–1/9d)		£38	

SOURCE

No.	Sheet Cylinder Nos.	Booklet Panes Nos.	Coils
M40	–	–	MV
M41	–	–	MV
M42	1	–	V
M43	–	–	H
M44	–	–	MV
M45	4,8	BP149	V,H
M46	4,8	BP148	–
M47	14	–	–
M48	–	BP156	–
M49	–	–	MV
M50	2	–	–
M51	3	–	–
M52	11	–	–
M53	2A–2B	–	–
M54	3A–2B	–	–
M55	5A–2B	–	–
M56	1A–1B	–	–
M57	1A–1B	–	–

Head Type A Flatter Base

Head Type B Curved Base

MACHIN STERLING HIGH VALUE DEFINITIVES 1969 – 70

Printers: Bradbury, Wilkinson & Co.   *Perf:* 12   *No Watermark*
Recess Printed

No.	Issued	Type	Colour	U/M	F/U

Type 25

Type 26

Type 27

Type 28

PVA Gum

No.	Issued	Type		Colour	U/M	F/U
M58	5/3/69	25	**2/6d**	Brown	1.00	15
M59	5/3/69	26	**5/–d**	Red	2.50	40
M60	5/3/69	27	**10/–d**	Blue	£30	7.00
M61	5/3/69	28	**£1**	Black	4.00	1.00
				Set of 4	£35	8.00
	5/3/69			**Presentation Pack**		
				4 stamps Nos. M58–61	£36	
				Presentation Pack		
				with German Text		
				4 stamps Nos. M58–61	£45	

MACHIN DECIMAL LOW VALUE DEFINITIVES 1971 –

Printers: Harrison & Sons in Photogravure   *Perf:* 15 x 14   *No Watermark*

SOURCE

All Type **29** with two phosphor bands except where stated

No.	Issued		Colour	U/M	F/U	No.	Sheet Cylinder Nos.	Booklet Panes Nos.	Coils
OCP/PVA						**OCP/PVA**			
M62	15/2/71	½p	Turquoise (I)	10	5	M62	2,4	DP1,3,7	–
M63	14/7/71	½p	Turquoise (II)	1.00	20	M63	–	DP11	–
M64	15/2/71	1p	Crimson	15	5	M64	1,3	DP2,12	V
M65	,,	1½p	Charcoal grey	15	5	M65	1	DP2,12	–
M66	,,	2p	Green	25	5	M66	4,5	DP1,11	–
M67	,,	2½p	Pink(I) CB	20	5	M67	5,6,7,8	–	V,H
M68	,,	2½p	Pink (II) CB	40	10	M68	–	DP4,5,8	–
M69	,,	2½p	Pink (II) SB(L)	2.50	1.00	M69	–	DP9	–
M70	,,	3p	Deep bright blue (I)	25	5	M70	2,4	DP6,9,10	–
M71	,,	3p	Deep bright blue (II)	4.00	1.00	M71	–	–	V,H
M72	,,	3½p	Grey Green	40	15	M72	1	–	–
M73	,,	4p	Light Sepia	20	10	M73	5	–	–
M74	,,	5p	Pale violet	20	10	M74	2	–	–
M75	,,	6p	Light green (I)	25	10	M75	1	–	–
M76	,,	7½p	Light brown (I)	25	15	M76	1	–	–
M77	,,	9p	Orange/black	1.50	25	M77	3A–2B	–	–
OCP/GA						**OCP/GA**			
M78	15/2/71	½p	Turquoise (I)	20	–	M78	–	–	MV
M79	,,	1p	Crimson	30	–	M79	–	–	MV
M80	,,	2p	Green	1.25	–	M80	–	–	MV
M81	,,	3p	Bright blue (II)	£35	–	M81	–	–	H
OCP/PVAD						**OCP/PVAD**			
M82	–/6/74	3½p	Deep grey green	£150	–	M82	11	–	–
FCP/PVA						**FCP/PVA**			
M83	27/8/71	½p	Turquoise (I)	50	–	M83	2	DP7,13,19,20	–
M84	6/10/71	½p	Turquoise (II)	75	–	M84	–	DP11	–
M85	24/5/72	½p	Turquoise (I) SB(L)	£65	£20	M85	–	DP20	–
M86	27/8/71	1p	Crimson	40	–	M86	1,3	DP12	–
M87	27/8/71	1½p	Charcoal grey	50	–	M87	4	DP12	–
M88	27/8/71	2p	Green	60	–	M88	4	DP11	–
M89	–/10/71	2½p	Pink (I) CB	60	10	M89	5,6,9,10,11,13,13A	DP16,18	–
M90	17/9/71	2½p	Pink (II) CB	75	–	M90	19	DP8,14,15,16	–
M91	24/5/72	2½p	Pink (I) SB(L)	£20	£10	M91	–	DP20 (Cyl.B22 only)	–
M92	17/9/71	2½p	Pink (II) SB(L)	1.75	75	M92	–	DP9	–
M93	24/5/72	2½p	Pink (III) SB(L)	2.00	1.00	M93	–	DP19,20	–
M94	24/5/72	2½p	Pink (I) SB(R)	7.00	3.00	M94	–	DP18	–
M95	24/5/72	2½p	Pink (III) SB(R)	6.75	3.00	M95	–	DP19	–
M96	17/9/71	3p	Bright blue (I)	30	10	M96	2,4,8,9,10,12,12A,21,22,24	DP6,9,10,17,18	–
M97	–/1/74	3p	Bright blue (I) CB	50	–	M97	31	DP21	–
M98	–/–/71	3½p	Grey green	1.25	–	M98	9,11	DP22	–
M99	–/–/71	4p	Light sepia	1.50	–	M99	4	–	–
M100	–/–/71	5p	Pale violet	2.00	–	M100	2,3	–	–
M101	–/–/71	6p	Light green (I)	£20	–	M101	4	–	–
M102	–/12/75	6½p	Peacock blue CB	£40	–	M102	4	–	–
M103	–/–/71	7½p	Light brown (I)	1.50	–	M103	1,3	–	–
M104	–/–/71	9p	Orange/black	2.50	–	M104	3A–3B,4A–4B	–	–
M105	11/8/71	10p	Orange/light orange	60	–	M105	3A–3B,5A–4B	–	–
FCP/GA						**FCP/GA**			
M106	22/9/72	½p	Turquoise (I)	15	–	M106	2	–	MV
M107	15/2/71	1p	Crimson	15	–	M107	–	–	V,MV
M108	–/9/72	2p	Green	1.25	–	M108	–	–	MV
M109	13/9/72	2½p	Pink (I) CB	15	–	M109	9,10,11	–	H
M110	23/8/72	3p	Bright blue (I)	35	–	M110	8,9,10	–	–
M111		3p	Bright blue (II)	3.00	–	M111	–	–	H
M112	10/9/73	3p	Bright blue (I) CB	20	–	M112	8,24,31	–	–
M113	–/11/72	4p	Light sepia	20	–	M113	4	–	–
M114	6/6/73	6p	Light green (I)	2.00	–	M114	4	–	–

MACHIN DECIMAL LOW VALUE DEFINITIVES 1971 –

Printers: Harrison & Sons in Photogravure   *Perf:* 15 x 14   *No Watermark*

Varieties (I) and (II) etc. are illustrated overleaf.

No.	Issued	Colour	U/M	F/U	No.	Sheet Cylinder Nos.	Booklet Panes Nos.	Coils
FCP/PVAD					**FCP/PVAD**			
M115	10/9/73	½p Turquoise (I)	5	5	M115	7,8	DP24	MV
M116	12/11/73	½p Turquoise (II)	35	15	M116	–	DP11	–
M117	14/12/77	½p Turquoise (CB)	5	5	M117	–	DP31	MV
M118	26/1/77	½p Turquoise (8 m/m)	25	10	M118	–	DP27,27A	–
M119	10/9/73	1p Crimson	5	5	M119	11,12	DP12,24	MV
M120	14/12/77	1p Crimson (CB)	10	5	M120	–	DP31	MV
M121	26/1/77	1p Crimson (8 m/m)	10	10	M121	–	DP27,27A	–
M122	5/6/74	1½p Charcoal grey	15	5	M122	9	DP12	–
M123	10/9/73	2p Green	5	5	M123	10,11	DP11	MV
M124	8/8/73	2½p Pink (II) CB	20	5	M124	19	–	–
M125	21/5/75	2½p Pink (II)	30	5	M125	19	–	–
M126	10/9/73	3p Bright blue (I) CB	10	5	M126	30,31,38	DP21	–
M127		3p Bright blue (II) CB	1.00	25	M127	–	–	V,H
M128	22/8/73	3½p Grey green	50	5	M128	9,11	DP22	V,H
M129		3½p Olive brown	£225	–	M129	9	–	–
M130	24/6/74	3½p Grey green CB	40	5	M130	9,11,12	DP22	H
M131	12/11/73	4p Light sepia	35	5	M131	12	–	–
M132	24/10/73	4½p Slate blue	35	5	M132	1,3,7	DP23	H
M133	13/11/74	4½p Slate blue AOP	65	30	M133	7	–	–
M134	5/6/74	5p Pale violet	10	5	M134	7,8	–	–
M135	13/12/73	5½p Deep purple	60	10	M135	2	–	–
M136	17/3/75	5½p Deep purple CB	40	10	M136	2,4	–	–
M137	30/10/73	6p Light green (II)	15	10	M137	4,8	DP24	–
M138	3/12/75	6p Light green (III)	35	10	M138	–	–	MV
M139	4/9/74	6½p Peacock blue	1.00	10	M139	2	–	–
M140	24/9/75	6½p Peacock blue CB	30	10	M140	2,4,5,9,11	DP25,25A	V,H
M141	26/1/77	6½p Peacock blue SB(L)	2.25	1.50	M141	–	DP27	–
M142	26/1/77	6½p Peacock blue SB(R)	3.25	1.75	M142	–	DP27A	–
M143	15/1/75	7p Red brown	50	10	M143	3,6	–	–
M144	13/6/77	7p Red brown CB	15	10	M144	8,14,20,21	DP28,28A,31	V,H,MV
M145	13/6/77	7p Red brown SB(L)	35	25	M145	–	DP30	–
M146	13/6/77	7p Red brown SB(R)	35	25	M146	–	DP30A	–
M147	15/11/78	7p Red brown (1 BAR)	25	20	M147	–	DP32	–
M148	–/1/74	7½p Light brown (I)	1.00	45	M148	3	–	–
M149		7½p Light brown (II)	20	10	M149	5	–	–
M150	24/10/73	8p Red	15	10	M150	3	–	–
M151	15/8/79	8p Red CB	15	10				
M152	24/9/75	8½p Yellow green	15	10	M152	4,6	DP26,26A	V,H
M153	24/3/76	8½p Yellow green AOP	65	25	M153	6	–	–
M154	26/1/77	8½p Yellow green (8 m/m)	25	10	M154	–	DP27,27A	–
M155	29/3/74	9p Orange/black	75	10	M155	8A–6B	–	–
M156		9p Dark orange/black	1.00	15	M156	4A–4B	–	–
M157	25/2/76	9p Blue	15	10	M157	11,12,16,27	DP29,29A	V,H
M158	25/2/76	9p Blue (varnished)	30	15	M158	12	–	–
M159	13/6/77	9p Blue (8 m/m)	15	10	M159	–	DP30,30A	–
M160	15/11/78	9p Blue (2 BARS)	30	20	M160	–	DP32	–
M161	25/2/76	9½p Purple	15	15	M161	13	–	–
M162	12/11/73	10p Orange/light orange	40	15	M162	5A–4B,8A–6B	–	–
M163	25/2/76	10p Beige	15	15	M163	3	–	–
M164	25/2/76	10½p Yellow	35	15	M164	1	–	–
M165	26/4/78	10½p Steel blue	15	15	M165	1	–	–
M166	25/2/76	11p Rose	15	15	M166	4	–	–
M167	15/8/79	11½p Light sepia	15	15				
M168	15/8/79	13p Grey green	20	20				
M169	15/8/79	15p Bright blue	22	22				
M170	25/2/76	20p Grey	25	25	M170	4	–	–
M171	2/2/77	50p Ochre	65	55	M171	4	–	–

The above issues have been re-numbered from M118 to provide for new varieties.

8 m/m denotes narrow phosphor bands – normally 9½ m/m.

1 BAR or 2 BARS denotes phosphor bands cover coloured portion of stamp only.

MACHIN DECIMAL LOW VALUE DEFINITIVES 1971 –

Type I
Original

Type II
Thicker

Type I
Original

Type II
Thicker

Type III
Thinner

Type I
Orginal

Type II
Thicker
ex coils only

Type I
Original

Type II
Thinner

Type III
Very Thin

Type I
Original

Type II
Thinner

PLEASE NOTE
The position of the value tablet in relation to the
corner of the bust varies within some values i.e. ½p,
1p, 2p, 2½p, 3p, 4½p, 6p,7p and 8½p.

Type 29

Issued	Detail	U/M
15/2/71	**Presentation Pack**	
	12 stamps (½p – 9p OCP/PVA)	5.50
15/4/71	**Presentation Pack**	
	(Scandinavia Edition)	
	12 stamps (½p – 9p OCP/PVA)	£25
25/11/71	**Presentation Pack**	
	18 stamps (½p – 10p	
	various papers and gums)	5.00
2/2/77	**Presentation Pack**	
	19 stamps (½p – 50p FCP/PVAD)	2.75

No.	Issued	Value	Detail	U/M	F/U
OCP/GA					
MV2	15/2/71	**5p**	(2p+½p+½p+1p+1p)	2.25	2.25
FCP/GA (with silicone coating)					
MV3	–/9/72	**5p**	(2p+½p+½p+1p+1p)	2.00	2.00
FCP/PVAD					
MV4	–/4/74	**5p**	(2p+½p+½p+1p+1p)	30	30
MV5	3/12/75	**10p**	(6p+2p+1p+½p+½p)	25	25
MV6	14/12/77	**10p**	(7p+1p+1p+½p+½p)	20	20
OCP/PVA					
MV7	–/–/77	**10p**	(6p+2p+1p+½p+½p)	1.50	1.50

MACHIN DECIMAL HIGH VALUE DEFINITIVES 1970 –

No Watermark

No.	Issued	Type		Colour	U/M	F/U

PRINTED BY BRADBURY, WILKINSON & CO.
Recess printed on thick (Post Office) paper.

PVA GUM Perf: 12

No.	Issued	Type		Colour	U/M	F/U
M180	17/6/70	30	10p	Cerise AOP	8.00	25
M181	17/6/70	30	20p	Olive green	4.00	15
M182	17/6/70	30	50p	Greyish blue	3.50	40
M183	1/2/73	30	50p	Greyish blue AOP	£10	3.00
M184	6/12/72	31	£1	Black	2.50	80
	17/6/70			**Presentation Pack** 3 stamps Nos.M180 – 182	£20	
	25/11/71			**Presentation Pack** 3 stamps Nos.M181,182 & 184	£12	

On thinner whiter (printers' own) paper

No.	Issued	Type		Colour	U/M	F/U
M185	30/11/73	30	20p	Olive green	1.00	15
M186	20/2/74	30	50p	Greyish blue	1.50	40
M187	27/9/73	31	£1	Black	2.00	80

PRINTED BY HARRISON & SONS in Photogravure
PVA DEXTRIN GUM Perf: 14 x 15

No.	Issued	Type		Colour	U/M	F/U
M188	2/2/77	32	£1	Olive green/ pale greenish yellow	1.25	60
				Gutter pair (Plain)	3.00	3.00
				Gutter pair (TL)	3.25	3.25
M189	2/2/77	33	£2	Purple brown/ pale green	2.50	1.25
				Gutter pair (Plain)	6.00	6.00
				Gutter pair (TL)	7.00	7.00
M190	2/2/77	34	£5	Royal blue/ pale pink	6.00	3.75
				Gutter pair (Plain)	£15	£15
				Gutter pair (TL)	£17	£17
	2/2/77			**Presentation Pack** 3 stamps Nos.M188 – 190	£10	

N.B. The above issues have been re-numbered.

Type 30

Type 31

Type 32

Type 33

Type 34

COMMEMORATIVE ISSUES 1953 – 60

Printers: Harrison & Sons in Photogravure   *Perf:* 15 x 14   *Paper:* Ordinary   *Watermark:* St. Edward's Crown (except where shown)

No.	Type		Colour	U/M	M/M	F/U

Type 1

Type 2

Type 3

Type 4

CORONATION Issued 3/6/53 (Wmk. Tudor Crown)

No.	Type		Colour	U/M	M/M	F/U
C1	1	2½d	Carmine red	30	20	15
C2	2	4d	Ultramarine	1.75	1.15	75
C3	3	1/3d	Olive green	9.00	6.00	3.50
C4	4	1/6d	Slate blue	£14	9.50	5.00
			Set of 4	£22	£15	8.50
			First Day Cover			£30

Type 5

Type 6

Type 7

WORLD SCOUT JUBILEE JAMBOREE Issued 1/8/57

No.	Type		Colour	U/M	M/M	F/U
C5	5	2½d	Red	20	15	15
C6	6	4d	Ultramarine	1.75	1.15	1.25
C7	7	1/3d	Olive green	£10	6.65	5.75
			Set of 3	£11	7.00	6.50
			First Day Cover			£18

Type 8

46th INTER-PARLIAMENTARY UNION CONFERENCE Issued 12/9/57

No.	Type		Colour	U/M	M/M	F/U
C8	8	4d	Light blue	2.00	1.30	2.25
			First Day Cover			£45

Type 9

Type 10

Type 11

SIXTH BRITISH EMPIRE AND COMMONWEALTH GAMES
Issued 18/7/58

No.	Type		Colour	U/M	M/M	F/U
C9	9	3d	Violet	20	15	10
C10	10	6d	Magenta	1.00	65	75
C11	11	1/3d	Green	6.00	4.00	5.00
			Set of 3	6.50	4.25	5.25
			First Day Cover			£30

Type 12

Type 13

**TERCENTENARY OF ESTABLISHMENT OF GENERAL
LETTER OFFICE** Issued 7/7/60

No.	Type		Colour	U/M	M/M	F/U
C12	12	3d	Purple violet	25	15	10
C13	13	1/3d	Green	£10.50	7.00	6.25
			(Wmk. Sideways)			
			Set of 2	£10.50	7.00	6.25
			First Day Cover			£18

COMMEMORATIVE ISSUES 1960 – 61

Printers: Harrison & Sons in Photogravure   *Perf:* 15 x 14   *Paper:* Chalky   *Watermark:* Multiple Crowns

No.	Type		Colour	U/M	M/M	F/U

Type 14   *Type 15*

Type 19   *Type 20*

1ST ANNIVERSARY EUROPEAN POSTAL AND
TELECOMMUNICATIONS CONFERENCE Issued 19/9/60

No.	Type		Colour	U/M	M/M	F/U
C14	14	6d	Green/redd. purple	1.50	1.00	1.00
C15	15	1/6d	Choc. brn./dp. blue	£11	7.00	5.75
			Set of 2	£12	7.25	6.25
			First Day Cover			£20

Type 21

C.E.P.T. CONFERENCE Issued 18/9/61

No.	Type		Colour	U/M	M/M	F/U
C21	19	2d	Pink/orange/brown	10	5	10
C22	20	4d	Lt. brown/pink/ult.	40	25	40
C23	21	10d	Yel. grn./tur./dp.blue	70	45	70
			Set of 3	1.10	70	1.10
			First Day Cover			4.50

Type 16

Type 22

Type 17   *Type 18*

CENTENARY POST OFFICE SAVINGS BANK Issued 28/8/61

Timson Press

No.	Type		Colour	U/M	M/M	F/U
C16	16	2½d	Black/red	25	15	15
			(Wmk. Sideways)			
C17	17	3d	Orange brown/pur.	25	15	15
C18	18	1/6d	Scarlet/dark blue	4.00	2.65	2.85
			Set of 3	4.25	2.75	3.00
			First Day Cover			£22

Thrissell Press

C19	16	2½d	Black/red	2.00	1.30	1.30
			(Wmk. Sideways)			
C20	17	3d	Orange brown/pur.	50	35	10

Type 23

COMMONWEALTH PARLIAMENTARY CONFERENCE
Issued 25/9/61

No.	Type		Colour	U/M	M/M	F/U
C24	22	6d	Gold/pur. magenta	60	40	35
C25	23	1/3	Blue black/green	4.25	2.80	3.25
			(Wmk. Sideways)			
			Set of 2	4.50	3.00	3.25
			First Day Cover			£18

COMMEMORATIVE ISSUES 1962–63

Printers: Harrison & Sons in Photogravure   *Perf:* 15 x 14   *Paper:* Chalky   *Watermark:* Multiple Crowns

No.	Type	Colour	U/M	M/M	F/U

PHOSPHOR LINES

All the following issues were also printed on an experimental basis with 3 vertical phosphor bands or 1 band where specially indicated. These experimental issues were distributed only from Post Offices in the Southampton area.

Type 24

Type 25

Type 26

NATIONAL PRODUCTIVITY YEAR Issued 14/11/62

Ordinary

No.	Type		Colour	U/M	M/M	F/U
C26	24	2½d	Myrtle grn./car. red (Wmk. Inverted)	15	10	10
C27	24	2½d	Dp. grn./bt.car.red. (Wmk. Inverted)	90	60	20
C28	24	2½d	Olive green/car. red (Wmk. Inverted)	30	20	15
C29	25	3d	Blue/violet (Wmk. Inverted)	30	20	10
C30	26	1/3d	Blue/car. red/green	3.00	2.00	2.45
			Set of 3	3.25	2.10	2.50
			First Day Cover			£14

Phosphor

No.	Type		Colour	U/M	M/M	F/U
C31	24	2½d	Olive green/car. red 1 band (Wmk. Invert.)	60	40	50
C32	25	3d	Blue/violet (Wmk. Inverted)	2.25	1.50	75
C33	26	1/3d	Blue/car. red/green	£30	£20	£16
			Set of 3	£30	£20	£16
			First Day Cover			£75

Type 27

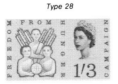

Type 28

FREEDOM FROM HUNGER Issued 21/3/63

Ordinary

No.	Type		Colour	U/M	M/M	F/U
C34	27	2½d	Crimson/pink (Wmk. Inverted)	20	15	15
C35	28	1/3d	Bistre brn./yellow (wmk. Inverted)	3.20	2.10	2.00
			Set of 2	3.25	2.15	2.00
			First Day Cover			£12

Phosphor

No.	Type		Colour	U/M	M/M	F/U
C36	27	2½d	Crimson/pink 1 band (Wmk. Invert.)	2.00	1.30	1.25
C37	28	1/3d	Bistre brn./yellow (Wmk. Inverted)	£26	£17	£15
			Set of 2	£26	£17	£15
			First Day Cover			£20

Type 29

CENTENARY OF PARIS POSTAL CONFERENCE Issued 7/5/63

Ordinary

No.	Type		Colour	U/M	M/M	F/U
C38	29	6d	Green/lilac (Wmk. Inverted)	1.90	1.25	1.25
			First Day Cover			5.00

Phosphor

No.	Type		Colour	U/M	M/M	F/U
C39	29	6d	Green/lilac (Wmk. Inverted)	4.50	3.00	4.25
			First Day Cover			£11

Type 30

Type 31

NATIONAL NATURE WEEK Issued 16/5/63

Ordinary

No.	Type		Colour	U/M	M/M	F/U
C40	30	3d	Multicoloured	10	5	10
C41	31	4½d	Multicoloured	55	40	55
			Set of 2	60	40	60
			First Day Cover			6.00

Phosphor

No.	Type		Colour	U/M	M/M	F/U
C42	30	3d	Multicoloured	60	40	40
C43	31	4½d	Multicoloured	2.75	1.80	2.35
			Set of 2	3.25	2.10	2.50
			First Day Cover			7.00

COMMEMORATIVE ISSUES 1963-64

Printers: Harrison & Sons in Photogravure   *Perf:* 15 x 14   *Paper:* Chalky   *Watermark:* Multiple Crowns

No.	Type		Colour	U/M	M/M	F/U

Type 32   Type 33

Type 34

9TH INTERNATIONAL LIFEBOAT CONFERENCE Issued 31/5/63

Ordinary

No.	Type		Colour	U/M	M/M	F/U
C44	32	2½d	Blue/red/black	15	10	10
C45	33	4d	Multicoloured	1.00	65	1.00
C46	34	1/6d	Yellow/brn./dk. blue	4.50	3.00	2.25
			Set of 3	5.25	3.50	3.00
			First Day Cover			£12

Phosphor

No.	Type		Colour	U/M	M/M	F/U
C47	32	2½d	Bl./red/blk. (1 band)	60	40	50
C48	33	4d	Multicoloured	2.00	1.30	2.00
C49	34	1/6d	Yellow/brn./dk. blue	£30	£20	£20
			Set of 3	£30	£20	£20
			First Day Cover			£30

Type 35

Type 36   Type 37

RED CROSS CENTENARY CONGRESS Issued 15/8/63

Ordinary

No.	Type		Colour	U/M	M/M	F/U
C50	35	3d	Red/violet	15	10	5
C51	36	1/3d	Red/blue/grey	4.75	3.15	3.00
C52	37	1/6d	Red/blue/bistre	5.50	3.65	2.50
			Set of 3	£10	6.50	5.00
			First Day Cover			£12

Phosphor

No.	Type		Colour	U/M	M/M	F/U
C53	35	3d	Red/violet	1.00	60	50
C54	36	1/3d	Red/blue/grey	£39	£26	£26
C55	37	1/6d	Red/blue/bistre	£39	£26	£26
			Set of 3	£75	£50	£50
			First Day Cover			£55

Type 38

OPENING OF COMMONWEALTH CABLE Issued 3/12/63

Ordinary

No.	Type		Colour	U/M	M/M	F/U
C56	38	1/6d	Black/blue	3.25	2.15	1.50
			First Day Cover			£10

Phosphor

No.	Type		Colour	U/M	M/M	F/U
C57	38	1/6d	Black/blue	£17	£11	£15
			First Day Cover			£18

Type 39   Type 40

Type 41   Type 42

Type 43

SHAKESPEARE FESTIVAL Issued 23/4/64

2/6d value only recess printed by Bradbury, Wilkinson & Co.
(Perf.: 11 x 12)

Ordinary

No.	Type		Colour	U/M	M/M	F/U
C58	39	3d	Lt. bistre/blk./vio. bl.	5	5	5
C59	40	6d	Multicoloured	22	15	15
C60	41	1/3d	Multicoloured	1.20	80	1.00
C61	42	1/6d	Multicoloured	1.50	1.00	75
C62	43	2/6d	Violet grey	2.40	1.55	2.00
C63	43	2/6d	Violet grey (Wmk. Inverted)	£100	£65	£65
C64	43	2/6d	Violet black	4.00	2.75	3.50
C65	43	2/6d	Black	£165	£110	£100
			Set of 5	4.75	3.20	3.50
			First Day Cover			6.00
			Presentation Pack	6.25		

COMMEMORATIVE ISSUES 1964

Printers: Harrison & Sons in Photogravure   *Perf:* 15 x 14   *Paper:* Chalky   *Watermark:* Multiple Crowns

No.	Type	Colour	U/M	M/M	F/U

SHAKESPEARE FESTIVAL (continued)

Phosphor

No.	Type	Colour	U/M	M/M	F/U
C66	39	**3d** Lt. bistre/blk./vio. bl.	20	12	20
C67	40	**6d** Multicoloured	60	40	60
C68	41	**1/3d** Multicoloured	6.75	4.50	6.75
C69	41	1/3d Multicoloured (Wmk. Inverted)	£70	£48	£48
C70	42	**1/6d** Multicoloured	9.25	6.25	7.50
		Set of 4	£15	£10	£14
		First Day Cover			£16

Type 44

Type 45

Type 46

Type 47

20TH INTERNATIONAL GEOGRAPHICAL CONGRESS Issued 1/7/64

Ordinary

No.	Type	Colour	U/M	M/M	F/U
C71	44	**2½d** Multicoloured	12	8	10
C72	45	**4d** Multicoloured	85	55	70
C73	46	**8d** Multicoloured	1.25	85	1.00
C74	46	8d Multicoloured (Wmk. Inverted)	£65	£45	£40
C75	47	**1/6d** Brown/black/pink	3.85	2.55	1.25
C76	47	1/6d Brown/black/pink (Wmk. Inverted)	£12	8.00	6.00
		Set of 4	5.50	3.65	2.90
		First Day Cover			9.00
		Presentation Pack	£45		

Phosphor

No.	Type	Colour	U/M	M/M	F/U
C77	44	**2½d** Multicoloured (1 band)	25	15	20
C78	45	**4d** Multicoloured	2.00	1.30	2.00
C79	46	**8d** Multicoloured	9.00	6.00	8.00
C80	47	**1/6d** Brown/black/pink	£18	£12	£12
		Set of 4	£28	£19	£20
		First Day Cover			£30

Type 48

Type 49

Type 50

Type 51

INTERNATIONAL BOTANICAL CONGRESS Issued 5/8/64

Ordinary

No.	Type	Colour	U/M	M/M	F/U
C81	48	**3d** Vio./blue/yel. green	12	8	5
C82	49	**6d** Multicoloured	40	25	15
C83	50	**9d** Multicoloured	2.00	1.30	1.60
C84	50	9d Multicoloured (Wmk. Inverted)	£45	£30	£30
C85	51	**1/3d** Multicoloured	3.75	2.50	2.65
C86	51	1/3d Multicoloured (Wmk. Inverted)	£75	£50	£50
		Set of 4	5.50	3.65	4.00
		First Day Cover			£10
		Presentation Pack	£45		

Phosphor

No.	Type	Colour	U/M	M/M	F/U
C87	48	**3d** Vio./blue/yel. green	25	15	20
C88	49	**6d** Multicoloured	2.00	1.30	2.00
C89	50	**9d** Multicoloured	£10	6.75	8.00
C90	51	**1/3d** Multicoloured	£17	£11	£12
		Set of 4	£28	£18	£20
		First Day Cover			£30

Type 52

Type 53

OPENING OF THE FORTH ROAD BRIDGE Issued 4/9/64

Ordinary

No.	Type	Colour	U/M	M/M	F/U
C91	52	**3d** Blk./ult./pur. mauve	10	5	5
C92	53	**6d** Black/blue/maroon	70	50	60
C93	53	6d Black/blue/maroon (Wmk. Inverted)	1.50	1.00	1.00
		Set of 2	70	50	60
		First Day Cover			4.00
		Presentation Pack	£185		

COMMEMORATIVE ISSUES 1964-65

Printers: Harrison & Sons in Photogravure   *Perf:* 15 x 14   *Paper:* Chalky   *Watermark:* Multiple Crowns

No.	Type		Colour	U/M	M/M	F/U

OPENING OF THE FORTH ROAD BRIDGE (continued)

Phosphor

No.	Type		Colour	U/M	M/M	F/U
C94	52	**3d**	Blk./ult./pur. mauve	60	40	40
C95	53	**6d**	Black/blue/maroon	4.00	2.65	3.25
C96	53	**6d**	Black/blue/maroon (Wmk. Inverted)	£28	£18	£20
			Set of 2	4.25	2.80	3.30
			First Day Cover			7.00

Type 54   *Type 55*

SIR WINSTON CHURCHILL MEMORIAL ISSUE Issued 8/7/65

Ordinary

No.	Type		Colour	U/M	M/M	F/U
C97	54	**4d**	Black/dp. brown (R)	10	5	10
C98	54	**4d**	Black/dp. brown (T)	10	5	10
C99	54	**4d**	Black/dp. brown (R) (Wmk. Inverted)	1.00	65	65
C100	55	**1/3d**	Black/slate grey	80	55	75
C101	55	**1/3d**	Black/slate grey (Wmk. Inverted)	£25	£15	£15
			Set of 2	80	55	75
			First Day Cover			5.00
			Presentation Pack	£12		

Phosphor

No.	Type		Colour	U/M	M/M	F/U
C102	54	**4d**	Black/dp. brown (R)	40	25	30
C103	55	**1/3d**	Black/slate grey	3.95	2.65	3.45
			Set of 2	4.00	2.70	3.50
			First Day Cover			7.00

(R) = Rembrandt Press
(T) = Timson Press

Type 56

Type 57

700TH ANNIVERSARY OF PARLIAMENT Issued 19/7/65

Ordinary

No.	Type		Colour	U/M	M/M	F/U
C104	56	**6d**	Olive green	20	15	20
C105	57	**2/6d**	Black/grey/ivory	1.80	1.35	1.10
C106	57	**2/6d**	Black/grey/ivory (Wmk. Inverted)	7.00	4.65	4.65
			Set of 2	1.85	1.40	1.15
			First Day Cover			6.00
			Presentation Pack	£18		

Phosphor

No.	Type		Colour	U/M	M/M	F/U
C107	56	**6d**	Olive green	1.35	90	90
			First Day Cover			6.00

Type 58   *Type 59*

CENTENARY OF THE SALVATION ARMY Issued 9/8/65

Ordinary

No.	Type		Colour	U/M	M/M	F/U
C108	58	**3d**	Multicoloured	15	10	10
C109	59	**1/6d**	Multicoloured	1.70	1.10	1.30
			Set of 2	1.75	1.15	1.35
			First Day Cover			6.00

Phosphor

No.	Type		Colour	U/M	M/M	F/U
C110	58	**3d**	Multicoloured (1 band)	50	35	45
C111	59	**1/6d**	Multicoloured	7.50	5.00	4.25
			Set of 2	7.75	5.25	4.50
			First Day Cover			8.00

Type 60   *Type 61*

COMMONWEALTH ARTS FESTIVAL Issued 1/9/65

Ordinary

No.	Type		Colour	U/M	M/M	F/U
C112	60	**6d**	Black/orange	30	20	25
C113	61	**1/6d**	Black/mauve	1.75	1.15	1.25
			Set of 2	1.80	1.20	1.35
			First Day Cover			5.00

Phosphor

No.	Type		Colour	U/M	M/M	F/U
C114	60	**6d**	Black/orange	75	50	55
C115	61	**1/6d**	Black/mauve	5.75	3.75	3.85
			Set of 2	6.00	4.00	4.00
			First Day Cover			6.00

COMMEMORATIVE ISSUES 1965

Printers: Harrison & Sons in Photogravure   *Perf:* 15 x 14   *Paper:* Chalky   *Watermark:* Multiple Crowns

No.	Type	Colour	U/M	M/M	F/U

Type 62

Type 68

Type 69

Type 63

Type 70

Type 71

JOSEPH LISTER CENTENARY Issued 1/9/65

Ordinary

No.	Type	Colour	U/M	M/M	F/U
C116	62	**4d** Brown/blue/grey	10	5	5
C117	63	**1/-d** Black/purple/blue	1.00	65	75
C118	63	**1/-d** Black/purple/blue (Wmk. Inverted)	£60	£40	£40
		Set of 2	1.00	65	75
		First Day Cover			3.00

Phosphor

C119	62	**4d** Brown/blue/grey	25	15	20
C120	63	**1/-d** Black/purple/blue	1.90	1.25	1.50
		Set of 2	2.00	1.30	1.60
		First Day Cover			5.00

25TH ANNIVERSARY OF THE BATTLE OF BRITAIN Issued 13/9/65

Ordinary

No.	Type	Colour	U/M	M/M	F/U
C121	64	**4d** Olive green/black	30	20	20
C122	65	**4d** Olive grn./grey/blk.	30	20	20
C123	66	**4d** Ol. grn./red/bl./grey	30	20	20
C124	67	**4d** Olive grn./grey/blk.	30	20	20
C125	68	**4d** Olive grn./grey/blk.	30	20	20
C126	69	**4d** Ol. grn./grey/bl./blk.	30	20	20
C121/6		4d Block of 6 se-tenant	4.00	2.65	4.00
C127	70	9d Black/orange/pur.	1.75	1.15	1.25
C128	70	9d Black/orange/pur. (Wmk. Inverted)	£15	£10	£10
C129	71	1/3d Multicoloured	1.75	1.15	1.25
C130	71	1/3d Multicoloured (Wmk. Inverted)	9.00	6.00	6.00
		Set of 8	7.00	4.65	6.00
		First Day Cover			8.50
		Presentation Pack	£22		

Phosphor

C131	64	**4d** Olive green/black	30	20	30
C132	65	**4d** Olive grn./grey/blk.	30	20	30
C133	66	**4d** Ol. grn./red/bl/grey	30	20	30
C134	67	**4d** Olive grn./grey/blk.	30	20	30
C135	68	**4d** Olive grn./grey/blk.	30	20	30
C136	69	**4d** Ol. grn. /grey/bl./blk.	30	20	30
C131/6		4d Block of 6 se-tenant	4.25	2.80	4.25
C137	70	9d Black/orange/pur.	2.00	1.30	1.50
C138	71	1/3d Multicoloured	2.25	1.45	1.75
C139	71	1/3d Multicoloured (Wmk. Inverted)	4.00	2.50	2.50
		Set of 8	8.00	5.30	7.00
		First Day Cover			9.00

Type 64

Type 65

Type 66

Type 67

 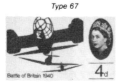

COMMEMORATIVE ISSUES 1965 – 66

Printers: Harrison & Sons in Photogravure   *Perf:* 15 x 14   *Paper:* Chalky   *Watermark:* Multiple Crowns

No.	Type	Colour	U/M	M/M	F/U

Type 72

Type 73

Type 76

Type 77

OPENING OF G.P.O. TOWER, LONDON Issued 8/10/65

Ordinary

No.	Type	Colour		U/M	M/M	F/U
C140	72	**3d**	Yel. bis./bl./olive grn.	10	5	5
C141	73	**1/3d**	Blue/grn./olive grn.	70	45	60
C142	73	**1/3d**	Blue/grn./olive grn.	£20	£15	£15
			(Wmk. Inverted)			
			Set of 2	70	45	60
			First day Cover			2.00
			Presentation Pack	1.50		

Phosphor

No.	Type	Colour		U/M	M/M	F/U
C143	72	**3d**	Yel. bis./bl./ol. grn.	15	10	15
			(1 band L.)			
C144	72	**3d**	Yel. bis./bl./ol. grn.	15	10	15
			(1 band R.)			
C143/4		3d	Pair	50	35	50
			(1 band L & 1 band R)			
C145	73	**1/3d**	Blue/grn./olive grn.	1.00	65	65
C146	73	**1/3d**	Blue/grn./olive grn.	£25	£15	£15
			(Wmk. Inverted)			
			Set of 2	1.40	90	1.00
			First Day Cover			2.25
			Presentation Pack	2.25		

CENTENARY OF INTERNATIONAL TELECOMMUNICATIONS UNION
Issued 15/11/65

Ordinary

No.	Type	Colour		U/M	M/M	F/U
C151	76	**9d**	Multicoloured	50	35	40
C152	76	**9d**	Multicoloured	3.50	2.25	2.25
			(Wmk. Inverted)			
C153	77	**1/6d**	Multicoloured	1.50	1.00	1.00
			Set of 2	1.75	1.15	1.25
			First Day Cover			3.00

Phosphor

No.	Type	Colour		U/M	M/M	F/U
C154	76	**9d**	Multicoloured	5.00	3.25	3.50
C155	76	**9d**	Multicoloured	£30	£20	£20
			(Wmk. Inverted)			
C156	77	**1/6d**	Multicoloured	£13	8.75	9.00
			Set of 2	£16	£11	£11
			First Day Cover			£12

Type 74

Type 75

Type 78

Type 79

20TH ANNIVERSARY OF UNITED NATIONS AND INTERNATIONAL CO-OPERATION YEAR Issued 25/10/65

Ordinary

No.	Type	Colour		U/M	M/M	F/U
C147	74	**3d**	Black/blue/orange	15	10	10
C148	75	**1/6d**	Black/magenta/blue	1.30	85	1.10
			Set of 2	1.30	85	1.10
			First Day Cover			3.00

Phosphor

No.	Type	Colour		U/M	M/M	F/U
C149	74	**3d**	Blk./bl./or. (1 band)	15	10	15
C150	75	**1/6d**	Black/magenta/blue	1.50	1.00	1.25
			Set of 2	1.50	1.00	1.25
			First Day Cover			3.50

ROBERT BURNS Issued 25/1/66

Ordinary

No.	Type	Colour		U/M	M/M	F/U
C157	78	**4d**	Blk/vio. blk./lt. blue	10	5	5
C158	79	**1/3d**	Blk./sl. blue/orange	75	50	70
			Set of 2	75	50	70
			First Day Cover			2.00
			Presentation Pack	£12		

Phosphor

No.	Type	Colour		U/M	M/M	F/U
C159	78	**4d**	Blk./vio. blk./lt. blue	20	15	20
C160	79	**1/3d**	Blk./sl. blue/orange	1.30	85	1.30
			Set of 2	1.40	90	1.40
			First Day Cover			3.50

COMMEMORATIVE ISSUES 1966

Printers: Harrison & Sons in Photogravure   *Perf:* 15 x 14   *Paper:* Chalky   *Watermark:* Multiple Crowns

No.	Type		Colour	U/M	M/M	F/U

Type 80   *Type 81*

900TH ANNIVERSARY WESTMINSTER ABBEY Issued 28/2/66
2/6d value recess printed by Bradbury, Wilkinson & Co. (Perf.: 11 x 12)

Ordinary

No.	Type		Colour	U/M	M/M	F/U
C161	80	**3d**	Black/chest./blue	10	5	5
C162	81	**2/6d**	Black	1.45	95	1.25
			Set of 2	1.45	95	1.25
			First Day Cover			3.50
			Presentation Pack	8.00		

Phosphor

No.	Type		Colour	U/M	M/M	F/U
C163	80	**3d**	Black/chest./blue (1 band)	30	20	30
			First Day Cover			3.00

Type 81   *Type 82*

Type 83   *Type 84*

LANDSCAPES OF THE BRITISH ISLES Issued 2/5/66

Ordinary

No.	Type		Colour	U/M	M/M	F/U
C164	81	**4d**	Black/yel. grn./blue	10	5	5
C165	82	**6d**	Blk./emer. grn./blue	15	10	15
C166	82	6d	Blk./emer. grn./blue (Wmk. Inverted)	1.75	1.20	1.20
C167	83	**1/3d**	Blk./yel. grn./sl. blue	40	25	40
C168	84	**1/6d**	Blk./orange/dp. blue	35	25	35
C169	84	1/6d	Blk./orange/dp. blue (Wmk. Inverted)	4.50	3.00	3.00
			Set of 4	90	60	90
			First Day Cover			2.50

Phosphor

No.	Type		Colour	U/M	M/M	F/U
C170	81	**4d**	Black/yel. grn./blue	15	10	10
C171	82	**6d**	Blk./emer. grn./blue	30	20	15
C172	82	6d	Blk./emer. grn./blue (Wmk. Inverted)	£18	£12	£12
C173	83	**1/3d**	Blk./yel. grn./sl. blue	80	50	40
C174	84	**1/6d**	Blk./orange/dp. blue	90	60	45
			Set of 4	2.00	1.30	1.00
			First Day Cover			3.50

Type 85

Type 86   *Type 87*

WORLD CUP FOOTBALL COMPETITION Issued 1/6/66

Ordinary

No.	Type		Colour	U/M	M/M	F/U
C175	85	**4d**	Multicoloured	5	5	5
C176	86	**6d**	Multicoloured	15	10	15
C177	86	6d	Multicoloured (Wmk. Inverted)	1.00	65	65
C178	87	**1/3d**	Multicoloured	35	25	35
C179	87	1/3	Multicoloured (Wmk. Inverted)	£35	£25	£25
			Set of 3	50	35	50
			First Day Cover			3.00
			Presentation Pack	2.25		

Phosphor

No.	Type		Colour	U/M	M/M	F/U
C180	85	**4d**	Multicoloured (2 bands)	10	5	10
C181	86	**6d**	Multicoloured	20	15	20
C182	87	**1/3**	Multicoloured	40	25	40
C183	87	1/3	Multicoloured (Wmk. Inverted)	1.75	1.15	1.15
			Set of 3	60	40	60
			First Day Cover			3.00

COMMEMORATIVE ISSUES 1966

Printers: Harrison & Sons in Photogravure   *Perf:* 15 x 14   *Paper:* Chalky   *Watermark:* Multiple Crowns

No.	Type	Colour	U/M	M/M	F/U

Type 88

Type 89

Type 93

Type 90

Type 91

Type 94

BRITISH BIRDS Issued 8/8/66

Ordinary

No.	Type		Colour	U/M	M/M	F/U
C184	88	**4d**	Multicoloured	15	10	15
C185	89	**4d**	Multicoloured	15	10	15
C186	90	**4d**	Multicoloured	15	10	15
C187	91	**4d**	Multicoloured	15	10	15
C184/7		4d	Block of 4 se-tenant	70	45	75
C188/91		4d	Block of 4 se-tenant	6.00	4.00	4.00
			(Wmk. Inverted)			
			First Day Cover			2.25
			Presentation Pack	2.25		

Phosphor

No.	Type		Colour	U/M	M/M	F/U
C192	88	**4d**	Multicoloured	15	10	15
C193	89	**4d**	Multicoloured	15	10	15
C194	90	**4d**	Multicoloured	15	10	15
C195	91	**4d**	Multicoloured	15	10	15
C192/5		4d	Block of 4 se-tenant	70	45	75
C196/9		4d	Block of 4 se-tenant	£35	£25	£25
			(Wmk. Inverted)			
			First Day Cover			2.25

Type 95

Type 96

Type 92

BRITISH TECHNOLOGY Issued 19/9/66

Ordinary

No.	Type		Colour	U/M	M/M	F/U
C201	93	**4d**	Black/yellow	5	5	5
C202	94	**6d**	Red/dp. bl./orange	10	5	10
C203	95	**1/3d**	Multicoloured	35	25	30
C204	96	**1/6d**	Multicoloured	35	25	30
			Set of 4	80	55	70
			First Day Cover			2.00
			Presentation Pack	2.25		

Phosphor

No.	Type		Colour	U/M	M/M	F/U
C205	93	**4d**	Black/yellow	15	10	10
C206	94	**6d**	Red/dp. bl./orange	30	20	20
C207	95	**1/3d**	Multicoloured	50	35	30
C208	96	**1/6d**	Multicoloured	60	40	35
			Set of 4	1.40	90	85
			First Day Cover			2.00

WORLD CUP FOOTBALL – ENGLAND WINNERS Issued 18/8/66

Ordinary

No.	Type		Colour	U/M	M/M	F/U
C200	92	**4d**	Multicoloured	10	5	20
			First Day Cover			70

COMMEMORATIVE ISSUES 1966

Printers: Harrison & Sons in Photogravure   *Perf:* 15 x 14   *Paper:* Chalky   *Watermark:* Multiple Crowns

No.	Type		Colour	U/M	M/M	F/U

900TH ANNIVERSARY OF BATTLE OF HASTINGS Issued 14/10/66

Ordinary

No.	Type		Colour	U/M	M/M	F/U
C209	97	4d	Multicoloured	15	10	10
C210	98	4d	Multicoloured	15	10	10
C211	99	4d	Multicoloured	15	10	10
C212	100	4d	Multicoloured	15	10	10
C213	101	4d	Multicoloured	15	10	10
C214	102	4d	Multicoloured	15	10	10
C209/214		4d	Strip of 6 se-tenant	1.50	1.00	90
C215/220		4d	Strip of 6 se-tenant (Wmk. Inverted)	8.00	5.50	5.50
C221	103	6d	Multicoloured	20	15	25
C222	103	6d	Multicoloured (Wmk. Inverted)	£25	£15	£15
C223	104	1/3d	Multicoloured (Wmk. Sideways)	40	25	40
C224	104	1/3d	Multicoloured (Wmk. Sideways Inv)	£18	£12	£12
			Set of 8	1.90	1.20	1.40
			First Day Cover			2.00
			Presentation Pack	2.75		

Phosphor

No.	Type		Colour	U/M	M/M	F/U
C225	97	4d	Multicoloured	20	15	15
C226	98	4d	Multicoloured	20	15	15
C227	99	4d	Multicoloured	20	15	15
C228	100	4d	Multicoloured	20	15	15
C229	101	4d	Multicoloured	20	15	15
C230	102	4d	Multicoloured	20	15	15
C225/230		4d	Strip of 6 se-tenant	1.75	1.15	1.50
C231/6		4d	Strip of 6 se-tenant (Wmk. Inverted)	5.00	3.50	3.50
C237	103	6d	Multicoloured	30	20	30
C238	103	6d	Multicoloured (Wmk. Inverted)	£25	£15	£15
C239	104	1/3d	Multicoloured (Wmk. Sideways)	60	40	60
C240	104	1/3d	Multicoloured (Wmk. Sideways Inv)	3.50	2.50	2.50
			Set of 8	2.30	1.50	2.20
			First Day Cover			2.75

Type 97   *Type 98*
Type 99   *Type 100*
Type 101   *Type 102*
Type 103
Type 104

CHRISTMAS 1966 Issued 1/12/66

Ordinary

No.	Type		Colour	U/M	M/M	F/U
C241	105	3d	Multicoloured	5	5	5
C242	106	1/6d	Multicoloured	35	25	35
C243	106	1/6d	Multicoloured (Wmk. Inverted)	3.50	2.25	2.25
			Set of 2	35	25	35
			First Day Cover			50
			Presentation Pack	2.25		

Phosphor

No.	Type		Colour	U/M	M/M	F/U
C244	105	3d	Multicoloured (1 band L.)	10	5	5
C245	105	3d	Multicoloured (1 band R.)	10	5	5
C244/5	105	3d	Pair (1 band L & 1 band R)	25	15	25

No.	Type		Colour	U/M	M/M	F/U
C246	106	1/6d	Multicoloured (2 bands)	35	25	35
C247	106	1/6d	Multicoloured (Wmk. Inverted)	£15	£10	£10
			Set of 2	55	35	55
			First Day Cover			75

Type 106
Type 105

COMMEMORATIVE ISSUES 1967

Printers: Harrison & Sons in Photogravure   *Perf:* 15 x 14   *Paper:* Chalky   *Watermark:* Multiple Crowns

No.	Type		Colour	U/M	M/M	F/U

Type 107   *Type 108*

EUROPEAN FREE TRADE ASSOCIATION Issued 20/2/67

Ordinary

No.	Type		Colour	U/M	M/M	F/U
C248	107	**9d**	Multicoloured	15	10	15
C249	107	9d	Multicoloured (Wmk. Inverted)	£12	8.00	8.00
C250	108	**1/6d**	Multicoloured	25	15	20
			Set of 2	35	25	30
			First Day Cover			60
			Presentation Pack	1.00		

Phosphor

C251	107	**9d**	Multicoloured	10	5	15
C252	107	9d	Multicoloured (Wmk. Inverted)	4.00	2.75	2.75
C253	108	**1/6d**	Multicoloured	15	10	20
C254	108	1/6d	Multicoloured (Wmk. Inverted)	£12	8.00	8.00
			Set of 2	25	15	30
			First Day Cover			60

Type 109   *Type 110*

Type 111   *Type 112*

Type 113   *Type 114*

BRITISH WILD FLOWERS Issued 24/4/67

Ordinary

No.	Type		Colour	U/M	M/M	F/U
C255	109	**4d**	Multicoloured	15	10	10
C256	110	**4d**	Multicoloured	15	10	10
C257	111	**4d**	Multicoloured	15	10	10
C258	112	**4d**	Multicoloured	15	10	10
C255/8		4d	Block of 4 se-tenant	90	60	60
C259/262		4d	Block of 4 se-tenant (Wmk. Inverted)	3.50	2.25	2.25
C263	113	**9d**	Multicoloured	20	15	15
C264	113	9d	Multicoloured (Wmk. Inverted)	70	45	45
C265	114	**1/9d**	Multicoloured	45	30	30
			Set of 6	1.45	95	95
			First Day Cover			1.50
			Presentation Pack	2.25		

Phosphor

C266	109	**4d**	Multicoloured	5	5	5
C267	110	**4d**	Multicoloured	5	5	5
C268	111	**4d**	Multicoloured	5	5	5
C269	112	**4d**	Multicoloured	5	5	5
C266/9		4d	Block of 4 se-tenant	35	25	50
C270/3		4d	Block of 4 se-tenant (Wmk. Inverted)	3.50	2.25	2.25
C274	113	**9d**	Multicoloured	15	10	15
C275	114	**1/9d**	Multicoloured	20	15	20
			Set of 6	60	45	75
			First Day Cover			1.00
			Presentation Pack	95		

PHOSPHOR LINES

All the following issues were printed with vertical phosphor bands only, but many also exist with the phosphor omitted in error. All were printed on unwatermarked paper except C280/285

Type 116

Type 115   *Type 117*

BRITISH PAINTINGS 1967 Issued 10/7/67

No.	Type		Colour	U/M	M/M	F/U
C276	115	**4d**	Multicoloured	5	5	5
C277	116	**9d**	Multicoloured	15	10	20
C278	117	**1/6d**	Multicoloured	15	10	15
			Set of 3	30	20	35
			First Day Cover			75
			Presentation Pack	1.75		

COMMEMORATIVE ISSUES 1967 – 68

Printers: Harrison & Sons in Photogravure   *Perf:* 15 x 14   *Paper:* Chalky   *Unwatermarked*

No.	Type	Colour	U/M	M/M	F/U	No.	Type	Colour	U/M	F/U

Type 118

Type 123

Type 124

SIR FRANCIS CHICHESTER Issued 24/7/67

C279	118	**1/9d** Multicoloured	15	10	15
		First Day Cover			40

IMPORTANT NOTE

From this issue all stamps have only 2 vertical phophor bands except where stated. The price column for Mounted Mint stamps (M/M) is omitted from this date, as most collectors now insist on Unmounted Mint (U/M) in modern issues.

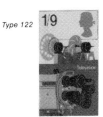

Type 125

CHRISTMAS 1967 Issued 18/10/67 (4d only) and 27/11/67

C286	123	**3d** Multicoloured (1 band)	5	5
C287	124	**4d** Multicoloured	5	5
C288	125	**1/6d** Multicoloured	20	20
		Set of 3	25	25
		First Day Cover 18/10/67		15
		First Day Cover 27/11/67		35

SPECIAL GIFT PACK Issued 27/11/67

C248/288		Presentation Pack	2.50

Type 119

Type 120

Type 122 **1/9**

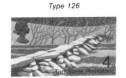

Type 126

Type 127

Type 121

BRITISH SCIENTIFIC DISCOVERIES Issued 19/9/67
(Wmk. Multiple Crowns)

			U/M	F/U
C280	119	**4d** Yellow/blk./red (3 bands)	5	5
C281	120	**1/–d** Multicoloured	10	10
C282	120	**1/–d** Multicoloured (Wmk. Inverted)	£10	8.00
C283	121	**1/6d** Multicoloured	15	15
C284	121	**1/6d** Multicoloured (Wmk. Inverted)	£15	£10
C285	122	**1/9d** Multicoloured (Wmk. Sideways)	20	20
		Set of 4	45	45
		First Day Cover		80
		Presentation Pack	1.10	

Type 128

Type 129

BRITISH BRIDGES Issued 29/4/68

			U/M	F/U
C289	126	**4d** Multicoloured	5	5
C290	127	**9d** Multicoloured	10	10
C291	128	**1/6d** Multicoloured	15	15
C292	129	**1/9d** Multicoloured	20	20
		Set of 4	45	45
		First Day Cover		80
		Presentation Pack	1.10	

COMMEMORATIVE ISSUES 1968

Printers: Harrison & Sons in Photogravure   *Perf:* 15 x 14   *Paper:* Chalky   *Unwatermarked*

No.	Type	Colour	U/M	F/U

Type 130

Type 131

Type 132

Type 133

BRITISH ANNIVERSARIES 1968 Issued 29/5/68

No.	Type		Colour	U/M	F/U
C293	130	**4d**	Multicoloured	5	5
C294	131	**9d**	Blk./vio./Bl.grey	10	10
C295	132	**1/–d**	Multicoloured	15	15
C296	133	**1/9d**	Blk. brn./yel. brn.	20	20
			Set of 4	45	
			First Day Cover		1.20
			Presentation Pack	1.00	

Type 134

Type 135

Type 136   *Type 137*

BRITISH PAINTINGS 1968 Issued 12/8/68

No.	Type		Colour	U/M	F/U
C297	134	**4d**	Multicoloured	5	5
C298	135	**1/–d**	Multicoloured	10	10
C299	136	**1/6d**	Multicoloured	20	20
C300	137	**1/9d**	Multicoloured	20	20
			Set of 4	50	50
			First Day Cover		75
			Presentation Pack	85	

COLLECTORS PACK 1968 Issued 16/9/68

C280/300		Presentation Pack	4.00

GIFT PACK Issued 16/9/68

C289/300		Presentation Pack	4.00

Type 138

Type 139

Type 140

CHRISTMAS 1968 Issued 25/11/68

No.	Type		Colour	U/M	F/U
C301	138	**4d**	Multicoloured (1 band)	5	5
C302	139	**9d**	Multicoloured	10	10
C303	140	**1/6d**	Multicoloured	20	20
			Set of 3	30	30
			First Day Cover		50
			Presentation Pack	85	

COMMEMORATIVE ISSUES 1969

Printers: Harrison & Sons in Photogravure   *Perf:* 15 x 14   *Paper:* Chalky   *Unwatermarked*

No.	Type	Colour	U/M	F/U

Type 141

Type 142

Type 143

Type 144

Type 145

Type 146

FAMOUS BRITISH SHIPS Issued 15/1/69

No.	Type	Colour	U/M	F/U
C304	141	**5d** Multicoloured (1 band horizontal)	5	5
C305	142	**9d** Multicoloured	20	20
C306	143	**9d** Multicoloured	20	20
C307	144	**9d** Multicoloured	20	20
C305/7		9d Strip of 3 se-tenant	75	85
C308	145	**1/–d** Multicoloured	20	20
C309	146	**1/–d** Multicoloured	20	20
C308/9		1/–d Pair se-tenant	50	60
		Set of 6	1.10	1.35
		First Day Cover		2.00
		Presentation Pack	1.75	

No.	Type	Colour	U/M	F/U

Type 147

Type 148

Type 149

FIRST FLIGHT OF CONCORDE Issued 3/3/69

No.	Type	Colour	U/M	F/U
C310	147	**4d** Multicoloured	5	5
C311	148	**9d** Multicoloured	10	15
C312	149	**1/6d** Lt. bl./dk. bl./silver	20	15
		Set of 3	30	30
		First Day Cover		75
		Presentation Pack	1.00	

Type 150

Type 151

Type 152

Type 153

Type 154

BRITISH ANNIVERSARIES 1969 Issued 2/4/69

No.	Type	Colour	U/M	F/U
C313	150	**5d** Black/blue/brown	5	5
C314	151	**9d** Blue/green/black	10	15
C315	152	**1/–d** Mauve/red/blue	10	10
C316	153	**1/6d** Multicoloured	15	15
C317	154	**1/9d** Yellow/green/sepia	20	20
		Set of 5	55	60
		First Day Cover		1.25
		Presentation Pack	1.25	

COMMEMORATIVE ISSUES 1969

Printers: Harrison & Sons in Photogravure   *Perf:* 15 x 14   *Paper:* Chalky   *Unwatermarked*

No.	Type		Colour	U/M	F/U

Type 155

Type 156

Type 157

Type 158

Type 159

Type 160

BRITISH ARCHITECTURE (CATHEDRALS) Issued 28/5/69

No.	Type		Colour	U/M	F/U
C318	155	**5d**	Blk./or./sepia/violet	5	10
C319	156	**5d**	Blk./or./sepia/violet	5	10
C320	157	**5d**	Blk./or./sepia/violet	5	10
C321	158	**5d**	Blk./or./sepia/violet	5	10
C318/21		5d	Block of 4 se-tenant	35	45
C322	159	**9d**	Multicoloured	15	20
C323	160	**1/6d**	Multicoloured	20	20
			Set of 6	65	75
			First Day Cover		90
			Presentation Pack	1.00	

Type 161   *Type 162*

No.	Type		Colour	U/M	F/U

Type 163

Type 164

Type 165

INVESTITURE OF H.R.H. THE PRINCE OF WALES Issued 1/7/69

No.	Type		Colour	U/M	F/U
C324	161	**5d**	Multicoloured	5	5
C325	162	**5d**	Multicoloured	5	5
C326	163	**5d**	Multicoloured	5	5
C324/6		5d	Strip of 3 se-tenant	40	40
C327	164	**9d**	Grey/black/gold	15	15
C328	165	**1/-d**	Black/gold	15	15
			Set of 5	60	60
			First Day Cover		75
			Presentation Pack	1.00	

Type 166

GANDHI CENTENARY YEAR Issued 13/8/69

No.	Type		Colour	U/M	F/U
C329	166	**1/6d**	Green/orange/black	15	15
			First Day Cover		35

COLLECTORS PACK 1969 Issued 15/9/69
C301/329			Presentation Pack	£15	

Printers: Harrison & Sons in Photogravure   *Perf:* 15 x 14   *Paper:* Chalky   *Unwatermarked*

No.	Type	Colour	U/M	F/U

Type 167   *Type 168*

Type 174   *Type 175*

Type 169   *Type 170*

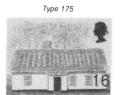

Type 176   *Type 177*

POST OFFICE TECHNOLOGY Issued 1/10/69
Printed by Lithography (De La Rue) Perf.:13½ x 14

No.	Type		Colour	U/M	F/U
C330	167	**5d**	Bl./lavender/blk.	5	5
C331	168	**9d**	Green/vio. bl./blk.	10	15
C332	169	**1/–d**	Grn./lavender/blk.	10	10
C333	170	**1/6d**	Rose/blue/black	20	20
			Set of 4	40	45
			First Day Cover		60
			Presentation Pack	1.75	

BRITISH RURAL ARCHITECTURE Issued 11/2/70

No.	Type		Colour	U/M	F/U
C337	174	**5d**	Multicoloured	5	5
C338	175	**9d**	Multicoloured	20	20
C339	176	**1/–d**	Multicoloured	20	20
C340	177	**1/6d**	Multicoloured	25	25
			Set of 4	65	65
			First Day Cover		80
			Presentation Pack	2.00	

Type 171   *Type 172*

Type 178   *Type 179*

Type 180

Type 181   *Type 182*

Type 173

CHRISTMAS 1969 Issued 26/11/69

No.	Type		Colour	U/M	F/U
C334	171	**4d**	Multicoloured	5	5
			(1 band)		
C335	172	**5d**	Multicoloured	5	5
C336	173	**1/6d**	Multicoloured	20	20
			Set of 3	25	25
			First Day Cover		50
			Presentation Pack	1.75	

ANNIVERSARIES Issued 1/4/70

No.	Type		Colour	U/M	F/U
C341	178	**5d**	Multicoloured	5	5
C342	179	**9d**	Multicoloured	20	20
C343	180	**1/–d**	Multicoloured	20	15
C344	181	**1/6d**	Multicoloured	25	20
C345	182	**1/9d**	Multicoloured	30	30
			Set of 5	90	80
			First Day Cover		1.00
			Presentation Pack	2.00	

COMMEMORATIVE ISSUES 1970

Printers: Harrison & Sons in Photogravure   *Perf:* 15 x 14   *Paper:* Chalky   *Unwatermarked*

No.	Type	Colour	U/M	F/U

Type 183   *Type 184*

Type 185

Type 186   *Type 187*

LITERARY ANNIVERSARIES Issued 3/6/70

No.	Type		Colour	U/M	F/U
C346	183	**5d**	Multicoloured	10	10
C347	184	**5d**	Multicoloured	10	10
C348	185	**5d**	Multicoloured	10	10
C349	186	**5d**	Multicoloured	10	10
C346/9		5d	Block of 4 se-tenant	60	60
C350	187	**1/6d**	Multicoloured	30	30
			Set of 5	80	80
			First Day Cover		1.00
			Presentation Pack	1.60	

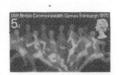

Type 188   *Type 189*

Type 190

9TH COMMONWEALTH GAMES Issued 15/7/70 Perf.: 13½ x 14

No.	Type		Colour	U/M	F/U
C351	188	**5d**	Multicoloured	5	5
C352	189	**1/6d**	Brn./bl./pur./bl. grey	30	25
C353	190	**1/9d**	Pink/mauve/or./brn.	35	35
			Set of 3	65	60
			First Day Cover		80
			Presentation Pack	1.60	

No.	Type	Colour	U/M	F/U

COLLECTORS PACK 1970 Issued 14/9/70

C330/353		Presentation Pack	£15

Type 191   *Type 192*   *Type 193*

INTERNATIONAL PHILATELIC EXHIBITION (PHILYMPIA)
Issued 18/9/70

No.	Type		Colour	U/M	F/U
C354	191	**5d**	Black/grey/brown	5	5
C355	192	**9d**	Black/grey/green	35	25
C356	193	**1/6d**	Black/grey/car./bl.	40	25
			Set of 3	75	50
			First Day Cover		75
			Presentation Pack	1.60	

Type 194   *Type 195*

Type 196

CHRISTMAS 1970 Issued 25/11/70

No.	Type		Colour	U/M	F/U
C357	194	**4d**	Multicoloured	5	5
			(1 band)		
C358	195	**5d**	Multicoloured	5	5
C359	196	**1/6d**	Multicoloured	30	30
			Set of 3	35	35
			First Day Cover		50
			Presentation Pack	1.60	

COMMEMORATIVE ISSUES 1971 – DECIMAL CURRENCY

Printers: Harrison & Sons in Photogravure   *Perf:* 15 x 14   *Paper:* Chalky   *Unwatermarked*

No.	Type	Colour	U/M	F/U

Type 197

Type 198

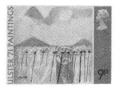

Type 199

ULSTER 71 Issued 16/6/71

C360	197	**3p**	Multicoloured	20	5
C361	198	**7½p**	Multicoloured	1.95	90
C362	199	**9p**	Multicoloured	2.40	1.10
			Set of 3	4.25	2.00
			First Day Cover		3.25
			Presentation Pack	6.50	

Type 200

Type 201

Type 202

LITERARY ANNIVERSARIES Issued 28/7/71

C363	200	**3p**	Black/gold/blue	15	5
C364	201	**5p**	Black/gold/green	1.50	75
C365	202	**7½p**	Black/gold/brown	1.75	90
			Set of 3	3.00	1.50
			First Day Cover		3.25
			Presentation Pack	4.75	

No.	Type	Colour	U/M	F/U

Type 203

Type 204

Type 205

GENERAL ANNIVERSARIES Issued 25/8/71

C366	203	**3p**	Multicoloured	20	5
C367	204	**7½p**	Multicoloured	2.50	90
C368	205	**9p**	Multicoloured	2.75	1.10
			Set of 3	5.00	2.00
			First Day Cover		3.25
			Presentation Pack	6.50	

Type 206

Type 207

Type 208

Type 209

BRITISH ARCHITECTURE SERIES:
MODERN UNIVERSITY BUILDINGS Issued 22/9/71

C369	206	**3p**	Multicoloured	20	10
C370	207	**5p**	Multicoloured	55	45
C371	208	**7½p**	Multicoloured	1.50	1.10
C372	209	**9p**	Multicoloured	2.25	1.50
			Set of 4	4.25	3.00
			First Day Cover		3.75
			Presentation Pack	6.50	

COMMEMORATIVE ISSUES 1971 – 72

Printers: Harrison & Sons in Photogravure   *Perf:* 15 x 14   *Paper:* Chalky   *Unwatermarked*

No.	Type	Colour	U/M	F/U

COLLECTORS PACK 1971 Issued 29/9/71

No.	Type	Colour	U/M	F/U
C354/372		Presentation Pack	£22	

Type 210

Type 211

Type 212

CHRISTMAS 1971 Issued 13/10/71

No.	Type	Colour	U/M	F/U
C373	210	**2½p** Multicoloured (1 band)	15	5
C374	211	**3p** Multicoloured	15	5
C375	212	**7½p** Multicoloured	80	95
		Set of 3	1.00	1.00
		First Day Cover		1.25
		Presentation Pack	1.75	

Type 215

Type 216

BRITISH POLAR EXPLORERS Issued 16/2/72

No.	Type	Colour	U/M	F/U
C376	213	**3p** Multicoloured	15	10
C377	214	**5p** Multicoloured	60	50
C378	215	**7½p** Multicoloured	1.50	1.10
C379	216	**9p** Multicoloured	2.25	1.50
		Set of 4	4.25	3.00
		First Day Cover		3.50
		Presentation Pack	5.50	

Type 217

Type 213

Type 214

Type 218

Type 219

GENERAL ANNIVERSARIES Issued 26/4/72

No.	Type	Colour	U/M	F/U
C380	217	**3p** Multicoloured	15	5
C381	218	**7½p** Multicoloured	60	45
C382	219	**9p** Multicoloured	75	60
		Set of 3	1.25	1.00
		First Day Cover		1.25
		Presentation Pack	2.25	

COMMEMORATIVE ISSUES 1972

Printers: Harrison & Sons in Photogravure   *Perf:* 15 x 14   *Paper:* Chalky   *Unwatermarked*

No.	Type	Colour	U/M	F/U

Type 220

Type 221

Type 223

Type 222

Type 224

OLD VILLAGE CHURCHES Issued 21/6/72

No.	Type		Colour	U/M	F/U
C383	220	**3p**	Multicoloured	20	10
C384	221	**4p**	Multicoloured	1.00	55
C385	222	**5p**	Multicoloured	1.00	55
C386	223	**7½p**	Multicoloured	2.50	1.65
C387	224	**9p**	Multicoloured	2.75	1.95
			Set of 5	6.75	4.50
			First Day Cover		5.25
			Presentation Pack	8.50	

SOUVENIR PACK "BELGICA 72" Issued 24/6/72

C373/5 +		Presentation Pack	£11
C383/7			

Type 225

Type 226

Type 227

Type 228

50TH ANNIVERSARY OF THE B.B.C. AND 75TH ANNIVERSARY OF THE 1ST RADIO TRANSMISSION ACROSS BRISTOL CHANNEL
Issued 13/9/72

No.	Type		Colour	U/M	F/U
C388	225	**3p**	Multicoloured	10	5
C389	226	**5p**	Multicoloured	35	25
C390	227	**7½p**	Multicoloured	1.00	75
C391	228	**9p**	Multicoloured	1.25	1.00
			Set of 4	2.35	2.00
			First Day Cover		2.50
			Presentation Pack	3.75	
			B.B.C. Staff Pack	£24	

Type 229

Type 230

Type 231

CHRISTMAS 1972 Issued 18/10/72

No.	Type		Colour	U/M	F/U
C392	229	**2½p**	Multicoloured	5	5
			(1 band)		
C393	230	**3p**	Multicoloured	10	10
C394	231	**7½p**	Multicoloured	50	50
			Set of 3	60	60
			First Day Cover		80
			Presentation Pack	1.60	

COMMEMORATIVE ISSUES 1972 – 73

Printers: Harrison & Sons in Photogravure   *Perf:* 15 x 14   *Paper:* Chalky   *Unwatermarked*

No.	Type	Colour	U/M	F/U

Type 232

Type 233

Type 235

TREE PLANTING YEAR Issued 28/2/73

No.	Type	Colour	U/M	F/U
C401	235	**9p** Green/brown/grey	35	35
		First Day Cover		60
		Presentation Pack	1.50	

ROYAL SILVER WEDDING Issued 20/11/72

Rembrandt Printing

No.	Type	Colour	U/M	F/U
C395	232	**3p** Silver/brn./steel bl.	15	10
C396	233	**20p** Silver/brown/purple	75	75
		Set of 2	80	80
		First Day Cover		1.00
		Presentation Pack	2.00	
		Souvenir Pack	2.25	

Gemini Printing

No.	Type	Colour	U/M	F/U
C397	232	**3p** Silver/brn./steel bl.	15	10
C397 (x2)		Gutter pair (Plain)	3.00	3.00
C397 (x2)		Gutter pair (TL)	£18	£18

GUTTER PAIRS

Two different printing presses were used for the 3p values of the Royal Silver Wedding Issue. These can easily be distinguished in sheet form, as the Gemini printing provided a plain gutter through the centre of the sheet – thus providing a new variety for collectors in the form of a gutter pair. This sheet form became standard for all Commemorative stamps from the Horse Chestnut Tree 9p issue on 27th February 1974, but both values of the Royal Wedding issue on 14th November 1973 were also printed with gutters.

COLLECTORS PACK 1972 Issued 20/11/72

C373/396		Presentation Pack	£20

Type 236

Type 239

Type 238

Type 237

Type 240

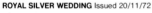

Type 234

ENTRY INTO THE EUROPEAN COMMUNITIES Issued 3/1/73

No.	Type	Colour	U/M	F/U
C398	234	**3p** Multicoloured	15	5
C399	234	**5p** Multicoloured	40	40
C400	234	**5p** Multicoloured	40	40
C399/400		5p Pair se-tenant	95	95
		Set of 3	1.00	95
		First Day Cover		1.20
		Presentation Pack	2.00	

FROM THIS ISSUE STAMPS WERE PRINTED ALL OVER PHOSPHOR UNLESS STATED

BRITISH EXPLORERS Issued 18/4/73

No.	Type	Colour	U/M	F/U
C402	236	**3p** Multicoloured	25	10
C403	237	**3p** Multicoloured	25	10
C402/3		3p Pair se-tenant	1.00	1.00
C404	238	**5p** Multicoloured	50	50
C405	239	**7½p** Multicoloured	1.25	1.25
C406	240	**9p** Multicoloured	2.00	2.00
		Set of 5	4.25	4.25
		First Day Cover		4.50
		Presentation Pack	6.50	

Printers: Harrison & Sons in Photogravure   *Perf:* 15 x 14   *Paper:* Chalky   *Unwatermarked*

No.	Type	Colour	U/M	F/U	No.	Type	Colour	U/M	F/U

Type 242

Type 241

Type 243

Type 248

Type 249

Type 250

Type 251

COUNTY CRICKET CENTENARY Issued 16/5/73

No.	Type		Colour	U/M	F/U
C407	241	**3p**	Ochre/black/gold	10	5
C408	242	**7½p**	Green/black/gold	40	40
C409	243	**9p**	Blue/black/gold	50	50
			Set of 3	90	90
			First Day Cover		1.10
			Presentation Pack	2.00	
			Souvenir Pack	2.75	

400TH ANNIVERSARY OF BIRTH OF INIGO JONES Issued 15/8/73

No.	Type		Colour	U/M	F/U
C414	248	**3p**	Purple/black/gold	10	10
C415	249	**3p**	Sepia/Black/Gold	10	10
C414/5			3p Pair se-tenant	35	35
C416	250	**5p**	Blue/black/gold	25	25
C417	251	**5p**	Blue/black/gold	25	25
C416/7			5p Pair se-tenant	55	55
			Set of 4	85	85
			First Day Cover		1.10
			Presentation Pack	2.00	

Type 244

Type 245

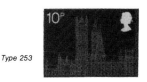

Type 252

Type 246

Type 247

Type 253

BRITISH PAINTINGS 1973 Issued 4/7/73

No.	Type		Colour	U/M	F/U
C410	244	**3p**	Multicoloured	10	5
C411	245	**5p**	Multicoloured	20	20
C412	246	**7½p**	Multicoloured	30	30
C413	247	**9p**	Multicoloured	35	35
			Set of 4	90	85
			First Day Cover		1.10
			Presentation Pack	2.00	

19TH COMMONWEALTH PARLIAMENTARY ASSOCIATION CONFERENCE Issued 12/9/73

No.	Type		Colour	U/M	F/U
C418	252	**8p**	Black/grey/buff	40	40
C419	253	**10p**	Black/gold	45	45
			Set of 2	80	80
			First Day Cover		1.00
			Presentation Pack	2.00	
			Souvenir Pack	4.75	

COMMEMORATIVE ISSUES 1973

Printers: Harrison & Sons in Photogravure   *Perf:* 15 x 14   *Paper:* Chalky   *Unwatermarked*

No.	Type	Colour		U/M	F/U	No.	Type	Colour		U/M	F/U

Type 254

Type 259

Type 255

Type 260

ROYAL WEDDING Issued 14/11/73

C420	254	**3½p**	Violet/silver	10	5
C421	255	**20p**	Light brown/silver	75	75
			Set of 2	80	75
			Set of gutter prs. (P)	£75	£75
			Set of gutter prs. (TL)	£425	£425
			First Day Cover		1.00
			Presentation Pack	2.00	

Type 261

Type 256

CHRISTMAS 1973 Issued 28/11/73

All 3p values have one phosphor band.

PVA Dextrin Gum

C422	256	**3p**	Multicoloured	10	5
C423	257	**3p**	Multicoloured	10	5
C424	258	**3p**	Multicoloured	10	5
C425	259	**3p**	Multicoloured	10	5
C426	260	**3p**	Multicoloured	10	5
C422/6		3p	Strip of 5 se-tenant	1.00	1.00
C427	261	**3½p**	Multicoloured	10	5
			Set of 6	1.05	1.00

Gum Arabic

C428	256	3p	Multicoloured	10	–
C429	257	3p	Multicoloured	10	–
C430	258	3p	Multicoloured	10	–
C431	259	3p	Multicoloured	10	–
C432	260	3p	Multicoloured	10	–
C428/432		3p	Strip of 5 se-tenant	1.00	–

PVA Gum

C433	261	3½p	Multicoloured	15	–
			First Day Cover		1.25
			Presentation Pack	2.00	
			(may contain stamps with any of the different gums)		

Type 257

Type 258

COLLECTORS PACK 1973 Issued 28/11/73

C398/427		Presentation Pack	£14

COMMEMORATIVE ISSUES 1974

Printers: Harrison & Sons in Photogravure   *Perf:* 15 x 14   *Paper:* Chalky   *Unwatermarked*

No.	Type	Colour	U/M	F/U

Type 262

PVA DEXTRIN GUM USED ON ALL FOLLOWING ISSUES (unless stated)

THE HORSE CHESTNUT TREE Issued 27/2/74

C434	262	**10p**	Multicoloured	25	25
			Gutter pair (Plain)	£10	£10
			Gutter pair (TL)	£40	£40
			First Day Cover		50
			Presentation Pack	1.00	

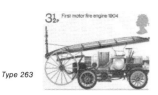

Type 263

Type 264

Type 265   *Type 266*

200TH ANNIVERSARY OF THE FIRE SERVICE Issued 24/4/74

C435	263	**3½p**	Multicoloured	10	5
C436	263	**3½p**	Multicoloured (PVA)	£10	–
C437	264	**5½p**	Multicoloured	25	25
C438	265	**8p**	Multicoloured	45	45
C439	266	**10p**	Multicoloured	70	70
			Set of 4	1.35	1.35
			Set of gutter prs. (P)	£25	£25
			Set of gutter prs. (TL)	£150	£150
			First Day Cover		1.75
			Presentation Pack	2.00	

Type 267

Type 268

Type 269

Type 270

UPU CENTENARY Issued 12/6/74

C440	267	**3½p**	Blk./grey/pink/gold	10	5
C441	268	**5½p**	Blk./or./green/gold	25	25
C442	269	**8p**	Blk./bl./brown/gold	45	45
C443	270	**10p**	Blk./grey/or./gold	70	70
			Set of 4	1.35	1.35
			Set of gutter prs. (P)	£25	£25
			Set of gutter prs. (TL)	£70	£70
			First Day Cover		1.75
			Presentation Pack	2.00	

Type 271

Type 272

Type 273

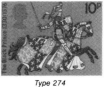
Type 274

GREAT BRITONS Issued 10/7/74

C444	271	**4½p**	Multicoloured	20	10
C445	272	**5½p**	Multicoloured	50	40
C446	273	**8p**	Multicoloured	1.20	80
C447	274	**10p**	Multicoloured	1.80	1.20
			Set of 4	3.50	2.25
			Set of gutter prs. (P)	£75	£75
			Set of gutter prs. (TL)	£200	£200
			First Day Cover		3.00
			Presentation Pack	4.25	

COMMEMORATIVE ISSUES 1974 – 75

Printers: Harrison & Sons in Photogravure   *Perf:* 15 x 14   *Paper:* Chalky   *Unwatermarked*

No.	Type	Colour	U/M	F/U

Type 275

Type 276

Type 277

Type 278

CENTENARY OF BIRTH OF SIR WINSTON CHURCHILL
Issued 9/10/74

No.	Type		Colour	U/M	F/U
C448	275	4½p	Green/blue/silver	10	10
C449	276	5½p	Lt. grey/grey/silver	45	45
C450	277	8p	Pink/red/silver	30	30
C451	277	8p	Pink/red/silver (PVA)	2.50	–
C452	278	10p	Buff/brown/silver	30	30
			Set of 4	1.00	1.00
			Set of gutter prs. (P)	£30	£30
			Set of gutter prs. (TL)	£90	£90
			First Day Cover		1.50
			Presentation Pack	2.00	
			Souvenir Pack	3.00	

Type 279

Type 280

Type 281

Type 282

CHRISTMAS 1974 Issued 27/11/74

No.	Type		Colour	U/M	F/U
C453	279	3½p	Multicoloured (1 band at right)	5	5
C454	279	3½p	Multicoloured (CB)	20	10
C455	280	4½p	Multicoloured	15	5
C456	281	8p	Multicoloured	30	30
C457	282	10p	Multicoloured	35	35
			Set of 4	75	70
			Set of gutter prs. (P)	£15	£15
			Set of gutter prs. (TL)	£50	£50
C454		3½p	Gutter pair (Plain)	60	60
C454		3½p	Gutter pair (TL)	6.75	6.75
			First Day Cover		90
			Presentation Pack	1.50	

COLLECTORS PACK 1974 Issued 27/11/74

C434/457		Presentation Pack	9.50	

Type 283

CHARITY ISSUE Issued 22/1/75

No.	Type		Colour	U/M	F/U
C458	283	4½+1½p	Lt.blue/dk.blue	15	15
			Gutter pair (Plain)	50	50
			Gutter pair (TL)	2.50	2.50
			First Day Cover		60

Type 284

Type 285

Type 286

Type 287

200TH ANNIVERSARY OF BIRTH OF J. W. TURNER Issued 19/2/75

No.	Type		Colour	U/M	F/U
C459	284	4½p	Multicoloured	10	5
C460	285	5½p	Multicoloured	15	15
C461	286	8p	Multicoloured	25	25
C462	287	10p	Multicoloured	35	35
			Set of 4	80	75
			Set of gutter prs. (P)	3.00	3.00
			Set of gutter prs. (TL)	£14	£14
			First Day Cover		1.00
			Presentation Pack	1.40	

COMMEMORATIVE ISSUES 1975

Printers: Harrison & Sons in Photogravure   *Perf:* 15 x 14   *Paper:* Chalky   *Unwatermarked*

No.	Type	Colour	U/M	F/U

Type 288

Type 289

Type 290

Type 291

Type 292

EUROPEAN ARCHITECTURAL HERITAGE YEAR Issued 23/4/75

No.	Type	Colour	U/M	F/U
C463	288	**7p** Multicoloured	15	10
C464	289	**7p** Multicoloured	15	10
C463/4		**7p** Pair se-tenant	60	60
C465	290	**8p** Multicoloured	20	20
C466	291	**10p** Multicoloured	20	20
C467	292	**12p** Multicoloured	25	25
		Set of 5	1.15	1.15
		Set of gutter prs. (P)	3.25	3.25
		Set of gutter prs. (TL)	£14	£14
		First Day Cover		1.30
		Presentation Pack	1.75	

Type 293   Type 294

Type 295

Type 296

SAILING Issued 11/6/75

No.	Type	Colour	U/M	F/U
C468	293	**7p** Multicoloured	15	15
C469	294	**8p** Multicoloured	20	20
C470	295	**10p** Multicoloured	25	25
C471	296	**12p** Multicoloured	70	70
		Set of 4	1.15	1.15
		Set of gutter prs. (P)	6.00	6.00
		Set of gutter prs. (TL)	£75	£75
		First Day Cover		2.00
		Presentation Pack	1.85	

Type 297

Type 298

Type 299

Type 300

150TH ANNIVERSARY OF FIRST PUBLIC STEAM RAILWAY
Issued 13/8/75

No.	Type	Colour	U/M	F/U
C472	297	**7p** Multicoloured	15	10
C473	298	**8p** Multicoloured	30	30
C474	299	**10p** Multicoloured	40	40
C475	300	**12p** Multicoloured	50	50
		Set of 4	1.20	1.20
		Set of gutter prs. (P)	3.00	3.00
		Set of gutter prs. (TL)	£12	£12
		First Day Cover		1.50
		Presentation Pack	1.75	
		Souvenir Pack	2.75	

COMMEMORATIVE ISSUES 1975 – 76

Printers: Harrison & Sons in Photogravure   *Perf:* 15 x 14   *Paper:* Chalky   *Unwatermarked*

No.	Type		Colour	U/M	F/U

Type 301

INTER PARLIAMENTARY UNION CONFERENCE Issued 3/9/75

No.	Type		Colour	U/M	F/U
C476	301	**12p**	Multicoloured	35	25
			Gutter pair (Plain)	80	80
			Gutter pair (TL)	6.75	6.75
			First Day Cover		60
			Presentation Pack	85	

Type 302   *Type 303*

Type 304   *Type 305*

BICENTENARY OF THE BIRTH OF JANE AUSTEN Issued 22/10/75

No.	Type		Colour	U/M	F/U
C477	302	**8½p**	Multicoloured	15	10
C478	303	**10p**	Multicoloured	30	30
C479	304	**11p**	Multicoloured	30	30
C480	305	**13p**	Multicoloured	35	35
			Set of 4	1.00	1.00
			Set of gutter prs. (P)	3.00	3.00
			Set of gutter prs. (TL)	£12	£12
			First Day Cover		1.50
			Presentation Pack	1.75	

Type 306   *Type 307*

Type 308   *Type 309*

CHRISTMAS 1975 Issued 26/11/75

No.	Type		Colour	U/M	F/U
C481	306	**6½p**	Multicoloured (1 band)	15	5
C482	306	**6½p**	Multicoloured (1 band) PVA	40	–
C483	307	**8½p**	Multicoloured (phosphor inked)	15	10
C484	308	**11p**	Multicoloured	35	35
C485	309	**13p**	Multicoloured	40	40
			Set of 4	90	85
			Set of gutter prs. (P)	2.50	2.50
			Set of gutter prs. (TL)	£11	£11
			First Day Cover		1.20
			Presentation Pack	1.50	

COLLECTORS PACK 1975 Issued 26/11/75

No.					
C458/485			Presentation Pack	7.00	

Type 310   *Type 311*

Type 312   *Type 313*

CENTENARY OF ALEXANDER GRAHAM BELL'S FIRST TELEPHONE TRANSMISSION Issued 10/3/76

No.	Type		Colour	U/M	F/U
C486	310	**8½p**	Magenta/blk./bl./tur.	15	10
C487	311	**10p**	Blk./olive/turquoise	30	30
C488	312	**11p**	Car./blk./mve./bl.	30	30
C489	313	**13p**	Scarlet/blk./or./brn.	35	35
			Set of 4	1.00	1.00
			Set of gutter prs. (P)	2.50	2.50
			Set of gutter prs. (TL)	£40	£40
			First Day Cover		1.30
			Presentation Pack	1.50	

COMMEMORATIVE ISSUES 1976

Printers: Harrison & Sons in Photogravure   *Perf:* 15 x 14   *Paper:* Chalky   *Unwatermarked*

No.	Type	Colour	U/M	F/U

Type 314   *Type 315*

Type 316   *Type 317*

SOCIAL REFORMERS Issued 28/4/76

No.	Type		Colour	U/M	F/U
C490	314	8½p	Multicoloured	15	10
C491	315	10p	Multicoloured	35	35
C492	316	11p	Multicoloured	35	35
C493	317	13p	Multicoloured	40	40
			Set of 4	1.10	1.10
			Set of gutter prs. (P)	2.50	2.50
			Set of gutter prs. (TL)	£40	£40
			First Day Cover		1.35
			Presentation Pack	1.60	

Type 318

BICENTENARY OF AMERICAN INDEPENDENCE Issued 2/6/76

No.	Type		Colour	U/M	F/U
C494	318	11p	Multicoloured	45	45
			Gutter pair (Plain)	3.50	3.50
			Gutter pair (TL)	£11	£11
			First Day Cover		1.00
			Presentation Pack	1.75	

Type 319

Type 320

Type 321

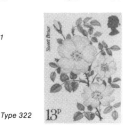

Type 322

CENTENARY OF THE ROYAL NATIONAL ROSE SOCIETY
Issued 30/6/76

No.	Type		Colour	U/M	F/U
C495	319	8½p	Multicoloured	15	10
C496	320	10p	Multicoloured	35	35
C497	321	11p	Multicoloured	35	35
C498	322	13p	Multicoloured	40	40
			Set of 4	1.10	1.10
			Set of gutter prs. (P)	2.50	2.50
			Set of gutter prs. (TL)	£11	£11
			First Day Cover		1.35
			Presentation Pack	1.50	

Type 323

Type 324

Type 325

Type 326

BRITISH CULTURE Issued 4/8/76

No.	Type		Colour	U/M	F/U
C499	323	8½p	Multicoloured	15	10
C500	324	10p	Multicoloured	30	30
C501	325	11p	Multicoloured	30	30
C502	326	13p	Multicoloured	35	35
			Set of 4	1.00	1.00
			Set of gutter prs. (P)	2.50	2.50
			Set of gutter prs. (TL)	£10	£10
			First Day Cover		1.25
			Presentation Pack	1.50	

COMMEMORATIVE ISSUES 1976 – 77

Printers: Harrison & Sons in Photogravure   *Perf:* 15 x 14   *Paper:* Chalky   *Unwatermarked*

No.	Type	Colour	U/M	F/U

Type 327   8½ᵖ

Type 328   10ᵖ

Type 329   11ᵖ

Type 330   13ᵖ

500TH ANNIVERSARY OF THE FIRST PRINTING IN BRITAIN
Issued 29/9/76

No.	Type	Value	Colour	U/M	F/U
C503	327	8½p	Multicoloured	15	10
C504	328	10p	Multicoloured	35	35
C505	329	11p	Multicoloured	35	35
C506	330	13p	Multicoloured	40	40
			Set of 4	1.10	1.10
			Set of gutter prs. (P)	2.50	2.50
			Set of gutter prs. (TL)	6.00	6.00
			First Day Cover		1.35
			Presentation Pack	1.50	

Type 331   6½ᵖ

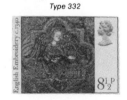

Type 332   8½ᵖ

Type 333   11ᵖ

Type 334   13ᵖ

CHRISTMAS 1976 Issued 24/11/76

No.	Type	Value	Colour	U/M	F/U
C507	331	6½p	Multicoloured (1 band)	10	10
C508	332	8½p	Multicoloured	20	10
C509	333	11p	Multicoloured	30	30
C510	334	13p	Multicoloured	40	40
			Set of 4	90	85
			Set of gutter prs. (P)	3.50	3.50
			Set of gutter prs. (TL)	£10	£10
			First Day Cover		1.10
			Presentation Pack	1.50	

COLLECTORS PACK Issued 24/11/76

No.				U/M	F/U
C486/510			Presentation Pack	7.00	

8½p   10p

Type 335   Type 336

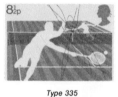

11p   13p

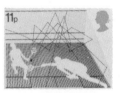

Type 337   Type 338

RACKET SPORTS Issued 12/1/77

No.	Type	Value	Colour	U/M	F/U
C511	335	8½p	Multicoloured	15	10
C512	336	10p	Multicoloured	25	25
C513	337	11p	Multicoloured	25	25
C514	338	13p	Multicoloured	30	30
			Set of 4	85	85
			Set of gutter prs. (P)	3.75	3.75
			Set of gutter prs. (TL)	9.00	9.00
			First Day Cover		1.10
			Presentation Pack	1.25	

Printers: Harrison & Sons in Photogravure   *Perf:* 15 x 14   Paper: Chalky   *Unwatermarked*

No.	Type	Colour	U/M	F/U

Type 339

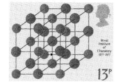

Type 340

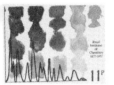

Type 341

Type 342

SILVER JUBILEE Issued 11/5/77 and 15/6/77 (9p only)

No.	Type		Colour	U/M	F/U
C519	343	8½p	Multicoloured	15	10
C520	343	9p	Multicoloured	15	10
C521	343	10p	Multicoloured	20	20
C522	343	11p	Multicoloured	20	20
C523	343	13p	Multicoloured	30	30
			Set of 5	90	85
			Set of gutter prs. (P)	2.20	2.20
			Set of gutter prs. (TL)	3.25	3.25
			First Day Cover 11/5/77		2.25
			First Day Cover 15/6/77 (9p only)		50
			Presentation Pack (excludes 9p)	1.25	
			Souvenir Pack (excludes 9p)	2.00	

Type 343

Type 344

HEADS OF GOVERNMENT Issued 8/6/77

			Colour	U/M	F/U
C524	344	13p	Bt.red/blk./grn./sil.	30	30
			Gutter pair (Plain)	1.00	1.00
			Gutter pair (TL)	7.00	7.00
			First Day Cover		50
			Presentation Pack	70	

CHEMISTRY Issued 2/3/77

No.	Type		Colour	U/M	F/U
C515	339	8½p	Multicoloured	15	10
C516	340	10p	Multicoloured	25	25
C517	341	11p	Multicoloured	25	25
C518	342	13p	Multicoloured	30	30
			Set of 4	90	85
			Set of gutter prs. (P)	2.20	2.20
			Set of gutter prs. (TL)	3.75	3.75
			First Day Cover		1.00
			Presentation Pack	1.25	

Type 345

Type 346

Type 347

Type 348

Type 349

BRITISH WILDLIFE Issued 5/10/77

No.	Type		Colour	U/M	F/U
C525	345	9p	(Hedgehog) Multi.	15	15
C526	346	9p	(Hare) Multicoloured	15	15
C527	347	9p	(Red Squirrel) Multi.	15	15
C528	348	9p	(Otter) Multicoloured	15	15
C529	349	9p	(Badger) Multi.	15	15

BRITISH WILDLIFE (Continued)

	U/M	F/U
Strip of 5 se-tenant	1.00	1.00
Strip of 10 se-tenant with gutter (Plain)	2.25	2.25
Strip of 10 se-tenant with gutter (TL)	3.00	3.00
First Day Cover		1.25
Presentation Pack	1.25	

COMMEMORATIVE ISSUES 1977 – 78

Printers: Harrison & Sons in Photogravure   *Perf:* 15 x 14   *Paper:* Chalky   *Unwatermarked*

No.	Type	Colour	U/M	F/U

Type 350

Type 351

Type 356

Type 352

Type 353

Type 357

Type 354

Type 355

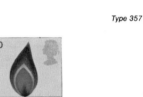

Type 358

Type 359

CHRISTMAS 1977 Issued 23/11/77

No.	Type	Value	Colour	U/M	F/U
C530	350	7p	Multicoloured (I.B.)	10	10
C531	351	7p	Multicoloured (I.B.)	10	10
C532	352	7p	Multicoloured (I.B.)	10	10
C533	353	7p	Multicoloured (I.B.)	10	10
C534	354	7p	Multicoloured (I.B.)	10	10
C530/4		7p	Strip of 5 se-tenant	65	65
C535	355	9p	Multicoloured	15	15
			Set of 6	70	70
			Set of gutter prs. (P)	1.70	1.70
			Set of gutter prs. (TL)	2.50	2.50
			First Day Cover		1.00
			Presentation Pack	95	

COLLECTORS PACK 1977 Issued 23/11/77

C511/535		Presentation Pack	5.00	

ENERGY Issued 25/1/78

No.	Type	Value	Colour	U/M	F/U
C536	356	9p	Multicoloured	13	13
C537	357	10½p	Multicoloured	18	18
C538	358	11p	Multicoloured	18	18
C539	359	13p	Multicoloured	20	20
			Set of 4	65	65
			Set of gutter prs. (P)	1.50	1.50
			Set of gutter prs. (TL)	3.00	3.00
			First Day Cover		1.00
			Presentation Pack	90	

COMMEMORATIVE ISSUES 1978

Printers: Harrison & Sons in Photogravure   *Perf:* 15 x 14   *Paper:* Chalky   *Unwatermarked*

Type 360

Type 361

Type 362

Type 363

Type 364

No.	Type	Colour	U/M	F/U
BRITISH ARCHITECTURE – HISTORIC BUILDINGS Issued 1/3/78				
C540	360	**9p** Multicoloured	13	13
C541	361	**10½p** Multicoloured	18	18
C542	362	**11p** Multicoloured	18	18
C543	363	**13p** Multicoloured	20	20
		Set of 4	65	65
		Set of gutter prs. (P)	1.50	1.50
		Set of gutter prs. (TL)	3.00	3.00
		First Day Cover		1.00
		Presentation Pack	90	
C544	364	**9p** **10½p** **11p** **13p** Miniature sheet (in original P.O.pack)	6.50	6.50
		First Day Cover		7.00

COMMEMORATIVE ISSUES 1978

Printers: Harrison & Sons in Photogravure   *Perf:* 15 x 14   *Paper:* Chalky   *Unwatermarked*

No.	Type	Colour	U/M	F/U

Type 365

Type 366

Type 367

Type 368

25TH ANNIVERSARY OF H.M. THE QUEEN'S CORONATION
Issued 31/5/78

No.	Type		Colour	U/M	F/U
C545	365	9p	Royal blue/gold	13	13
C546	366	10½p	Carmine lake/gold	18	18
C547	367	11p	Deep green/gold	18	18
C548	368	13p	Reddish violet/gold	20	20
			Set of 4	65	65
			Set of gutter prs. (P)	1.50	1.50
			Set of gutter prs. (TL)	3.50	3.50
			First Day Cover		1.00
			Presentation Pack	90	
			Souvenir Pack	2.00	

Type 369

Type 370

Type 371

Type 372

HORSES – CENTENARY OF THE SHIRE HORSE SOCIETY
Issued 5/7/78

No.	Type		Colour	U/M	F/U
C549	369	9p	Multicoloured	13	13
C550	370	10½p	Multicoloured	18	18
C551	371	11p	Multicoloured	18	18
C552	372	13p	Multicoloured	20	20
			Set of 4	65	65
			Set of gutter prs. (P)	1.50	1.50
			Set of gutter prs. (TL)	5.00	5.00
			First Day Cover		1.00
			Presentation Pack	90	

Type 373

Type 374

Type 375

Type 376

CYCLING – CENTENARY OF THE CYCLISTS' TOURING CLUB
Issued 2/8/78

No.	Type		Colour	U/M	F/U
C553	373	9p	Multicoloured	13	13
C554	374	10½p	Multicoloured	18	18
C555	375	11p	Multicoloured	18	18
C556	376	13p	Multicoloured	20	20
			Set of 4	65	65
			Set of gutter prs. (P)	1.50	1.50
			Set of gutter prs. (TL)	3.00	3.00
			First Day Cover		1.00
			Presentation Pack	80	

Printers: Harrison & Sons in Photogravure   Perf: 15 x 14   Paper: Chalky   Unwatermarked

No.	Type	Colour	U/M	F/U

Type 377

Type 378

Type 379   Type 380

CHRISTMAS 1978 Issued 22/11/78

No.	Type	Colour	U/M	F/U
C557	377	**7p** Multicoloured (1 band)	10	10
C558	378	**9p** Multicoloured	13	13
C559	379	**11p** Multicoloured	18	18
C560	380	**13p** Multicoloured	20	20
		Set of 4	60	60
		Set of gutter prs. (P)	1.40	1.40
		Set of gutter prs. (TL)	2.00	2.00
		First Day Cover		90
		Presentation Pack	80	

COLLECTORS PACK 1978 Issued 22/11/78

C540/543 C545/560	Presentation Pack	4.00

Type 381

Type 382

Type 383   Type 384

No.	Type	Colour	U/M	F/U

DOGS Issued 7/2/79

No.	Type		Colour	U/M	F/U
C561	381	**9p**	Multicoloured	13	13
C562	382	**10½p**	Multicoloured	18	18
C563	383	**11p**	Multicoloured	18	18
C564	384	**13p**	Multicoloured	20	20
			Set of 4	65	65
			Set of gutter prs. (P)	1.50	1.50
			Set of gutter prs. (TL)	4.00	4.00
			First Day Cover		1.00
			Presentation Pack	80	

Type 385

Type 387

Type 386

Type 388

BRITISH FLOWERS Issued 21/3/79

C565	385	**9p**	Multicoloured	13	13
C566	386	**10½p**	Multicoloured	18	18
C567	387	**11p**	Multicoloured	18	18
C568	388	**13p**	Multicoloured	20	20
			Set of 4	65	65
			Set of gutter prs. (P)	1.50	1.50
			Set of gutter prs. (TL)	2.50	2.50
			First Day Cover		1.00
			Presentation Pack	80	

COMMEMORATIVE ISSUES 1979

Printers: Harrison & Sons in Photogravure   *Perf:* 15 x 14   *Paper:* Chalky   *Unwatermarked*

No.	Type	Colour	U/M	F/U

Type 389

Type 391

Type 390

Type 392

DIRECT ELECTIONS TO THE EUROPEAN ASSEMBLY Issued 9/5/79

No.	Type		Colour	U/M	F/U
C569	389	9p	Multicoloured	13	13
C570	390	10½p	Multicoloured	18	18
C571	391	11p	Multicoloured	18	18
C572	392	13p	Multicoloured	20	20
			Set of 4	65	65
			Set of gutter prs. (P)	1.50	1.50
			Set of gutter prs. (TL)	2.50	2.50
			First Day Cover		1.00
			Presentation Pack	80	

Saddling Malmaison for The Derby 1936

Type 393

Type 395

The Liverpool Great National Steeple Chase 1899

Type 394

Type 396

The First Spring Meeting, Newmarket 1793

Racing at Dorsett Ferry, Windsor 1684

HORSE RACING Issued 6/6/79

No.	Type		Colour	U/M	F/U
C573	393	9p	Multicoloured	13	13
C574	394	10½p	Multicoloured	18	18
C575	395	11p	Multicoloured	18	18
C576	396	13p	Multicoloured	20	20
			Set of 4	65	65
			Set of gutter prs. (P)	1.50	1.50
			Set of gutter prs. (TL)	2.25	2.25
			First Day Cover		1.00
			Presentation Pack	80	

Type 397

Type 398

The Tale of Peter Rabbit *The Year of the Child*

The Wind in the Willows *The Year of the Child*

Type 399

Type 400

Winnie-the-Pooh *The Year of the Child*

Alice's Adventures in Wonderland *The Year of the Child*

UNITED NATIONS' "YEAR OF THE CHILD" Issued 11/7/79

No.	Type		Colour	U/M	F/U
C577	397	9p	Multicoloured	13	13
C578	398	10½p	Multicoloured	18	18
C579	399	11p	Multicoloured	18	18
C580	400	13p	Multicoloured	20	20
			Set of 4	65	65
			Set of gutter prs. (P)	1.50	1.50
			Set of gutter prs. (TL)	2.25	2.25
			First Day Cover		1.50
			Presentation Pack	80	

FORTHCOMING ISSUES

22/8/79	Postal History – Centenary of the death of Sir Rowland Hill (Stamps only)
26/9/79	The Metropolitan Police Force – 150th Anniversary
–/10/79	Postal History – Centenary of the death of Sir Rowland Hill (Miniature Sheet)
21/11/79	Christmas 1979
–/1/80	British Birds
–/3/80	Railways
–/5/80	London 1980 International Stamp Exhibition (Stamps and Miniature Sheet)
–/6/80	Famous People (Europa theme)
–/8/80	Sport
–/9/80	Music
–/11/80	Christmas 1980

POST OFFICE PICTURE CARDS

These enlarged colour reproductions of certain commemorative stamps were first issued in July 1973, and subsequently for random values. Since June 1976 every commemorative stamp has been reproduced on a postcard.

First Day of Issue refers to cards with the matching stamp on the face or reverse, postmarked with F.D.I. circular stamp or special postmark. The cards are normally available from main Post Offices a few days in advance of the equivalent stamps.

No.	Issued	Type	Mint	F.D.I.
PHQ1	–/7/72	**County Cricket Centenary** 3p	£35	–
PHQ2	15/8/73	**400th Anniversary of Birth of Inigo Jones** 3p	£25	£50
PHQ3	12/9/73	**19th Commonwealth Parliamentary Conference** 8p	£20	£45
PHQ4	14/11/73	**Royal Wedding** 3½p	3.25	£18
PHQ5	27/2/74	**The Horse Chestnut Tree** 10p	£55	£45
PHQ6	24/4/74	**200th Anniversary of the Fire Service** 3½p	£60	£60
PHQ7	10/7/74	**Great Britons**	6.00	£20
		4½p, 5½p, 8p, 10p, set of four		
PHQ8	9/10/74	**Centenary of Birth of Sir Winston Churchill** 5½p	1.75	£10
PHQ9	19/2/75	**200th Anniversary of Birth of J.W. Turner** 5½p	3.00	£10
PHQ10	23/4/75	**European Architectural Heritage Year**	3.00	9.50
		7p x 2, 8p x 1, set of three		
PHQ11	11/6/75	**Sailing** 8p	2.25	7.50
PHQ12	13/8/75	**150th Anniversary of First Public Steam Railway**	£18	£20
		7p, 8p, 10p, 12p, set of four		
PHQ13	22/10/75	**Bicentenary of Birth of Jane Austen**	4.75	£12
		8½p, 10p, 11p, 13p, Set of four		
PHQ14	28/4/76	**Social Reformers** 8½p	1.75	6.50
PHQ15	2/6/76	**Bicentenary of American Independence** 11p	1.75	£10
PHQ16	30/6/76	**Centenary of the Royal National Rose Society**	4.00	8.00
		8½p, 10p, 11p, 13p, Set of four		
PHQ17	4/8/76	**British Culture** 8½p, 10p, 11p, 13p, Set of four	2.00	6.00
PHQ18	29/9/76	**500th Anniversary of the First Printing in Britain**	2.00	6.00
		8½p, 10p, 11p, 13p, Set of four		
PHQ19	24/11/76	**Christmas 1976** 6½p, 8½p, 11p, 13p, Set of four	1.20	5.00
PHQ20	12/1/77	**Racket Sports** 8½p, 10p, 11p, 13p, Set of four	1.75	5.00
PHQ21	2/3/77	**Chemistry** 8½p, 10p, 11p, 13p, Set of four	1.75	5.00
PHQ22	11/5/77	**Silver Jubilee** 8½p, 10p, 11p, 13p, Set of four	2.00	6.00
PHQ22E	15/6/77	**Silver Jubilee** 9p	35	75
PHQ23	8/6/77	**Heads of Government** 13p	1.75	4.00
PHQ25	5/10/77	**British Wildlife** 9p x 5, set of five	1.50	4.00
PHQ26	23/11/77	**Christmas 1977** 7p x 5, 9p x 1, Set of six	80	2.75
PHQ27	25/1/78	**Energy** 9p, 10½p, 11p, 13p, Set of four	75	1.25
PHQ28	1/3/78	**Historic Buildings** 9p, 10½p, 11p, 13p, Set of four	75	1.25
PHQ29	31/5/78	**25th Anniversary of HM Queen's Coronation**	1.00	1.75
		9p, 10½p, 11p, 13p, Set of four		
PHQ30	5/7/78	**Horses** 9p, 10½p, 11p, 13p, Set of four	50	1.25
PHQ31	2/8/78	**Cycling** 9p, 10½p, 11p, 13p, Set of four	50	1.25
PHQ32	22/11/78	**Christmas 1978** 7p, 9p, 11p, 13p, Set of four	50	1.20
PHQ33	7/2/79	**British Dogs** 9p, 10½p, 11p, 13p, Set of four	50	1.25
PHQ34	21/3/79	**British Flowers** 9p, 10½p, 11p, 13p, Set of four	50	1.25
PHQ35	9/5/79	**D.E.E.A.** 9p, 10½p, 11p, 13p, Set of four	50	1.25
PHQ36	6/6/79	**Horse Racing** 9p, 10½p, 11p, 13p, Set of four	50	1.25
PHQ37	11/7/79	**U.N. 'Year of the Child'** 9p, 10½p, 11p, 13p, Set of four	50	1.25

REGIONAL ISSUES – NORTHERN IRELAND   1958 –

Printers: Harrison & Sons in Photogravure   *Perf:* 15 x 14   *No Watermark* unless marked MC = Multiple Crowns

No.	Issued	Type		Colour	Phosphor	Wmk.	U/M	F/U
STERLING VALUES								
Gum Arabic								
U1	18/5/58	R1	**3d**	Reddish violet		MC	15	10
U2	9/6/67		**3d**	Reddish violet	CB	MC	10	10
U3	7/2/66		**4d**	Dull ultramarine		MC	10	10
U4	2/10/67		**4d**	Dull ultramarine	2B	MC	10	10
U5	27/6/68		**4d**	Dull ultramarine	2B		10	15
U6	29/9/58	R2	**6d**	Claret		MC	20	15
U7	1/3/67		**9d**	Deep green	2B	MC	35	25
U8	29/9/58	R3	**1/3d**	Green		MC	30	25
U9	1/3/67		**1/6d**	Grey blue	2B	MC	40	30
PVA Gum								
U10	23/10/68	R1	**4d**	Dull ultramarine	2B		9.50	–
U11	4/9/68		**4d**	Sepia	CB		10	15
U12	26/2/69		**4d**	Vermilion	CB		30	10
U13	4/9/68		**5d**	Deep blue	2B		35	10
U14	20/5/69	R3	**1/6d**	Grey blue	2B		4.25	2.00
Presentation Pack								
	9/12/70			7 stamps Nos. U2, 7, 8, 9, 11, 12, 13			3.00	
DECIMAL VALUES								
OCP/PVA								
U15	7/7/71	R4	**2½p**	Magenta	CB		25	15
U16	7/7/71		**3p**	Dull ultramarine	2B		25	15
U17	7/7/71		**5p**	Bright violet	2B		50	30
U18	7/7/71		**7½p**	Chestnut	2B		1.00	75
FCP/PVA								
U19	–/6/73	R4	**2½p**	Magenta	CB		1.75	30
U20	–/4/73		**3p**	Dull ultramarine	2B		1.75	40
U21	–/4/74		**3p**	Dull ultramarine	CB		30	–
FCP/PVAD								
U22	23/1/74	R4	**3p**	Dull ultramarine	CB		40	10
U23	23/1/74		**3½p**	Bronze green	2B		25	15
U24	6/11/74		**3½p**	Bronze green	CB		25	15
U25	6/11/74		**4½p**	Steel blue	2B		25	15
U26	23/1/74		**5½p**	Violet	2B		20	15
U27	21/5/75		**5½p**	Violet	CB		20	15
U28	14/1/76		**6½p**	Greenish blue	CB		20	10
U29	18/1/78		**7p**	Red brown	CB		12	10
U30	23/1/74		**8p**	Rose red	2B		25	15
U31	14/1/76		**8½p**	Yellow green	2B		15	15
U32	18/1/78		**9p**	Blue	2B		14	12
U33	20/10/76		**10p**	Orange brown	2B		15	15
U34	18/1/78		**10½p**	Steel blue	2B		15	15
U35	20/10/76		**11p**	Red	2B		16	16
Presentation Packs								
	7/7/71			4 stamps Nos. U15–18			2.50	
	29/5/74			4 stamps Nos. U21, 23, 26, 30			1.50	
	6/11/74			5 stamps Nos U21, 23, 25, 26, 30			1.50	
	20/10/76			4 stamps Nos. U28, 31, 33, 35			80	

Type R1

Type R2

Type R3

Type R4

REGIONAL ISSUES – SCOTLAND 1958 –

Printers: Harrison & Sons in Photogravure   *Perf:* 15 x 14   *No Watermark* unless marked MC = Multiple Crowns

No.	Issued	Type		Colour	Phosphor	Wmk.	U/M	F/U
STERLING VALUES								
Gum Arabic								
S1	18/8/58	R5	**3d**	Reddish violet		MC	10	8
S2	29/1/63		**3d**	Reddish violet	2B	MC	4.00	1.75
S3	30/4/65		**3d**	Reddish violet	SB(L)	MC	20	25
S4	30/4/65		**3d**	Reddish violet	SB(R)	MC	20	25
S5	6/11/67		**3d**	Reddish violet	CB	MC	15	15
S6	16/5/68		**3d**	Reddish violet	CB		10	15
S7	7/2/66		**4d**	Dull ultramarine		MC	10	10
S8	7/2/66		**4d**	Dull ultramarine	2B	MC	10	10
S9	28/11/67		**4d**	Dull ultramarine	2B		10	10
S10	29/9/58	R6	**6d**	Claret		MC	10	10
S11	29/1/63		**6d**	Claret	2B	MC	25	25
S12	1/3/67		**9d**	Deep green	2B	MC	30	30
S13	29/9/58	R7	**1/3d**	Green		MC	30	20
S14	29/1/63		**1/3d**	Green	2B	MC	30	40
S15	1/3/67		**1/6d**	Grey	2B	MC	40	40
PVA Gum								
S16	11/7/68	R5	**3d**	Reddish violet	CB		10	15
S17	25/7/68		**4d**	Dull ultramarine	2B		10	10
S18	4/9/68		**4d**	Sepia	CB		10	8
S19	26/2/69		**4d**	Vermilion	CB		30	10
S20	4/9/68		**5d**	Deep blue	2B		30	10
S21	28/9/70	R6	**9d**	Deep green	2B		9.50	5.00
S22	12/12/68	R7	**1/6d**	Grey blue	2B		3.00	1.35
Presentation Pack								
	9/12/70			8 stamps			£18	
				Nos. S10, 14, 16, 18, 19, 20, 21, 22.				
DECIMAL VALUES								
OCP/PVA								
S23	7/7/71	R8	**2½p**	Magenta	CB		30	15
S24	7/7/71		**3p**	Dull ultramarine	2B		35	15
S25	7/7/71		**5p**	Bright violet	2B		50	30
S26	7/7/71		**7½p**	Chestnut	2B		1.00	70
FCP/GA								
S27	22/9/72	R8	**2½p**	Magenta	CB		20	15
S28	14/12/72		**3p**	Dull ultramarine	2B		20	15
FCP/PVA								
S29	–/6/73	R8	**2½p**	Magenta	CB		2.00	15
S30	–/–/73		**3p**	Dull ultramarine	2B		1.00	–
S31	23/1/74		**3p**	Dull ultramarine	CB		20	–
S32	23/1/74		**3½p**	Bronze green	2B		£15	–
S33	–/6/73		**5p**	Bright violet	2B		2.50	75
S34	–/11/73		**7½p**	Chestnut	2B		£25	2.00
FCP/PVAD								
S35	–/9/74	R8	**3p**	Dull ultramarine	CB		50	10
S36	23/1/74		**3½p**	Bronze green	2B		25	15
S37	6/11/74		**3½p**	Bronze green	CB		25	15
S38	6/11/74		**4½p**	Steel blue	2B		25	15
S39	23/1/74		**5½p**	Violet	2B		20	15
S40	21/5/75		**5½p**	Violet	CB		20	15
S41	14/1/76		**6½p**	Greenish blue	CB		20	10
S42	18/1/78		**7p**	Red brown	CB		12	10
S43	23/1/74		**8p**	Rose red	2B		60	15
S44	14/1/76		**8½p**	Yellow green	2B		15	15
S45	18/1/78		**9p**	Blue	2B		14	12
S46	20/10/76		**10p**	Orange brown	2B		15	15
S47	18/1/78		**10½p**	Steel blue	2B		15	15
S48	20/10/76		**11p**	Red	2B		16	16

Type R5

Type R6

Type R7

Type R8

Presentation Packs

7/7/71	4 stamps Nos. S23–26	2.50
29/5/74	4 stamps Nos. S31, 36, 39, 43	1.50
6/11/74	5 stamps Nos. S31, 36, 38, 39, 43	1.50
20/10/76	4 stamps Nos. S41, 44, 46, 48	80

REGIONAL ISSUES – WALES 1958 –

Printers: Harrison & Sons in Photogravure   *Perf:* 15 x 14   *No Watermark* unless marked MC = Multiple Crowns

No.	Issued	Type		Colour	Phosphor	Wmk.	U/M	F/U
STERLING VALUES								
Gum Arabic								
WA1	18/8/58	R9	**3d**	Reddish violet		MC	15	5
WA2	16/5/67		**3d**	Reddish violet	CB	MC	10	20
WA3	6/12/67		**3d**	Reddish violet	CB		10	10
WA4	7/2/66		**4d**	Dull ultramarine		MC	15	5
WA5	–/10/67		**4d**	Dull ultramarine	2B	MC	10	5
WA6	29/9/58	R10	**6d**	Claret		MC	30	15
WA7	1/3/67		**9d**	Deep green	2B	MC	30	25
WA8	29/9/58	R11	**1/3d**	Green		MC	35	25
WA9	1/3/67		**1/6d**	Grey blue	2B	MC	40	20
PVA Gum								
WA10	21/6/68	R9	**4d**	Dull ultramarine	2B		10	10
WA11	4/9/68		**4d**	Sepia	CB		10	10
WA12	26/2/69		**4d**	Vermilion	CB		30	10
WA13	4/9/68		**5d**	Deep blue	2B		25	10
WA14	1/8/69	R11	**1/6d**	Grey blue	2B		4.00	1.75
Presentation Pack								
	9/12/70			6 stamps Nos. WA3, 7, 9, 11, 12, 13			3.00	
DECIMAL VALUES								
OCP/PVA								
WA15	7/7/71	R12	**2½p**	Magenta	CB		20	15
WA16	7/7/71		**3p**	Dull ultramarine	2B		15	15
WA17	7/7/71		**5p**	Bright violet	2B		50	30
WA18	7/7/71		**7½p**	Chestnut	2B		1.00	75
FCP/GA								
WA19	22/9/72	R12	**2½p**	Magenta	CB		30	15
WA20	6/6/73		**3p**	Dull ultramarine	2B		2.50	15
FCP/PVA								
WA21	–/–/73	R12	**2½p**	Magenta	CB		1.50	–
WA22	–/2/73		**3p**	Dull ultramarine	2B		1.50	–
WA23	23/1/74		**3p**	Dull ultramarine	CB		30	10
WA24	–/6/73		**5p**	Bright violet	2B		1.75	50
FCP/PVAD								
WA25	23/1/74	R12	**3½p**	Bronze green	2B		25	15
WA26	6/11/74		**3½p**	Bronze green	CB		25	15
WA27	6/11/74		**4½p**	Steel blue	2B		25	15
WA28	23/1/74		**5½p**	Violet	2B		20	15
WA29	21/5/75		**5½p**	Violet	CB		20	15
WA30	14/1/76		**6½p**	Greenish blue	CB		20	10
WA31	18/1/78		**7p**	Red brown	CB		14	10
WA32	23/1/74		**8p**	Rose red	2B		25	15
WA33	14/1/76		**8½p**	Yellow green	2B		15	15
WA34	18/1/78		**9p**	Blue	2B		14	12
WA35	20/10/76		**10p**	Orange brown	2B		16	15
WA36	18/1/78		**10½p**	Steel blue	2B		16	15
WA37	20/10/76		**11p**	Red	2B		16	16
Presentation Packs								
	7/7/71			4 stamps Nos. WA15–18			2.50	
	29/6/74			4 stamps Nos. WA23, 25, 28, 32			1.50	
	6/11/74			5 stamps Nos. WA23, 25, 27, 28, 32			1.50	
	20/10/76			4 stamps Nos. WA30, 33, 35, 37			80	

Type R9

Type R10

Type R11

Type R12

ALL REIGNS 1904 – 1978

Type BP2 and BP4

Type BP59

Type BP95

Type BP106

Type BP107

Baked Stuffed
Haddock

2 Fillets of fresh haddock
(about ½ lb each)
2 large sliced tomatoes
2 skinned and chopped
tomatoes
2 level tbsps chopped
parsley
2 level tbsps chopped
celery
3 oz melted butter
¼ lb fresh white
breadcrumbs
½ level tsp salt
Milk

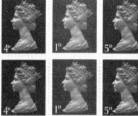

Type BP142

Type BP110 and BP130

Type BP110 and BP130

Type BP143 and 144

Type BP145

Type BP146

Type BP154 and BP161

ALL REIGNS 1904 – 1935

The prices are for unmounted mint or fine used panes with **full perforations all round plus selvedge.** Lightly mounted panes 15% less. Panes with **clipped perforations** are usually obtainable from 30% – 60% off listed prices dependent on how many stamps are affected. Panes with cylinder numbers are worth considerably more, up to 150% in some cases.

No.	Issued	Panes of	Value	Detail		Printer	Upright	Inverted
KING EDWARD VII								
BP1	1904	6	½d × 6	Yellow green		De La Rue	£10	£50
BP2	1906	6	½d × 5	Yellow green		De La Rue	£150	£150
			Label	"ST. ANDREW'S CROSS"				
BP3	1911	6	½d × 6	Yellow green		Harrison Perf. 14	£30	£60
BP4	1911	6	½d × 5	Yellow green		Harrison Perf. 14	£225	£250
			Label	"ST. ANDREW'S CROSS"				
BP5	1904	6	1d × 6	Red		De La Rue	5.00	£14
BP6	1911	6	1d × 6	Red		Harrison Perf. 14	£14	£60
KING GEORGE V					Die No.	Wmk.		
BP7	1911	6	½d × 6	Green	Die 1B	IC	£20	£45
BP8	1912	6	½d × 6	Green	Die 1B	RC	£85	£85
BP9	1911	6	1d × 6	Carmine	Die 1B	IC	£20	£45
BP10	1912	6	1d × 6	Scarlet	Die 1B	IC	£100	£100
BP11	1912	6	1d × 6	Aniline scarlet	Die 1B	IC	£950	£1150
BP12	1912	6	1d × 6	Scarlet	Die 1B	RC	£55	£55
BP13	1913	6	½d × 6	Green		RC	4.00	6.50
BP14	1913	6	1d × 6	Red		RC	4.00	6.50
BP15	1918	6	1½d × 6	Red brown		RC	4.00	8.00
BP16	1924	6	1½d × 4	Red brown		RC	£200	£200
			Label × 2	Advertisements				
BP17	1921	6	2d × 6	Orange	Die I	RC	£15	£55
BP18	1921	6	2d × 6	Orange	Die II	RC	£45	£150
BP19	1924	6	½d × 6	Green		BC	4.00	7.50
BP20	1924	6	1d × 6	Red		BC	4.00	£25
BP21	1924	6	1½d × 6	Red brown		BC	7.50	£15
BP22	1924	6	1½d × 4	Red brown		BC	£75	£75
			Label × 2	Advertisements				
BP23	1924	6	1½d × 4	Red brown		BC Sideways		£850
			Label × 2	Advertisements				
POSTAL UNION CONGRESS ISSUE								
BP24	1929	6	½d × 6	Green			£35	£125
BP25	1929	6	1d × 6	Scarlet			£35	£150
BP26	1929	6	1½d × 6	Red brown			£15	£60
BP27	1929	6	1½d × 4	Red brown			£90	£120
			Label × 2	Advertisements				
PHOTOGRAVURE ISSUE						Format		
BP28	1935	6	½d × 6	Green		Intermediate	£45	£175
BP29	1935	6	½d × 6	Green		Small	£10	£45
BP30	1935	6	1d × 6	Red		Intermediate	£35	£150
BP31	1935	6	1d × 6	Red		Small	£10	£45
BP32	1935	6	1½d × 6	Red brown		Intermediate	£30	£90
BP33	1935	6	1½d × 4	Red brown		Intermediate	£150	£150
			Label × 2	Advertisements				
BP34	1935	6	1½d × 6	Red brown		Small	7.50	£20
BP35	1935	6	1½d × 4	Red brown		Small	£30	£30
			Label × 2	Advertisements				
SILVER JUBILEE								
BP36	1935	4	½d × 4	Green	Type II Wmk. Inverted, Type III Wmk. Upright		£20	£30
BP37	1935	4	1d × 4	Scarlet	Type II Wmk. Inverted, Type III Wmk. Upright		£30	£40
BP38	1935	4	1½d × 4	Red brown	Type II Wmk. Inverted, Type III Wmk. Upright		£15	£15

ALL REIGNS 1936 – 1954

No.	Issued	Panes of	Value	Detail		Upright	Inverted

KING EDWARD VIII

No.	Issued	Panes of	Value	Detail	Upright	Inverted
BP39	1936	6	½**d** x 6	Green	2.50	£18
BP40	1936	6	1**d** x 6	Red	4.50	£40
BP41	1936	6	1½**d** x 6	Red brown	2.00	£15
BP42	1936	6	1½**d** x 4	Red brown	£15	£20
			Label x 2	Advertisements		
BP43	1936	2	1½**d** x 2	Red brown	2.50	6.00

KING GEORGE VI

No.	Issued	Panes of	Value	Detail	UPR.	INV.	S/W
BP44	1937	6	½**d** x 6	Green	2.50	£15	–
BP45	1940	4	½**d** x 4	Green	–	–	£15
BP46	1938	2	½**d** x 2	Green	2.50	6.00	–
BP47	1942	6	½**d** x 6	Pale green	2.00	£22	–
BP48	1947	2	½**d** x 2	Pale green	75	–	–
BP49	1951	6	½**d** x 6	Orange	1.25	2.00	–
BP50	1951	4	½**d** x 4	Orange	1.25	1.75	–
BP51	1951	2	½**d** x 2	Orange	50	–	–
BP52	1937	6	1**d** x 6	Scarlet	3.00	£275	–
BP53	1940	4	1**d** x 4	Scarlet	–	–	£50
BP54	1938	2	1**d** x 2	Scarlet	5.00	£95	–
BP55	1947	2	1**d** x 2	Pale scarlet	1.00	–	–
BP56	1953	6	1**d** x 6	Ultramarine	1.25	£20	–
BP57	1951	4	1**d** x 4	Ultramarine	1.00	£14	–
BP58	1951	2	1**d** x 2	Ultramarine	75	–	–
BP59	1952	6	1**d** x 3	Ultramarine			
			Label x 3	"MINIMUM INLAND PRINTED PAPER RATE 1½d" (Overall height of slogan 17 mm.)	7.50	7.50	–
BP60	1953	6	1**d** x 3	Ultramarine			
			Label x 3	"MINIMUM INLAND PRINTED PAPER RATE 1½d" (Overall height of slogan 15 mm)	£25	£25	–
BP61	1954	6	1**d** x 3	Ultramarine	£10	£10	–
			Label x 3	"SHORTHAND IN ONE WEEK"			
BP62	1937	6	1½**d** x 6	Red brown	2.50	£15	–
BP63	1937	6	1½**d** x 4	Red brown	£25	£100	–
			Label x 2	Advertisements			
BP64	1938	2	1½**d** x 2	Red brown	2.00	6.00	–
BP65	1947	2	1½**d** x 2	Pale red brown	2.00	–	–
BP66	1952	6	1½**d** x 6	Green	6.00	£18	–
BP67	1951	4	1½**d** x 4	Green	4.00	£12	–
BP68	1951	2	1½**d** x 2	Green	2.00	–	–
BP69	1937	6	2**d** x 6	Orange	6.00	£375	–
BP70	1941	6	2**d** x 6	Pale orange	6.00	£42	–
BP71	1951	6	2**d** x 6	Pale red brown	£10	£45	–
BP72	1937	6	2½**d** x 6	Ultramarine	5.50	£260	–
BP73	1941	6	2½**d** x 6	Light ultramarine	4.00	£30	–
BP74	1951	6	2½**d** x 6	Scarlet	4.50	£10	–

QUEEN ELIZABETH II 1953 – 1960

No.	Panes of	Value	Detail	UPR.	INV.	S/W
1953 – 55 WILDING ISSUES – WATERMARK: TUDOR CROWN						
BP75	6	½d x 6	Orange red	75	2.80	–
BP76	4	½d x 4	Orange red	80	2.40	–
BP77	2	½d x 2	Orange red	40	–	–
BP78	6	1d x 6	Deep ultramarine	1.20	£19	–
BP79	4	1d x 4	Deep ultramarine	1.20	£13	–
BP80	2	1d x 2	Deep ultramarine	50	–	–
BP81	6	1d x 3	Deep ultramarine	£48	£48	–
		Label x 3	"MINIMUM INLAND PRINTED PAPER RATE 1½d"			
BP82	6	1d x 3	Deep ultramarine	9.50	£13	–
		Label x 3	"PLEASE POST EARLY IN THE DAY"			
BP83	6	1d x 3	Deep ultramarine			
		Label	"PACK YOUR PARCELS SECURELY"	9.50	£13	–
		Label	"ADDRESS YOUR LETTERS CORRECTLY"			
		Label	"AND POST EARLY IN THE DAY"			
BP84	6	1½d x 6	Green	60	2.80	–
BP85	4	1½d x 4	Green	80	2.60	–
BP86	2	1½d x 2	Green	60	–	–
BP87	6	2d x 6	Red brown	2.80	£96	–
BP88	6	2½d x 6	Carmine red	3.60	4.80	–
1955 – 58 WILDING ISSUES – WATERMARK: ST. EDWARD'S CROWN						
BP89	6	½d x 6	Orange red	90	2.00	–
BP90	4	½d x 4	Orange red	85	3.20	–
BP91	2	½d x 2	Orange red	75	–	–
BP92	6	1d x 6	Deep ultramarine	1.00	4.50	–
BP93	4	1d x 4	Deep ultramarine	80	3.25	–
BP94	2	1d x 2	Deep ultramarine	75	–	–
BP95	6	1d x 3	Deep ultramarine			
		Label	"PACK YOUR PARCELS SECURELY"	9.00	8.00	–
		Label	"ADDRESS YOUR LETTERS CORRECTLY"			
		Label	"POST EARLY IN THE DAY"			
BP96	6	1½d x 6	Green	3.50	3.60	–
BP97	4	1½d x 4	Green	3.00	3.60	–
BP98	2	1½d x 2	Green	90	–	–
BP99	6	2d x 6	Red brown	3.60	£48	–
BP100	6	2d x 6	Light red brown	1.60	£13	–
BP101	6	2½d x 6	Carmine red	2.00	2.50	–
BP102	6	3d x 6	Deep violet	1.50	£12	–
BP103	4	3d x 4	Deep violet	3.00	£10	–
1958 – 60 WILDING ISSUES – WATERMARK: MULTIPLE CROWNS						
BP104	6	½d x 6	Orange red	55	2.40	–
BP105	4	½d x 4	Orange red	80	2.00	1.20
BP106	4	½d x 3	Orange red	5.00	5.00	–
		2½d x 1	Carmirle red			
BP107	4	½d x 2	Orange red	–	–	1.60
		2½d x 2	Carmine red			
BP108	6	1d x 6	Deep ultramarine	55	3.00	–
BP109	4	1d x 4	Deep ultramarine	80	2.00	2.25
BP110	4	1d x 2	Deep ultramarine (L.H. or R.H. format)	–	–	1.60
		3d x 2	Deep violet			
BP111	6	1½d x 6	Green	80	6.00	–
BP112	4	1½d x 4	Green	55	4.00	–
BP113	4	1½d x 4	Green	–	–	£30
BP114	6	2d x 6	Red brown	£10	£360	–
BP115	6	2½d x 6	Carmine red	40	£12	–
BP116	4	2½d x 4	Carmine red	2.00	2.00	–
BP117	6	3d x 6	Deep violet	65	1.50	–
BP118	4	3d x 4	Deep violet	1.20	1.80	1.25
BP119	6	4d x 6	Deep ultramarine	1.20	2.20	–
BP120	4	4d x 4	Deep ultramarine	–	–	1.60

QUEEN ELIZABETH II 1958 – 1970

No.	Issued	Panes of	Value	Detail	Phosphor	Gum	UPR.	INV.	S/W
1958–59 WILDING ISSUES – WATERMARK: MULTIPLE CROWNS WITH GRAPHITE LINES									
BP121		6	½**d** x 6	Orange red			£17	£17	–
BP122		6	1**d** x 6	Deep ultramarine			6.50	6.00	–
BP123		6	1½**d** x 6	Green			£475	£175	–
BP124		6	2½**d** x 6	Carmine red			£50	£290	–
BP125		6	3**d** x 6	Deep violet			3.25	2.50	–
1960 – 67 WILDING ISSUES – WATERMARK: MULTIPLE CROWNS WITH PHOSPHOR BANDS									
BP126		6	½**d** x 6	Orange red			75	2.25	–
BP127		4	½**d** x 4	Orange red			–	–	£18
BP128		6	1**d** x 6	Deep ultramarine			80	1.50	–
BP129		4	1**d** x 4	Deep ultramarine			–	–	4.80
BP130		4	1**d** x 2	Deep ultramarine (L.H. or R.H. format)			–	–	4.50
			3**d** x 2	Deep violet					
BP131		6	1½**d** x 6	Green			75	£20	–
BP132		4	1½**d** x 4	Green			–	–	£30
BP133		6	2½**d** x 6	Carmine red	2B		4.80	£650	–
BP134		6	2½**d** x 6	Carmine red	1B		5.00	£60	–
BP135		6	3**d** x 6	Deep violet	2B		3.60	4.25	–
BP136		4	3**d** x 4	Deep violet	2B		–	–	4.80
BP137		6	3**d** x 6	Deep violet	1B		4.80	£16	–
BP138		6	3**d** x 6	Deep violet	CB		3.20	7.25	–
BP139		6	4**d** x 6	Deep ultramarine			1.10	1.60	–
BP140		4	4**d** x 4	Deep ultramarine			–	–	1.00
1967 – 70 MACHIN STERLING ISSUES								No Wmk.	
BP141	1/5/68	6	1**d**(B) x 6	Olive	2B	PVA			80
BP142	1/12/69	16	1**d**(B) x 6	Olive	2B	PVA			
			4**d**(B) x 3	Vermilion	SB(L)				
			4**d**(B) x 3	Vermilion	SB(R)				£10
			5**d**(B) x 3	Royal blue	2B				
			Label	"BAKED STUFFED HADDOCK"					
BP143	16/9/68	6	1**d**(B) x 4	Olive	CB	PVA			3.00
			4**d**(B) x 2	Olive brown	CB				
BP144	6/1/69	6	1**d**(B) x 4	Olive	2B	PVA			3.00
			4**d**(B) x 2	Vermilion	SB(L)				
BP145	6/4/68	4	1**d**(B) x 2	Olive (at left)	2B	PVA			2.00
			3**d**(B) x 2	Violet	2B				
BP146	6/4/68	4	1**d**(B) x 2	Olive (at right)	2B	PVA			2.00
			3**d**(B) x 2	Violet	2B				
BP147	25/3/68	6	3**d**(B) x 6	Violet	CB	PVA			8.00
BP148	21/9/67	6	4**d**(A) x 6	Olive sepia	2B	GA			3.00
BP149	–/2/68	6	4**d**(A) x 6	Olive brown	2B	GA			3.00
BP150	1/5/68	6	4**d**(A) x 6	Olive brown/olive sepia	2B	PVA			1.00
BP151	6/4/68	4	4**d**(B) x 4	Olive brown	2B	PVA			1.00
BP152	16/9/68	6	4**d**(A) x 6	Olive brown	CB	PVA			1.00
BP153	16/9/68	4	4**d**(B) x 4	Olive brown	CB	PVA			80
BP154	16/9/68	4	4**d**(B) x 2	Olive brown	CB	PVA			
			Label	"£4,315 FOR YOU AT AGE 55"					1.00
			Label	"SEE OTHER PAGES"					
BP155	6/1/69	6	4**d**(A) x 6	Vermilion	CB	PVA			1.00
BP156	20/2/69	6	4**d**(A) x 6	Vermilion	CB	GA			£90
BP157	6/1/69	6	4**d**(B) x 6	Vermilion	CB	PVA			90
BP158	3/3/69	4	4**d**(B) x 4	Vermilion	CB	PVA			75
BP159	1/12/69	16	4**d**(B) x 15	Vermilion	CB	PVA			3.50
			Label	"STUFFED CUCUMBER" etc.					
BP160	1/12/69	16	4**d**(B) x 15	Vermilion	CB	PVA			3.50
			Label	"METHOD" etc.					
BP161	3/3/69	4	4**d**(B) x 2	Vermilion	CB	PVA			
			Label	"£4,315 FOR YOU AT AGE 55"					75
			Label	"SEE OTHER PAGES"					
BP162	16/9/68	6	5**d**(B) x 6	Royal blue	2B	PVA			1.00
BP163	1/12/69	16	5**d**(B) x 15	Royal blue	2B	PVA			3.25
			Label	"METHOD" etc.					

Type DP1

Type DP2

Type DP3

Type DP4

Type DP5

Type DP6

Type DP7

Type DP8

Type DP9

Type DP11

Type DP12

Type DP13

Type DP14

Type DP15

Type DP16

Some facts about Wedgwood

A first edition copy of the Portland Vase made in the late eighteenth century realised £20,000 at Sotheby's on 30th November 1971 – a world record auction price for an English ceramic.

Josiah Wedgwood paid the third Duke of Portland £100, a handsome hiring fee in those days, for the loan of the Barberini (or Portland) vase in order to model his famous Jasper reproductions.

Josiah Wedgwood equipped dairies with his ceramic products – from the tiling for the walls to settling pans for the cream.

In 1784 Wedgwood made a Jasper chess set. Flaxman the artist used Sarah Siddons as his model for the Queen.

It is recorded that Catherine the Great paid just over £2,700 for her 952-piece Wedgwood dinner and dessert service.

Type DP18

Some facts about Wedgwood

A monument to Josiah Wedgwood, executed by the famous artist, John Flaxman, is in Stoke Parish Church. The inscription states he: 'converted a rude and inconsiderable Manufactory into an elegant Art and an important part of the National Commerce.'

The foundation of Sydney was marked by the issue, in 1789, of the Sydney Cove medallion. This included some Australian clay brought back from Botany Bay by Captain James Cook in the *Endeavour*.

Early Jasper vases were often made in sets, to form a *garniture de cheminée*. Such vases were particularly admired by late 19th century collectors, many of whom left their collections to museums.

Canals interested Josiah Wedgwood, and he was a pioneer in promoting this form of transport in England.

Type DP19

ALL REIGNS 1904 – 1978 (continued)

Inland letter rates (and to the Irish Republic and Channel Islands)

Not over	First class	Second class	Not over	First class	Second class
2oz	3p	2½p	14oz	15p	9½p
4oz	4p	3½p	1lb 6oz	17p	11½p
6oz	6p	5½p	1lb 8oz	24p	13½p (max)
8oz	8p	6½p	2lb 0oz	34p	
10oz	10p	7½p	Each additional		
12oz	13p	8½p	1lb	17p	

Overseas rates: Air

Europe: for letters and postcards surface rates apply.

Outside Europe
Zone A: N. Africa, Israel, Lebanon and neighbouring countries.
Zone B: Americas, most of Africa, India and neighbouring countries, S.E. Asia.
Zone C: China, Japan, Australasia.

	Zone A	Zone B	Zone C
Letters (per ½oz)	5p	7½p	9p
Printed papers (per ½oz)	3p	4p	5p
Postcards	3p	4p	5p
Letter forms	5p: 6½p	5p: 6½p	5p: 6½p

Overseas rates: Surface

Foreign includes Europe except Cyprus, Gibraltar and Malta.

Weight step	Letters		Printed papers	
	For-eign	Common-wealth	Ordin-ary	Re-duced
up to 1oz	5p	3p	3p	1½p
1–2oz	9p	8p	4p	2p
2–4oz	12p	7½p	5p	2½p
4–8oz	30p	10p	8p	4p
8oz–1lb	50p	20p	15p	8p
1–2lb	80p	38p	25p	15p
2–4lb	130p	70p	40p	25p

Postcards to all countries: 3p.

For full details see leaflet or P.O. Guide at any Post Office. These rates apply at time of printing.
Edition date: May 1972.

Type DP20

Type DP21

Type DP22

Type DP23

The rates shown here were correct at the time of going to press, March 1978.

Type DP24

Type DP27

Type DP27A

Type DP30

Type DP30A

remember the postcode

Type DP31

DP32

MACHIN DECIMAL ISSUES 1971 – 1972

The DP series of code numbers, for the Decimal Booklet Panes listed below, are the copyright of the Decimal Stamp Book Study Circle, and we acknowledge with thanks their assistance in granting permission to use their system of identification.

The panes are found with a variety of different perforations in respect of the selvedge. The prices shown below represent the cheapest variety of perforation type, but with the stamps having full perforations.

No.	Issued	Panes of	Value	Detail	Phosphor	Gum	U/M
DP1	15/2/71	4	½p(I) x 2	Turquoise	2B	OCP/PVA	3.00
			2p x 2	Green (se-tenant vertical)	2B		
DP2	15/2/71	4	1p x 2	Crimson	2B	OCP/PVA	3.00
			1½p x 2	Grey (se-tenant vertical)	2B		
DP3	15/2/71	6	½p(I) x 5	Turquoise	2B	OCP/PVA	3.00
			Label	"B. ALAN LTD."			
DP4	15/2/71	6	2½p(II) x 4	Pink	CB	OCP/PVA	3.75
			Label	"UNIFLO"			
			Label	"STICK FIRMLY"			
DP5	15/2/71	6	2½p(II) x 5	Pink	CB	OCP/PVA	3.75
			Label	"STICK FIRMLY"			
DP6	15/2/71	6	3p(I) x 5	Blue	2B	OCP/PVA	3.50
			Label	"£4,315 FOR YOU AT AGE 55"			
	1/10/71	6	3p(I) x 5	Blue	2B	FCP/PVA	2.25
			Label	"£4,315 FOR YOU AT AGE 55"			
DP7	15/2/71	6	½p(I) x 5	Turquoise	2B	OCP/PVA	2.50
			Label	"LICK"			
	17/9/71	6	½p(I) x 5	Turquoise	2B	FCP/PVA	2.50
			Label	"LICK"			
DP8	15/2/71	6	2½p(II) x 5	Pink	CB	OCP/PVA	3.75
			Label	"TEAR OFF"			
	17/9/71	6	2½p(II) x 5	Pink	CB	FCP/PVA	3.50
			Label	"TEAR OFF"			
DP9	15/2/71	6	3p x 4	Blue	2B	OCP/PVA	4.75
			2½p(II) x 2	Pink	SB(L)		
	13/3/72	6	3p x 4	Blue	2B	FCP/PVA	3.50
			2½p(II) x 2	Pink	SB(L)		
DP10	15/2/71	6	3p x 6	Blue	2B	OCP/PVA	4.50
	17/9/71	6	3p x 6	Blue	2B	FCP/PVA	3.00
DP11	14/7/71	4	½p(II) x 2	Turquoise	2B	OCP/PVA	4.00
			2p x 2	Green (se-tenant horizontal)	2B		
	6/10/71	4	½p(II) x 2	Turquoise	2B	FCP/PVA	2.75
			2p x 2	Green (se-tenant horizontal)	2B		
	12/11/73	4	½p(II) x 2	Turquoise	2B	FCP/PVAD	1.50
			2p x 2	Green (se-tenant horizontal)	2B		
DP12	14/7/71	4	1p x 2	Crimson	2B	OCP/PVA	2.75
			1½p x 2	Grey (se-tenant horizontal)	2B		
	6/10/71	4	1p x 2	Crimson	2B	FCP/PVA	2.25
			1½p x 2	Grey (se-tenant horizontal)	2B		
	12/11/73	4	1p x 2	Crimson	2B	FCP/PVAD	1.75
			1½p x 2	Grey (se-tenant horizontal)	2B		
DP13	24/12/71	6	½p(I) x 5	Turquoise	2B	FCP/PVA	3.00
			Label	"RUSHSTAMPS"			
DP14	24/12/71	6	2½p(II) x 5	Pink	CB	FCP/PVA	4.25
			Label	"RUSHSTAMPS"			
DP15	24/12/71	6	2½p(II) x 4	Pink	CB	FCP/PVA	3.75
			Lable	"DO YOU COLLECT GB STAMPS"			
			Label	"RUSHSTAMPS"			
DP16	24/12/71	6	2½p(II) x 5	Pink	CB	FCP/PVA	3.50
			Label	"B. ALAN"			
	24/12/71	6	2½p(II) x 5	Pink	CB	FCP/PVA	6.00
			Label	"B. ALAN"			
DP17	24/5/72	13	3p x 12	Blue	2B	FCP/PVA	6.00
			Label	"SOME FACTS ABOUT WEDGWOOD"			

MACHIN DECIMAL ISSUES 1972 – 1978

No.	Issued	Panes of	Value	Detail	Phosphor	Gum	U/M
DP18	24/5/72	13	2½p(I) x 3	Pink	CB	FCP/PVA	
			2½p(I) x 3	Pink	SB(R)		
			3p x 6	Blue	2B		£25
			Label	"SOME FACTS ABOUT WEDGWOOD"			
DP19	24/5/72	13	2½p(III) x 3	Pink	SB(R)	FCP/PVA	
			2½p(III) x 3	Pink	SB(L)		
			2½p(III) x 3	Pink	CB		£25
			½p(I) x 3	Turquoise	2B		
			Label	"SOME FACTS ABOUT WEDGWOOD"			
DP20	24/5/72	7	½p(I) x 3	Turquoise	2B	FCP/PVA	
			½p(I) x 1	Turquoise	SB(L)		
			2½p(III) x 2	Pink	SB(L)		£75
			Label	"INLAND LETTER RATES"			
DP21	14/11/73	6	3p x 5	Blue	CB	FCP/PVA	7.50
			Label	Blank			
	14/11/73	6	3p x 5	Blue	CB	FCP/PVAD	3.75
			Label	Blank			
DP22	14/11/73	6	3½p x 5	Grey green	2B	FCP/PVA	7.50
			Label	Blank			
	14/11/73	6	3½p x 5	Grey green	2B	FCP/PVAD	3.00
			Label	Blank			
	23/10/74	6	3½p x 5	Grey green	CB	FCP/PVAD	3.75
			Label	Blank			
DP23	9/10/74	6	4½p x 5	Slate blue	2B	FCP/PVAD	6.00
			Label	Blank			
DP24	10/3/76	6	½p(I) x 2	Turquoise	2B	FCP/PVAD	
			1p x 3	Crimson	2B		50
			6p(II) x 1	Light green	2B		
DP25	14/7/76	10	6½p x 10	Peacock blue (margin on left)	CB	FCP/PVAD	2.00
DP25A	14/7/76	10	6½p x 10	Peacock blue (margin on right)	CB	FCP/PVAD	2.00
DP26	14/7/76	10	8½p x 10	Yellow green (margin on left)	2B	FCP/PVAD	2.00
DP26A	14/7/76	10	8½p x 10	Yellow green (margin on right)	2B	FCP/PVAD	2.00
DP27	26/1/77	10	6½p x 2	Peacock blue (at left)	SB(L)	FCP/PVAD	
			8½p x 4	Yellow green	2B		
			1p x 2	Crimson	2B		6.00
			½p x 2	Turquoise	2B		
DP27A	26/1/77	10	6½p x 2	Peacock blue (at right)	SB(R)	FCP/PVAD	
			8½p x 4	Yellow green	2B		
			1p x 2	Crimson	2B		6.00
			½p x 2	Turquoise	2B		
DP28	13/6/77	10	7p x 10	Red brown (margin on left)	CB	FCP/PVAD	1.10
DP28A	13/6/77	10	7p x 10	Red brown (margin on right)	CB	FCP/PVAD	1.10
DP29	13/6/77	10	9p x 10	Blue (margin on left)	2B	FCP/PVAD	1.40
DP29A	13/6/77	10	9p x 10	Blue (margin on right)	2B	FCP/PVAD	1.40
DP30	13/6/77	8	7p x 3	Red brown (at left)	SB(L)	FCP/PVAD	
			9p x 3	Blue	2B		
			1p x 2	Crimson	2B		1.00
DP30A	13/6/77	8	7p x 3	Red brown (at right)	SB(R)	FCP/PVAD	
			9p x 3	Blue	2B		
			1p x 2	Crimson	2B		1.00
DP31	8/2/78	6	½p x 2	Turquoise	CB	FCP/PVAD	
			1p x 2	Crimson	CB		
			7p x 1	Red brown	CB		15
			Label	"REMEMBER THE POSTCODE"			
DP32	15/11/78	20	7p x 10	Red brown	1 BAR	FCP/PVAD	4.75
			9p x 10	Blue	2 BARS		

NOTE:- Miscut panes have occured fairly regularly from DP22 onwards and these sell at a premium.

POSTAGE DUE STAMPS

Printed in Typography Nos. P1 – P80   *Perf:* All 14 x 15

Watermarks: Are always Sideways, normally with the Crown pointing to the left as viewed from the front. Many of the values are found with the Crown pointing to the right and occasionally reversed. These are not separately catalogued but they do sell at a considerable premium.

Type 1   Type 2

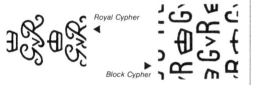

Royal Cypher

Block Cypher

1914–23 WATERMARK: ROYAL CYPHER SIDEWAYS
Printed by Somerset House & Harrison & Sons

No.	Type		Colour	U/M	M/M	F/U
P1	1	½d	Emerald	65	40	25
P2		1d	Carmine	65	40	10
P3			Pale carmine	65	40	20
P4		1½d	Chestnut	£55	£30	8.50
P5		2d	Agate	65	40	25
P6		3d	Violet	2.50	1.75	70
P7			Bluish violet	2.50	1.75	70
P8		4d	Grey green	7.00	5.00	1.00
P9		5d	Bistre brown	3.00	2.00	1.25
P10		1/–d	Bright blue	£30	£18	1.50
P11			Deep bright blue	£30	£18	1.50
			Set of 8	£100	£70	£14

STAMP NOS. P4, 8, 10 & 11 ONLY.
The Crown in the watermark normally points to the right, but varieties with the Crown pointing to the left are known and sell at a premium

1924 WATERMARK: ROYAL CYPHER SIDEWAYS
Printed by Waterlow & Sons

No.	Type		Colour	U/M	M/M	F/U
P12		1d	Car. (chalky paper)	5.50	4.00	2.00

1924–36 WATERMARK: BLOCK CYPHER SIDEWAYS
Printed by Waterlow & Sons and from 1934, Harrison & Sons

No.	Type		Colour	U/M	M/M	F/U
P13	1	½d	Emerald	65	40	25
P14		1d	Carmine	65	40	20
P15		1½d	Chestnut	£45	£27	8.00
P16		2d	Agate	1.00	60	20
P17		3d	Violet	2.50	1.75	25
P18		3d	Violet (experimental paper)	£40	£30	£30
P19		4d	Grey green	7.00	4.50	60
P20		5d	Bistre brown	£35	£20	£10
P21		1/–d	Deep blue	5.00	3.75	50
P22	2	2/6d	Purple/yellow	£35	£25	1.00
			Set of 9	£125	£85	£16

1936–37 WATERMARK: E8R SIDEWAYS
Printed by Harrison & Sons

No.	Type		Colour	U/M	M/M	F/U
P23	1	½d	Emerald	3.00	2.00	3.00
P24		1d	Carmine	1.00	60	1.00
P25		2d	Agate	1.25	80	1.00
P26		3d	Violet	1.00	60	60
P27		4d	Grey green	6.00	3.00	4.00
P28		5d	Bistre brown	5.00	3.50	4.00
P29			Yellow brown	£30	£15	£15
P30		1/–d	Deep blue	4.50	3.00	4.00
P31	2	2/6d	Purple/yellow	£90	£55	£10
			Set of 8	£100	£65	£25

1937–50 WATERMARK: GⱽIR SIDEWAYS
Printed by Harrison & Sons

No.	Type		Colour	U/M	M/M	F/U
P32	1	½d	Emerald	1.00	80	1.00
P33		1d	Carmine	2.00	70	30
P34		2d	Agate	1.00	60	20
P35		3d	Violet	2.00	1.00	20
P36		4d	Grey green	£12	7.50	1.75
P37		5d	Yellow brown	2.50	1.75	25
P38		1/–d	Deep blue	£10	7.00	50
P39	2	2/6d	Purple/yellow	£32	£24	1.75
			Set of 8	£52	£38	5.00

1951–54 WATERMARK: GⱽIR SIDEWAYS
Printed by Harrison & Sons

No.	Type		Colour	U/M	M/M	F/U
P40	1	½d	Orange	1.50	1.00	1.50
P41		1d	Violet blue	1.50	40	30
P42		1½d	Green	1.00	60	60
P43		4d	Blue	6.00	4.00	3.00
P44		1/–d	Bistre brown	£12	8.00	5.00
			Set of 5	£18	£12	9.50

1954–55 WATERMARK: TUDOR CROWN SIDEWAYS
Printed by Harrison & Sons

No.	Type		Colour	U/M	M/M	F/U
P45	1	½d	Orange	3.00	2.00	2.50
P46		2d	Agate	1.50	1.00	1.50
P47		3d	Violet	£25	£16	£12
P48		4d	Blue	8.00	4.50	5.00
P49		5d	Yellow brown	7.00	4.25	3.00
P50	2	2/6d	Purple/yellow	£80	£60	3.50
			Set of 6	£110	£80	£25

POSTAGE DUE STAMPS (continued)

No.	Type	Colour	U/M	M/M	F/U

Tudor Crown

St. Edward's Crown

Multiple Crown

Type 3

Type 4

1955–58 WATERMARK: ST. EDWARD'S CROWN SIDEWAYS
Printed by Harrison & Sons

No.	Type		Colour	U/M	M/M	F/U
P51	1	½d	Orange	3.00	2.25	3.00
P52		1d	Violet blue	5.00	2.00	1.00
P53		1½d	Green	4.00	3.00	3.50
P54		2d	Agate	£10	4.75	1.30
P55		3d	Violet	4.00	2.75	1.15
P56		4d	Blue	5.50	3.75	1.50
P57		5d	Brown ochre	5.50	3.75	1.75
P58		1/–d	Ochre	£13	9.00	2.25
P59	2	2/6d	Purple/yellow	£130	£95	4.00
P60		5/–d	Scarlet/yellow	£60	£40	£18
			Set of 10	£225	£150	£33

1959–68 WATERMARK: MULTIPLE CROWNS SIDEWAYS
Printed by Harrison & Sons

No.	Type		Colour	U/M	M/M	F/U
P61	1	½d	Orange	15	10	50
P62		1d	Violet blue	15	10	15
P63		1½d	Green	1.50	1.00	1.50
P64		2d	Agate	90	60	15
P65		3d	Violet	55	40	10
P66		4d	Blue	55	40	25
P67		5d	Yellow brown	55	40	40
P68		6d	Purple	55	40	10
P69		1/–d	Ochre	80	55	10
P70	2	2/6d	Purple/yellow	1.50	1.00	20
P71		5/–d	Scarlet/yellow	2.00	1.30	40
P72		10/–d	Blue/yellow	£10	6.75	2.25
P73		£1	Black/yellow	£28	£18	2.50
			Set of 13	£42	£27	7.00

1968–70 UNWATERMARKED CHALKY PAPER
Printed by Harrison & Sons
Gum Arabic

No.	Type		Colour	U/M		F/U
P74	1	2d	Agate	70		–
P75		4d	Blue	90		30

PVA Gum

No.	Type		Colour	U/M		F/U
P76	1	2d	Agate	3.00		30
P77		3d	Violet	80		30
P78		5d	Orange brown	4.00		2.75
P79		6d	Purple	2.00		50
P80		1/–d	Ochre	2.25		50
			Set of 6	£10		4.00

1968–70 UNWATERMARKED CHALKY PAPER
Printed in smaller format by Harrison & Sons in Photogravure
PVA Gum

No.	Type		Colour	U/M		F/U
P81		4d	Blue	6.00		3.00
P82		8d	Red	1.50		1.50
			Set of 2	7.00		4.25

1971–77 DECIMAL VALUES – UNWATERMARKED PAPER
Printed by Harrison & Sons in Photogravure
OCP/PVA

No.	Issued	Type		Colour	U/M	F/U
P83	15/2/71	3	½p	Turquoise	5	25
P84	,,	3	1p	Crimson	5	5
P85	,,	3	2p	Green	5	5
P86	,,	3	3p	Bright blue	6	6
P87	,,	3	4p	Light sepia	7	7
P88	,,	3	5p	Pale violet	10	10
P89	12/6/70	4	10p	Cerise	15	15
P90	,,	4	20p	Olive green	30	15
P91	,,	4	50p	Blue	75	40
P92	,,	4	£1	Black	1.50	40

FCP/PVA

No.	Issued	Type		Colour	U/M	F/U
P93	–/10/74	3	1p	Crimson	1.00	–
P94	,,	3	3p	Bright blue	1.00	–
P95	–/2/74	3	5p	Pale violet	2.25	–
P96	–/2/74	4	10p	Cerise	£30	–
P97	–/10/74	4	20p	Olive green	£50	–
P98	2/4/73	4	£5	Black/orange	7.50	3.00

FCP/PVAD

No.	Issued	Type		Colour	U/M	F/U
P99	–/12/74	3	1p	Crimson	5	5
P100	"	3	2p	Green	5	5
P101	–/6/75	3	3p	Bright blue	6	6
P102	–/–/78	3	4p	Light sepia	10	10
P103	–/1/76	3	5p	Pale violet	10	10
P104	21/8/74	3	7p	Red brown	12	20
P105	–/3/75	4	10p	Cerise	15	15
P106	18/6/75	4	11p	Brunswick green	16	35
P107	2/5/74	4	20p	Olive green	30	20
P108	–/12/74	4	50p	Blue	75	40
P109	–/–/78	4	£1	Black	1.50	40
P110	–/–/78	4	£5	Black/orange	7.00	–

Presentation Pack

3/11/71		10 stamps	5.50
		Nos. P83-92	

Presentation Pack

2/2/77		12 stamps Nos.P83,	3.25
		87,99-101,103-109	

OCCUPATION ISSUES 1941 – 5

Paper: White except where stated   *No Watermark*

No.	Issued	Type		Colour	U/M	M/M	F/U

Type 1

ARMS OF JERSEY
Printed in Typography by Evening Post, Jersey.
Perf.: 11

No.	Issued	Type		Colour	U/M	M/M	F/U
J1	29/1/42	1	½d	Bright green	2.25	1.45	75
J2			½d	Bright green (grey paper)	2.75	1.80	1.50
J3	1/4/41	1	**1d**	Scarlet	2.00	1.30	1.00
J4			1d	Scarlet (grey paper)	2.25	1.45	1.25
J5			1d	Scar. (chalky paper)	£30	£20	£20
	29/1/42			First Day Cover ½d			3.00
	1/4/41			First Day Cover 1d			4.00

Type 2   *Type 3*

Type 4   *Type 5*

Type 6   *Type 7*

VIEWS OF JERSEY
Printed in Typography by French Government Printing Works, Paris
Perf.: 13½

No.	Issued	Type		Colour	U/M	M/M	F/U
J6	1/6/43	2	**½d**	Green	2.25	1.45	1.75
J7	1/6/43	3	**1d**	Scarlet	25	15	25
J8			1d	Scarlet (on newsprint)	1.50	1.00	1.00
J9	8/6/43	4	**1½d**	Brown	60	40	60
J10	8/6/43	5	**2d**	Orange yellow	60	40	60
J11	29/6/43	6	**2½d**	Blue	1.50	1.00	1.00
J12			2½d	Blue (on newsprint)	1.50	1.00	1.00
J13	29/6/43	7	**3d**	Violet	1.25	80	1.25
				Set of 6	6.00	4.00	5.50
	1/6/43			First Day Cover (½d+1d)			2.50
	8/6/43			First Day Cover (½d+2d)			3.75
	29/6/43			First Day Cover (2½d+3d)			2.50

REGIONAL ISSUES 1958 – 69

Printers: Harrison & Sons in Photogravure
Paper: Ordinary except where stated
Watermark: Multiple Crowns   Phosphor bands where indicated

Type 8   *Type 9*

Gum Arabic

No.	Issued	Type		Colour	U/M	M/M	F/U
J14	8/6/64	8	**2½d**	Carmine red	65	45	45
J15	18/8/58	9	**3d**	Redd. violet	60	40	10
J16	9/6/67	9	**3d**	Redd. violet (CB)	10	5	15
J17	7/2/66	9	**4d**	Dull ultramarine	20	15	15
J18	5/9/67	9	**4d**	Dull ult. (2B)	10	5	15

NO WATERMARK (Chalky paper)

PVA Gum

No.	Issued	Type		Colour	U/M	M/M	F/U
J19	4/9/68	9	**4d**	Sepia (CB)	10	5	10
J20	26/2/69	9	**4d**	Vermillion (CB)	25	15	10
J21	4/9/68	9	**5d**	Deep blue (2B)	25	15	15

INDEPENDENT POSTAL ADMINISTRATION
Inaugurated on 1st October 1969

Type 10

Type 11

Type 12

Type 13

Type 14

Type 15

Type 16

Type 17

Type 18

Type 19

Type 20

Type 21

Type 22

Type 23

Type 24

1ST DEFINITIVE ISSUES 1969 – 70

Printers: Harrison, ½d – 1/9d ordinary paper, Perf. 14
Courvoisier, 2/6d – £1 granite paper, Perf. 12

No.	Issued	Type		Colour	U/M	F/U
J22	1/10/69	10	½d	Multicoloured	30	30
J23			½d	ditto (Thick paper)	1.00	1.00
J24		11	1d	Multicoloured	10	10
J25			1d	ditto (Thick paper)	30	30
J26		12	2d	Multicoloured	12	12
J27			2d	ditto (Thinner paper)	20	20
J28		13	3d	Multicoloured	15	15
J29			3d	ditto (Thinner paper)	25	25
J30		14	4d	Multicoloured	10	10
J31			4d	ditto (Thinner paper)	30	30
J32		15	5d	Multicoloured	12	12
J33			5d	ditto (Thinner paper)	30	30
J34		16	6d	Multicoloured	30	30
J35			6d	ditto (Thinner paper)	1.50	1.00
J36		17	9d	Multicoloured	75	75
J37			9d	ditto (Thinner paper)	75	75
J38		18	1/–d	Multicoloured	70	70
J39			1/–d	ditto (Thinner paper)	1.65	1.25
J40		19	1/6d	Multicoloured	1.50	1.50
J41			1/6d	ditto (Thinner paper)	2.50	2.00
J42		20	1/9d	Multicoloured	5.00	5.00
J43			1/9d	ditto (Thinner paper)	£10	8.00
J44		21	2/6d	Multicoloured	6.00	2.25
J45		22	5/–d	Multicoloured	£11	6.00
J46		23	10/–d	Multicoloured	£35	£22
J47		24	£1	Multicoloured	1.50	1.75
				Set of 15	£55	£34
				First Day Cover		£36
				Presentation		
				Packs (3)	£60	

Booklet Panes

J48				Pane of 1 x 1d	40	40
J49				Pane of 2 x 1d	50	50
J50				Pane of 1 x 4d	45	45
J51				Pane of 2 x 4d	70	70
J52				Pane of 2 x 5d	1.00	1.00
				First Day Cover		1.25
				1d+4d		
				First Day Cover		1.50
				1d+4d+5d		

INDEPENDENT POSTAL ADMINISTRATION (continued)
Sterling Issues 1969 – 70

All the following issues printed by Courvoisier in Photogravure on unwatermarked Granite paper, Perf. 11½ unless otherwise stated.

No.	Issued	Type	Colour	U/M	F/U

Type 25

Type 30

INAUGURATION OF POST OFFICE
Printers: Harrison ordinary paper, Perf. 14

No.	Issued	Type		Colour	U/M	F/U
J53	1/10/69	25	**4d**	Multicoloured	20	20
J54		25	**5d**	Multicoloured	40	40
J55		25	**1/6d**	Multicoloured	3.25	3.25
J56		25	**1/9d**	Multicoloured	3.50	3.25
				Set of 4	6.50	6.50
				First Day Cover		£10
				Presentation Pack	7.00	

Type 26

Type 27

Type 31

Type 32

Type 28

Type 29

Type 33

25th ANNIVERSARY OF LIBERATION

No.	Issued	Type		Colour	U/M	F/U
J57	9/5/70	26	**4d**	Multicoloured	15	10
J58		27	**5d**	Multicoloured	20	20
J59		28	**1/6d**	Multicoloured	2.75	2.25
J60		29	**1/9d**	Multicoloured	3.25	2.75
				Set of 4	5.50	4.75
				First Day Cover		5.50
				Presentation Pack	6.50	

BATTLE OF FLOWERS

No.	Issued	Type		Colour	U/M	F/U
J61	28/7/70	30	**4d**	Multicoloured	40	10
J62		31	**5d**	Multicoloured	60	20
J63		32	**1/6d**	Multicoloured	£14	3.85
J64		33	**1/9d**	Multicoloured	£16	4.95
				Set of 4	£28	8.25
				First Day Cover		8.50
				Presentation Pack	£30	

INDEPENDENT POSTAL ADMINISTRATION (continued)
Decimal Issues 1970 – 71

All the following issues printed by Courvoisier in Photogravure on unwatermarked Granite paper, Perf. 11½ unless otherwise stated.

No.	Issued	Type		Colour	U/M	F/U

Type 34

2ND DEFINITIVE ISSUES

Printers: Harrison & Sons(½p – 9p) in Photo   *Perf:* 14
Courvoisier (10p – 50p) in Photo   *Perf:* 12

No.	Issued	Type		Colour	U/M	F/U
J65	15/2/71	10	½p	Multicoloured	5	5
J66	,,	13	1p	Multicoloured	5	5
J67	,,	16	1½p	Multicoloured	5	5
J68	,,	14	2p	Multicoloured	5	5
J69	,,	15	2½p	Multicoloured	5	5
J70	,,	11	3p	Multicoloured	6	6
J71	,,	12	3½p	Multicoloured	6	6
J72	,,	17	4p	Multicoloured	8	8
J73	31/10/74	15	4½p	Multicoloured	10	10
J74	15/2/71	18	5p	Multicoloured	11	11
J75	31/10/74	16	5½p	Multicoloured	11	11
J76	15/2/71	34	6p	Multicoloured	12	12
J77	15/2/71	19	7½p	Multicoloured	14	14
J78	31/10/74	14	8p	Multicoloured	17	17
J79	15/2/71	20	9p	Multicoloured	20	20
J80	1/10/70	21	10p	Multicoloured	25	25
J81	1/10/70	22	20p	Multicoloured	40	40
J82	1/10/70	23	50p	Multicoloured	90	90
				Set of 18	2.70	2.70
	1/10/70			First Day Cover 10p – 50p		3.75
	15/2/71			First Day Cover ½p – 9p		2.50
				Presentation Packs (3)	4.00	

Booklet Panes

No.	Issued		Colour	U/M	F/U
J83			Pane of 1 x ½p	10	10
J84			Pane of 2 x 1p	10	10
J85			Pane of 4 x 1p	10	10
J86			Pane of 1 x 2p	60	60
J87			Pane of 2 x 2p	10	10
J88			Pane of 1 x 2½p	15	15
J89			Pane of 2 x 2½p	20	20
J90			Pane of 1 x 3p	10	10
J91			Pane of 2 x 3p	15	15
J92			Pane of 1 x 3½p	15	15
J93			Pane of 2 x 3½p	15	15
J94			Pane of 2 x 4p	15	15
J95			Pane of 4 x 4p	35	35
J96			Pane of 2 x 5p	25	25
J97			Pane of 4 x 5p	50	50
	15/2/71		First Day Cover ½+2+2½		1.25
	1/12/72		First Day Cover ½+2½+3p		1.50
	1/7/74		First Day Cover 3+3½p		1.25

Type 35

Type 36

Type 37

Type 38

WILDLIFE PRESERVATION TRUST 1971

No.	Issued	Type		Colour	U/M	F/U
J98	12/3/71	35	2p	Multicoloured	20	10
J99		36	2½p	Multicoloured	30	15
J100		37	7½p	Multicoloured	£13	3.75
J101		38	9p	Multicoloured	£16	4.85
				Set of 4	£28	8.00
				First Day Cover		8.25
				Presentation Pack	£30	

INDEPENDENT POSTAL ADMINISTRATION (continued)
Decimal Issues 1971 – 72

All the following issues printed by Courvoisier in Photogravure on unwatermarked Granite paper, Perf. 11½ unless otherwise stated.

No.	Issued	Type	Colour	U/M	F/U

Type 39

Type 40

PAINTINGS 1971

No.	Issued	Type		Colour	U/M	F/U
J106	5/10/71	43	**2p**	Multicoloured	10	10
J107		44	**2½p**	Multicoloured	15	15
J108		45	**7½p**	Multicoloured	4.75	3.00
J109		46	**9p**	Multicoloured	5.75	4.00
				Set of 4	£10	6.50
				First Day Cover		7.00
				Presentation Pack	10.50	

Type 41

Type 42

Type 47

BRITISH LEGION ANNIVERSARY

Printers: Questa Colour in Litho – ordinary paper, Perf. 14

No.	Issued	Type		Colour	U/M	F/U
J102	15/6/71	39	**2p**	Multicoloured	20	10
J103		40	**2½p**	Multicoloured	25	15
J104		41	**7½p**	Multicoloured	5.00	2.75
J105		42	**9p**	Multicoloured	6.75	3.75
				Set of 4	£11	6.50
				First Day Cover		7.00
				Presentation Pack	12.50	

Type 43

Type 44

Type 48

Type 49

Type 45

Type 46

Type 50

Type 45

WILD FLOWERS OF JERSEY

No.	Issued	Type		Colour	U/M	F/U
J110	18/1/72	47	**3p**	Multicoloured	20	20
J111		48	**5p**	Multicoloured	1.65	1.50
J112		49	**7½p**	Multicoloured	3.25	2.25
J113		50	**9p**	Multicoloured	5.00	3.00
				Set of 4	9.00	6.50
				First Day Cover		7.00
				Presentation Pack	9.50	

INDEPENDENT POSTAL ADMINISTRATION (continued)
Decimal Issues 1972

All the following issues printed by Courvoisier in Photogravure on unwatermarked Granite paper, Perf. 11½ unless otherwise stated.

No.	Issued	Type	Colour	U/M	F/U

Type 52

Type 51

Type 53

Type 54

WILDLIFE PRESERVATION TRUST 1972

No.	Issued	Type		Colour	U/M	F/U
J114	17/3/72	51	**2½p**	Multicoloured	15	10
J115		52	**3p**	Multicoloured	20	15
J116		53	**7½p**	Multicoloured	2.00	1.75
J117		54	**9p**	Multicoloured	2.75	2.50
				Set of 4	4.75	4.25
				First Day Cover		7.00
				Presentation Pack	6.00	

Type 55

Type 56

Type 57

Type 58

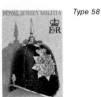

JERSEY MILITIA

No.	Issued	Type		Colour	U/M	F/U
J118	27/6/72	55	**2½p**	Multicoloured	15	10
J119		56	**3p**	Multicoloured	20	15
J120		57	**7½p**	Multicoloured	1.75	1.35
J121		58	**9p**	Multicoloured	2.25	1.95
				Set of 4	4.00	3.25
				First Day Cover		5.50
				Presentation Pack	5.25	

Type 60

Type 59

Type 61

Type 62

ROYAL SILVER WEDDING

No.	Issued	Type		Colour	U/M	F/U
J122	1/11/72	59	**2½p**	Multicoloured	10	10
J123		60	**3p**	Multicoloured	10	10
J124		61	**7½p**	Multicoloured	40	40
J125		62	**20p**	Multicoloured	70	70
				Set of 4	1.20	1.20
				First Day Cover		3.00
				Presentation Pack	2.75	

INDEPENDENT POSTAL ADMINISTRATION (continued)
Decimal Issues 1973

All the following issues printed by Courvoisier in Photogravure on unwatermarked Granite paper, Perf. 11½ unless otherwise stated.

No.	Issued	Type	Colour	U/M	F/U

Type 63

Type 64

Type 65

Type 66

JERSEY 9ᴾ

No.	Issued	Type	Colour	U/M	F/U

Type 71

Type 72

Type 73

Type 74

CENTENARY OF THE JERSEY SOCIETY

No.	Issued	Type		Colour	U/M	F/U
J126	23/1/73	63	2½p	Multicoloured	10	10
J127		64	3p	Multicoloured	10	10
J128		65	7½p	Multicoloured	55	50
J129		66	9p	Multicoloured	80	70
				Set of 4	1.40	1.20
				First Day Cover		1.70
				Presentation Pack	2.00	

CENTENARY OF THE JERSEY EASTERN RAILWAY

No.	Issued	Type		Colour	U/M	F/U
J134	6/8/73	71	2½p	Multicoloured	10	5
J135		72	3p	Multicoloured	10	10
J136		73	7½p	Multicoloured	50	40
J137		74	9p	Multicoloured	80	65
				Set of 4	1.30	1.10
				First Day Cover		1.50
				Presentation Pack	2.00	

Type 67

Type 68

Type 69

Type 70

Type 75

AVIATION HISTORY

No.	Issued	Type		Colour	U/M	F/U
J130	16/5/73	67	3p	Multicoloured	10	10
J131		68	5p	Multicoloured	20	20
J132		69	7½p	Multicoloured	55	50
J133		70	9p	Multicoloured	80	75
				Set of 4	1.50	1.30
				First Day Cover		1.70
				Presentation Pack	2.00	

ROYAL WEDDING

No.	Issued	Type		Colour	U/M	F/U
J138	14/11/73	75	3p	Multicoloured	10	10
J139		75	20p	Multicoloured	55	60
				Set of 2	60	65
				First Day Cover		90
				Presentation Pack	1.00	

INDEPENDENT POSTAL ADMINISTRATION (continued)
Decimal Issues 1973 – 74

All the following issues printed by Courvoisier in Photogravure on unwatermarked Granite paper, Perf. 11½ unless otherwise stated.

No.	Issued	Type		Colour	U/M	F/U

Type 76

Type 77

Type 78

Type 79

MARINE LIFE

No.	Issued	Type		Colour	U/M	F/U
J140	15/11/73	76	2½p	Multicoloured	5	5
J141		77	3p	Multicoloured	10	10
J142		78	7½p	Multicoloured	25	25
J143		79	20p	Multicoloured	30	30
				Set of 4	60	60
				First Day Cover		95
				Presentation Pack	1.00	

Type 80

Type 81

Type 82

Type 83

SPRING FLOWERS

No.	Issued	Type		Colour	U/M	F/U
J144	13/2/74	80	3p	Multicoloured	6	6
J145		81	5½p	Multicoloured	11	11
J146		82	8p	Multicoloured	16	16
J147		83	10p	Multicoloured	22	22
				Set of 4	50	50
				First Day Cover		75
				Presentation Pack	75	

Type 84

Type 85

Type 86

Type 87

CENTENARY OF THE UNIVERSAL POSTAL UNION

No.	Issued	Type		Colour	U/M	F/U
J148	7/6/74	84	2½p	Multicoloured	6	6
J149		85	3p	Multicoloured	8	8
J150		86	5½p	Multicoloured	17	17
J151		87	20p	Multicoloured	50	50
				Set of 4	75	75
				First Day Cover		90
				Presentation Pack	1.00	

INDEPENDENT POSTAL ADMINISTRATION (continued)
Decimal Issues 1974 – 75

All the following issues printed by Courvoisier in Photogravure on unwatermarked Granite paper, Perf. 11½ unless otherwise stated.

No.	Issued	Type	Colour	U/M	F/U

Type 88

Type 89

Type 94

Type 95

Type 90

Type 91

PAINTINGS 1974

No.	Issued	Type	Colour	U/M	F/U
J156	22/11/74	92	3½p Multicoloured	7	7
J157		93	5½p Multicoloured	12	12
J158		94	8p Multicoloured	18	18
J159		95	25p Multicoloured	50	50
			Set of 4	80	80
			First Day Cover		95
			Presentation Pack	1.00	

ANNIVERSARIES

Printers: De La Rue in Litho, Perf. 13 x 14

No.	Issued	Type	Colour	U/M	F/U
J152	31/7/74	88	3p Multicoloured	6	6
J153		89	3½p Multicoloured	7	7
J154		90	8p Multicoloured	25	25
J155		91	20p Multicoloured	40	40
			Set of 4	70	70
			First Day Cover		90
			Presentation Pack	1.00	

Type 96

Type 97

Type 92

Type 93

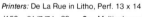

Type 98

Type 99

19TH CENTURY FARMING

No.	Issued	Type	Colour	U/M	F/U
J160	25/2/75	96	3p Multicoloured	6	6
J161		97	3½p Multicoloured	7	7
J162		98	8p Multicoloured	16	16
J163		99	10p Multicoloured	20	20
			Set of 4	50	50
			First Day Cover		80
			Presentation Pack	80	

INDEPENDENT POSTAL ADMINISTRATION (continued)
Decimal Issues 1975

All the following issues printed by Courvoisier in Photogravure on unwatermarked Granite paper, Perf. 11½ unless otherwise stated.

No.	Issued	Type	Colour	U/M	F/U

Type 100

Type 105

Type 106

ROYAL VISIT OF THE QUEEN MOTHER

No.	Issued	Type		Colour	U/M	F/U
J164	30/5/75	100	20p	Multicoloured	45	45
				First Day Cover		60
				Presentation Pack	55	

Type 107

Type 108

Type 101

Type 102

SEA BIRDS

No.	Issued	Type		Colour	U/M	F/U
J170	28/7/75	105	4p	Multicoloured	8	8
J171		106	5p	Multicoloured	10	10
J172		107	8p	Multicoloured	18	18
J173		108	25p	Multicoloured	50	50
				Set of 4	80	80
				First Day Cover		95
				Presentation Pack	1.00	

Type 103

Type 104

Type 109

Type 110

Type 111

Type 112

TOURISM

No.	Issued	Type		Colour	U/M	F/U
J165	6/6/75	101	5p	Multicoloured	10	10
J166		102	8p	Multicoloured	18	18
J167		103	10p	Multicoloured	20	20
J168		104	12p	Multicoloured	24	24
				Set of 4	65	65
				First Day Cover		80
				Presentation Pack	80	
J169				Miniature sheet	1.00	75
				(single of each value)		
				First Day Cover M/S		1.00

ANNIVERSARY OF THE ROYAL AIR FORCES ASSOCIATION

No.	Issued	Type		Colour	U/M	F/U
J174	30/10/75	109	4p	Multicoloured	7	7
J175		110	5p	Multicoloured	10	10
J176		111	10p	Multicoloured	18	18
J177		112	25p	Multicoloured	45	45
				Set of 4	75	75
				First Day Cover		90
				Presentation Pack	1.00	

INDEPENDENT POSTAL ADMINISTRATION (continued)
Decimal Issues 1976 – 77

 Type 113

 Type 114

 Type 115

 Type 116

 Type 117

Type 118

 Type 119

Type 120

 Type 121

Type 122

 Type 123

Type 124

 Type 125

Type 126

Type 127

  Type 128

 Type 129

 Type 130

Type 131

3RD DEFINITIVE ISSUES
Printers: Questa Colour ½p – 15p, in Litho, Perf. 14½
Courvoisier 20p – £2, in Photo, Perf. 12

No.	Issued	Type		Colour	U/M	F/U
J178	29/1/76	113	½p	Multicoloured	5	5
J179		114	1p	Multicoloured	5	5
J180		115	5p	Multicoloured	9	9
J181		116	6p	Multicoloured	10	10
J182		117	7p	Multicoloured	12	12
J183		118	8p	Multicoloured	13	13
J184		119	9p	Multicoloured	14	14
J185		120	10p	Multicoloured	15	15
J186		121	11p	Multicoloured	16	16
J187		122	12p	Multicoloured	18	18
J188		123	13p	Multicoloured	19	19
J189		124	14p	Multicoloured	21	21
J190		125	15p	Multicoloured	22	22
J191	20/8/76	126	20p	Multicoloured	30	30
J192		127	30p	Multicoloured	45	45
J193		128	40p	Multicoloured	60	60
J194		129	50p	Multicoloured	75	75
J195		130	£1	Multicoloured	1.50	1.50
J196	16/11/77	131	£2	Multicoloured	3.00	3.00
				Set of 19	7.50	7.50
				F.D.C. (low values)		2.20
				F.D.C. (high values)		3.50
				F.D.C. (£2)		3.25
				Presentation Packs (2)	2.00	
				(low values)		
				Presentation Packs (2)	6.75	
				(high values)		

Booklet Panes

J197				Pane 4 x 1p	8	8
J198				Pane 2 x 1p+2 labels	15	15
J199				Pane 4 x 5p	30	30
J200				Pane 4 x 7p	42	42
J200A				Pane 4 x 6p	40	
J200B				Pane 4 x 8p	55	
	5/4/76			First Day Cover		5.00
				(4 x 1p, 2 x 1p,		
				4 x 5p, 4 x 7p)		

INDEPENDENT POSTAL ADMINISTRATION (continued)
Decimal Issues 1976 – 77

All the following issues printed by Courvoisier in Photogravure on unwatermarked Granite paper, Perf. 11½ unless otherwise stated.

No.	Issued	Type	Colour	U/M	F/U

Type 132

Type 133

Type 134

Type 135

BICENTENARY OF AMERICAN INDEPENDENCE

No.	Issued	Type	Value	Colour	U/M	F/U
J201	29/5/76	132	5p	Multicoloured	10	10
J202		133	7p	Multicoloured	15	15
J203		134	11p	Multicoloured	20	20
J204		135	13p	Multicoloured	25	25
				Set of 4	65	65
				First Day Cover		95
				Presentation Pack	95	

Type 136

Type 137

Type 138  Type 139

BIRTH CENTENARY OF DR. LILIAN GRANDIN

No.	Issued	Type	Value	Colour	U/M	F/U
J205	25/11/76	136	5p	Multicoloured	10	10
J206		137	7p	Multicoloured	15	15
J207		138	11p	Multicoloured	20	20
J208		139	13p	Multicoloured	25	25
				Set of 4	60	60
				First Day Cover		75
				Presentation Pack	75	

Type 140

Type 141

Type 142

SILVER JUBILEE

No.	Issued	Type	Value	Colour	U/M	F/U
J209	7/2/77	140	5p	Multicoloured	10	10
J210		141	7p	Multicoloured	15	15
J211		142	25p	Multicoloured	40	40
				Set of 3	60	60
				First Day Cover		1.75
				Presentation Pack	90	

INDEPENDENT POSTAL ADMINISTRATION (continued)
Decimal Issues 1977

No.	Issued	Type	Colour	U/M	F/U

Type 143

Type 144

Type 145

Type 146

Type 147

Type 148

Type 149

Type 150

CENTENARY OF CURRENCY REFORM
Printers: Questa in Litho. *Perf:* 14

No.	Issued	Type		Colour	U/M	F/U
J212	25/3/77	143	**5p**	Multicoloured	9	9
J213		144	**7p**	Multicoloured	12	12
J214		145	**11p**	Multicoloured	16	16
J215		146	**13p**	Multicoloured	22	22
				Set of 4	55	55
				First Day Cover		80
				Presentation Pack	75	

CENTENARY OF ST. JOHN'S AMBULANCE ASSOCIATION
Printers: Questa in Litho. *Perf:* 14

No.	Issued	Type		Colour	U/M	F/U
J216	24/6/77	147	**5p**	Multicoloured	9	9
J217		148	**7p**	Multicoloured	12	12
J218		149	**11p**	Multicoloured	16	16
J219		150	**13p**	Multicoloured	22	22
				Set of 4	55	55
				First Day Cover		75
				Presentation Pack	70	

INDEPENDENT POSTAL ADMINISTRATION (continued)
Decimal Issues 1977 – 78

No.	Issued	Type	Colour	U/M	F/U

Type 151

Type 152

Type 153   *Type 154*

250TH ANNIVERSARY OF VICTORIA COLLEGE
Printers: Questa in Litho. *Perf:* 14½ x 14

No.	Issued	Type	Value	Colour	U/M	F/U
J220	29/9/77	151	**7p**	Multicoloured	12	12
J221		152	**10½p**	Multicoloured	16	16
J222		153	**11p**	Multicoloured	16	16
J223		154	**13p**	Multicoloured	22	22
				Set of 4	60	60
				First Day Cover		85
				Presentation Pack	75	

No.	Issued	Type	Colour	U/M	F/U

Type 155   *Type 156*

Type 157   *Type 158*

CENTENARY OF ROYAL JERSEY GOLF CLUB
Printers: Questa in Litho. *Perf:* 14

No.	Issued	Type	Value	Colour	U/M	F/U
J224	28/2/78	155	**6p**	Multicoloured	10	10
J225		156	**8p**	Multicoloured	11	11
J226		157	**11p**	Multicoloured	16	16
J227		158	**13p**	Multicoloured	22	22
				Set of 4	55	55
				First Day Cover		80
				Presentation Pack	75	

Type 159

Type 160   *Type 161*

EUROPA 1978
Printers: Courvoisier on granite paper in Photo. *Perf:* 11½

No.	Issued	Type	Value	Colour	U/M	F/U
J228	1/5/78	159	**6p**	Multicoloured	10	10
J229		160	**8p**	Multicoloured	11	11
J230		161	**10½p**	Multicoloured	16	16
				Set of 3	35	35
				First Day cover		55
				Presentation Pack	50	

INDEPENDENT POSTAL ADMINISTRATION (continued)
Decimal Issues 1978

All the following issues printed by Courvoisier in Photogravure on unwatermarked Granite paper, Perf. 11½ unless otherwise stated.

No.	Issued	Type	Colour	U/M	F/U

Type 162

Type 163

Type 169

Type 164

Type 165

Type 170   Type 171

Type 166

Type 172

JERSEY – LINKS WITH CANADA

No.	Issued	Type		Colour	U/M	F/U
J231	9/6/78	162	6p	Multicoloured	10	10
J232		163	8p	Multicoloured	11	11
J233		164	10½p	Multicoloured	16	16
J234		165	11p	Multicoloured	16	16
J235		166	13p	Multicoloured	22	22
				Set of 5	70	70
				First Day Cover		1.00
				Presentation Pack	90	

Type 173

Type 167

Type 168

25TH ANNIVERSARY OF THE CORONATION

No.	Issued	Type		Colour	U/M	F/U
J236	26/6/78	167	8p	Rose carmine/silver	11	11
J237		168	25p	New blue/silver	45	45
				Set of 2	50	50
				First Day Cover		75
				Presentation Pack	65	

BICENTENARY OF THE FIRST GOVERNMENT MAIL PACKET BETWEEN BRITAIN AND JERSEY
Printers: Harrison & Sons in Photo. *Perf:* 14

No.	Issued	Type		Colour	U/M	F/U
J238	18/10/78	169	6p	Pale yellow/black	10	10
J239		170	8p	Pale green/black	11	11
J240		171	10½p	Pale blue/black	16	16
J241		172	11p	Lilac/black	16	16
J242		173	13p	Pale pink/black	22	22
				Set of 5	70	70
				First Day Cover		1.00
				Presentation Pack	90	

INDEPENDENT POSTAL ADMINISTRATION (continued)
Decimal Issues 1979

All the following issues printed by Courvoisier in Photogravure on unwatermarked Granite paper, Perf. 11½ unless otherwise stated.

No.	Issued	Type		Colour	U/M	F/U

Type 174   Type 175

Type 176   Type 177

JERSEY Type 180

JERSEY Type 181

JERSEY Type 182

JERSEY Type 183

EUROPA (POSTS & TELEGRAPHS)
Printers: Questa in Litho. *Perf:* 14½

No.	Issued	Type		Colour	U/M	F/U
J243	1/3/79	174	**8p**	Multicoloured	13	13
J244		175	**8p**	Multicoloured	13	13
J243/4			**8p**	Pair se-tenant	30	30
J245		176	**10½p**	Multicoloured	18	18
J246		177	**10½p**	Multicoloured	18	18
J245/6			**10½p**	Pair se-tenant	40	40
				Set of 4	70	70
				First Day Cover		1.00
				Presentation Pack	90	

Type 178   Type 179

WORLD JERSEY CATTLE BUREAU CONFERENCE
Printers: Questa in Litho. *Perf:* 14½

No.	Issued	Type		Colour	U/M	F/U
J247	1/3/79	178	**6p**	Multicoloured	10	10
J248		179	**25p**	Multicoloured	45	45
				Set of 2	50	50
				First Day Cover		70
				Presentation Pack	70	

JERSEY Type 184

INTERNATIONAL AIR RALLY – 25TH ANNIVERSARY

No.	Issued	Type		Colour	U/M	F/U
J249	24/4/79	180	**6p**	Multicoloured	10	10
J250		181	**8p**	Multicoloured	11	11
J251		182	**10½p**	Multicoloured	16	16
J252		183	**11p**	Multicoloured	16	16
J253		184	**13p**	Multicoloured	22	22
				Set of 5	70	70
				First Day Cover		1.00
				Presentation Pack	90	

INDEPENDENT POSTAL ADMINISTRATION (continued)
Decimal Issues 1979

No.	Issued	Type	Colour	U/M	F/U		No.	Issued	Type	Colour	U/M	F/U

Type 185

Type 186

Type 3

Type 187   Type 188

Type 4

STERLING CURRENCY

No.	Issued	Type		Colour	U/M	F/U
JP1	1/10/69	1	1d	Violet blue	2.25	2.00
JP2			2d	Brown	1.75	1.75
JP3			3d	Rose red	2.25	1.75
JP4		2	1/–d	Green	7.25	4.50
JP5			2/6d	Olive grey	£22	£14
JP6			5/–d	Vermilion	£55	£35
				Set of 6	£80	£52
				First Day Cover		£200

150TH ANNIVERSARY OF BIRTH OF SIR JOHN MILLAIS RA AND THE YEAR OF THE CHILD

J254	13/8/79	185	8p	Multicoloured	11	11
J255		186	10½p	Multicoloured	16	16
J256		187	11p	Multicoloured	16	16
J257		188	25p	Multicoloured	45	45
				Set of 4	80	80
				First Day Cover		1.10
				Presentation Pack	1.00	

JERSEY WILDLIFE (THIRD SERIES)
To be issued on 15 November 1979

DECIMAL CURRENCY

No.	Issued	Type		Colour	U/M	F/U
JP7	15/2/71	3	½p	Black	5	5
JP8	15/2/71		1p	Blue	5	5
JP9	15/2/71		2p	Brown	5	5
JP10	15/2/71		3p	Pink	6	6
JP11	15/2/71		4p	Red	8	8
JP12	15/2/71		5p	Green	9	9
JP13	12/8/74		6p	Orange	10	10
JP14	12/8/74		7p	Yellow	12	12
JP15	1/5/75		8p	Light blue	14	14
JP16	15/2/71		10p	Grey green	15	15
JP17	1/5/75		11p	Light brown	17	17
JP18	15/2/71		14p	Purple	22	22
JP19	12/8/74		25p	Myrtle green	40	40
JP20	1/5/75		50p	Maroon	75	75
				Set of 14	2.25	2.25
	15/2/71			First Day Cover		£22
	12/8/74			First Day Cover		2.50
	1/5/75			First Day Cover		2.50
				Presentation Pks. (3)	2.50	

POSTAGE DUE STAMPS 1969 –

Printers: Bradbury, Wilkinson & Co. in Lithography   *Perf:* 13½

Type 1   Type 2

NEW DESIGNS – DIFFERENT PARISH ARMS AND VIEWS
Printers: Questa in Litho. *Perf:* 14

No.	Issued	Type		Colour	U/M	F/U
JP21	17/1/78	4	1p	Bright bl. grn./black	5	5
JP22			2p	Orange yellow/black	5	5
JP23			3p	Lake brown/black	6	6
JP24			4p	Orange ver./black	8	8
JP25			5p	Bright ult./black	10	10
JP26			10p	Brown olive/black	15	15
JP27			12p	New blue/black	17	17
JP28			14p	Bright orange/black	20	20
JP29			15p	Bright mag./black	20	20
JP30			20p	Apple green/black	30	30
JP31			50p	Bright yel. brn./black	75	75
JP32			£1	Bluish violet/black	1.50	1.50
				Set of 12	3.50	3.50
				First Day Cover		3.75
				Presentation Pack	3.75	

THE GUERNSEY BISECTS 1940 – 41

On the 27th December 1940, authority was given to bisect British stamps as the stores of 1d stamps were almost exhausted.

The locally printed 1d stamps were not issued until the 18th February 1941. Almost all examples of the bisects found are of a philatelic nature and genuine commercially used covers are of the utmost rarity and worth considerably more than the quoted prices.

GEORGE V			Price on cover
1912	**2d**	Orange (Wmk. Royal Cypher)	£150
1924	**2d**	Orange (Wmk. Block Cypher)	£150
1934	**2d**	Orange (Photo.)	£150
GEORGE VI			
1937	**1d**	Scarlet	£300
	2d	Orange	£12
Postal Centenary			
1940	**1d**	Scarlet	£300
	2d	Orange	£12
	2½d	Ultramarine	£400

OCCUPATIONAL ISSUES 1941 – 45
Arms of Guernsey

Printers: Guernsey Press Company   *Perf:* Rouletted

Type 1

No.	Issued	Type		Colour	U/M	M/M	F/U
UNWATERMARKED WHITE PAPER							
GY1	7/4/41	1	½d	**Light green**	2.25	1.45	1.00
GY2				Pale yellow green	2.25	1.45	1.25
GY3				Emerald green	2.75	1.80	1.50
GY4				Dull green	3.75	2.50	1.50
GY5				Bright green	£11	7.00	4.00
GY6				Bluish green	£18	£12	8.00
GY7				Olive green	£20	£13	8.00
GY8	18/2/41	1	**1d**	**Scarlet**	1.75	1.15	45
GY9				Pale vermilion	2.75	1.80	1.25
GY10				Carmine	6.00	4.00	2.00
GY11	12/4/44	1	**2½d**	**Ultramarine**	4.00	2.65	2.65
				Set of 3	7.50	5.00	3.75
				First Day Cover (½d)			3.00
				First Day Cover (1d)			5.00
				First Day Cover (2½)			6.00
BLUISH BANKNOTE PAPER WATERMARK: LOOPS							
GY12	11/3/42	1	½d	**Bright green**	8.00	5.25	£10
GY13	9/4/42	1	**1d**	**Scarlet**	6.00	4.00	9.00
				Set of 2	£13	9.00	£18
				First Day Cover (½d)			£60
				First Day Cover (1d)			£40

REGIONAL ISSUES 1958 – 69

Printers: Harrison & Sons in Photogravure
Paper: Ordinary except where stated
Watermark: Multiple Crowns
Phosphor bands where indicated

Type 2

Type 3

No.	Issued	Type		Colour	U/M	M/M	F/U
GUM ARABIC							
GY14	8/6/64	2	2½d	Carmine red	65	45	40
GY15	18/8/58	3	3d	Redd. violet	60	40	10
GY16	24/5/67	3	3d	Redd. violet (CB)	10	5	10
GY17	7/2/66	3	4d	Dull ultramarine	20	10	10
GY18	24/10/67	3	4d	Dull ultramarine (2B)	10	5	10
UNWATERMARKED CHALKY PAPER – PVA GUM							
GY19	16/4/68	3	4d	Dull ultramarine (2B)	15	10	10
GY20	4/9/68	3	4d	Sepia (CB)	15	10	10
GY21	26/2/69	3	4d	Vermilion (CB)	30	20	10
GY22	4/9/68	3	5d	Deep blue (2B)	25	15	10

INDEPENDENT POST OFFICE BOARD
Inaugurated on 1st October 1969

All the following issues were printed on unwatermarked paper.

Type 4

Type 5
Style A Latitude 40°30'N
Style B Latitude 49°30'N

Type 6

Type 7

Type 8

Type 9

Type 10

Type 11

Type 12

Type 13

Type 14
Style A Latitude 40°30'N
Style B Latitude 49°30'N

Type 15

Type 16

Type 17

Type 18

Type 19

INDEPENDENT POST OFFICE BOARD (continued)
1st Definitive Issues – Sterling 1969

All the following issues were printed on unwatermarked paper.

No.	Issued	Type		Colour	U/M	F/U
Printers: Harrison in Photo. (½d–2/6d) Perf. 14						
Delrieu in Photo. (5/–d–£1) Perf. 12½						
GY23	1/10/69	4	½d	Multicoloured	10	10
GY24			½d	ditto (Thin paper)	1.00	1.00
GY25	1/10/69	5	1d	Multicol. (Style A)	15	15
GY26			1d	ditto (Thin paper)	40	40
GY27	12/12/69	5	1d	Multicol. (Style B)	15	15
GY28			1d	ditto (Thick paper)	20	20
GY29	1/10/69	6	1½d	Multicoloured	15	15
GY30	1/10/69	7	2d	Multicoloured	15	15
GY31			2d	ditto (Thin paper)	25	25
GY32	1/10/69	8	3d	Multicoloured	15	15
GY33			3d	ditto (Thin paper)	20	20
GY34	1/10/69	9	4d	Multicoloured	15	15
GY35	1/10/69	10	5d	Multicoloured	20	20
GY36	1/10/69	11	6d	Multicoloured	30	30
GY37			6d	ditto (Thin paper)	50	50
GY38	1/10/69	12	9d	Multicoloured	70	70
GY39			9d	ditto (Thin paper)	70	70
GY40	1/10/69	13	1/–d	Multicoloured	50	50
GY41			1/–d	ditto (Thin paper)	1.00	1.00
GY42	1/10/69	14	1/6d	Multicol. (Style A)	40	40
GY43			1/6d	ditto (Thin paper)	1.25	1.25
GY44	4/2/70	14	1/6d	Multicol. (Style B)	£10	2.00
GY45	1/10/69	15	1/9d	Multicoloured	3.75	2.25
GY46			1/9d	ditto (Thin paper)	3.75	2.25
GY47	1/10/69	16	2/6d	Multicoloured	8.50	4.25
GY48			2/6d	ditto (Thin paper)	£11	7.00
GY49	1/10/69	17	5/–d	Multicoloured	7.75	4.25
GY50	1/10/69	18	10/–d	Multicol. (Perf. 12½)	£30	£22
GY51	17/3/70		10/–d	ditto (Perf. 13)	£150	£95
GY52	1/10/69	19	£1	Multicol. (Perf. 12½)	£10	8.50
GY53	17/3/70		£1	Multicol. (Perf. 13)	2.30	2.30
				Set of 18 (includes	£60	£35
				Perf. 13 £1)		
				First Day Cover		£40
				Presentation Packs (3)	£65	

Definitive Gutter Pairs

No.		Type		Colour	U/M	F/U
GY54		4	½d	Multicoloured	1.00	1.00
GY55		5	1d	ditto (Style A)	2.00	2.00
GY56		5	1d	ditto (Style B)	2.25	2.25
GY57		6	1½d	Multicoloured	1.25	1.25
GY58		7	2d	Multicoloured	2.50	2.50
GY59		8	3d	Multicoloured	2.50	2.50
GY60		9	4d	Multicoloured	9.00	9.00
GY61		10	5d	Multicoloured	9.00	9.00
GY62		11	6d	Multicoloured	£10	£10
GY63		12	9d	Multicoloured	£10	£10
GY64		13	1/–d	Multicoloured	£25	£25
GY65		14	1/6d	ditto (Style A)	£40	£40
GY66		14	1/6d	ditto (Style B)	£40	£40
GY67		15	1/9d	Multicoloured	£60	£60
GY68		16	2/6d	Multicoloured	£175	£175
GY68A			5/–d	Multicoloured	£600	£600
GY69		18	10/–d	ditto (Perf. 13)	£650	£650
GY69A			10/–d	ditto (Perf. 12½)	£650	£650
GY70		19	£1	ditto (Perf. 13)	£700	£700
GY70A			£1	ditto (Perf.12½)	£450	£450

Booklet Panes

No.	Issued	Type	Colour	U/M	F/U
GY71	12/12/69		Pane of 1 x 1d	25	25
GY72			Pane of 1 x 4d	30	30
GY73			Pane of 1 x 5d	40	40
			First Day Cover		1.25

Type 20

Type 21

Type 22

Type 23

BICENTENARY OF BIRTH OF GENERAL SIR ISAAC BROCK
Printers: Format Int. in Litho. Perf. 14 x 13½

No.	Issued	Type		Colour	U/M	F/U
GY74	1/12/69	20	4d	Multicoloured	20	10
GY75		21	5d	Multicoloured	30	15
GY76		22	1/9d	Multicoloured	2.75	1.60
GY77		23	2/6d	Multicoloured	4.50	2.60
				Set of 4	7.00	4.00
				Set of gutter pairs	£400	£400
				First Day Cover		4.25
				Presentation Pack	7.50	

INDEPENDENT POST OFFICE BOARD (continued)
Sterling Issues 1970

All the following issues were printed on unwatermarked paper.

No.	Issued	Type		Colour	U/M	F/U

Type 24

Type 25

Type 26

25TH ANNIVERSARY OF LIBERATION
Printers: Courvoisier in Photo. Granite paper
Perf. 11½

No.	Issued	Type		Colour	U/M	F/U
GY78	9/5/70	24	**4d**	Multicoloured	25	15
GY79		25	**5d**	Multicoloured	35	25
GY80		26	**1/6d**	Multicoloured	5.10	4.20
				Set of 3	5.20	4.25
				First Day Cover		4.50
				Presentation Pack	6.75	

Type 27

Type 28

Type 29

Type 30

AGRICULTURE AND HORTICULTURE
Printers: Courvoisier in Photo. Granite paper. Perf. 11½

No.	Issued	Type		Colour	U/M	F/U
GY81	12/8/70	27	**4d**	Multicoloured	20	10
GY82		28	**5d**	Multicoloured	25	15
GY83		29	**9d**	Multicoloured	5.50	3.00
GY84		30	**1/6d**	Multicoloured	9.00	5.00
				Set of 4	£14	7.50
				First Day Cover		8.00
				Presentation Pack	£18	

Type 31

Type 32

Type 33

Type 34

CHRISTMAS 1970
Printers: Courvoisier in Photo. Granite paper. Perf. 11½

No.	Issued	Type		Colour	U/M	F/U
GY85	11/11/70	31	**4d**	Multicoloured	15	10
GY86		32	**5d**	Multicoloured	25	15
GY87		33	**9d**	Multicoloured	2.50	1.75
GY88		34	**1/6d**	Multicoloured	4.75	2.75
				Set of 4	7.00	4.25
				First Day Cover		4.75
				Presentation Pack	8.50	

INDEPENDENT POST OFFICE BOARD (continued)
2nd Definitive Issues – Decimal 1971 – 73

All the following issues were printed on unwatermarked paper.

No.	Issued	Type		Colour	U/M	F/U

Printers: Harrison in Photo. (½p–10p) Perf. 14
Delrieu in Photo. (20p–50p) Perf. 13
Designs as 1st Definitive Issues but with decimal currency values. New design for 10p only.

No.	Issued	Type		Colour	U/M	F/U
GY89	15/2/71	4	½p	Multicoloured	5	5
GY90	,,	5	1p	Multicoloured	5	5
GY91	,,	6	1½p	Multicoloured	6	6
GY92	,,	9	2p	Multicoloured	8	8
GY93	,,	10	2½p	Multicoloured	10	10
GY94	,,	8	3p	Multicoloured	10	10
GY95	,,	15	3½p	Multicoloured	12	12
GY96	,,	7	4p	Multicoloured	15	15
GY97	,,	5	5p	Multicoloured	18	18
GY98	,,	11	6p	Multicoloured	20	20
GY99	,,	13	7½p	Multicoloured	30	30
GY100	,,	12	9p	Multicoloured	2.00	2.00
GY101	6/1/71	35	10p	ditto (chalky paper)	2.00	2.00
GY102	1/9/72	35	10p	ditto (ordinary paper)	1.50	1.50
GY103	6/1/71	17	20p	ditto (tur. blue sky)	1.75	1.75
GY104	25/1/73	17	20p	ditto (tur. green sky)	60	60
GY105	6/1/71	18	50p	Multicoloured	1.50	1.50
				Set of 15	6.50	6.50
				First Day Cover		8.50
				Presentation Pack	6.75	

Definitive Gutter Pairs

GY106		4	½p	Multicoloured	£30	£30
GY107		5	1p	Multicoloured	75	75
GY108		6	1½p	Multicoloured	75	75
GY109		9	2p	Multicoloured	2.25	2.25
GY110		10	2½p	Multicoloured	1.75	1.75
GY111		8	3p	Multicoloured	1.75	1.75
GY112		15	3½p	Multicoloured	2.25	2.25
GY113		7	4p	Multicoloured	6.00	6.00
GY114		5	5p	Multicoloured	2.50	2.50
GY115		11	6p	Multicoloured	2.50	2.50
GY116		13	7½p	Multicoloured	3.00	3.00
GY117		12	9p	Multicoloured	£11	£11
GY118		35	10p	ditto (chalky paper)	£50	£50
GY119		35	10p	ditto (ordinary paper)	£12	£12

Booklet Panes

GY120				Pane of 1 x ½p	10	10
				(glazed paper)		
GY121				Pane of 1 x ½p	10	10
				(non–glazed)		
GY122				Pane of 1· x 2p	15	15
				(glazed paper)		
GY123				Pane of 1 x 2p	15	15
				(non–glazed)		
GY124				Pane of 1 x 2½p	15	15
				(glazed paper)		
GY125				Pane of 1 x 2½p	15	15
				(non–glazed)		
				First Day Cover		1.25
				½p+2p+2½p		

Type 36

Type 37

Type 38

Type 39

THOMAS DE LA RUE COMMEMORATION

Printers: De La Rue in Recess. Perf. 14 x 13½

GY126	2/6/71	36	2p	Multicoloured	30	10
GY127		37	2½p	Multicoloured	40	15
GY128		38	4p	Multicoloured	9.00	2.50
GY129		39	7½p	Multicoloured	£13	3.50
				Set of 4	£20	5.50
				First Day Cover		5.75
				Presentation Pack	£22	

Type 35

INDEPENDENT POST OFFICE BOARD (continued)
Decimal Issues 1971 – 72

All the following issues were printed on unwatermarked paper.

No.	Issued	Type	Colour	U/M	F/U

Type 40

Type 41

Type 46

Type 42

Type 43

Type 47

ALL FURTHER ISSUES UNLESS STATED WERE PRINTED BY COURVOISIER IN PHOTOGRAVURE ON GRANITE PAPER. Perf. 11½

CHRISTMAS 1971

No.	Issued	Type		Colour	U/M	F/U
GY130	27/10/71	40	**2p**	Multicoloured	15	10
GY131		41	**2½p**	Multicoloured	20	15
GY132		42	**5p**	Multicoloured	3.50	2.25
GY134		43	**7½p**	Multicoloured	4.75	3.50
				Set of 4	7.75	5.50
				Set of gutter pairs	£75	£75
				First Day Cover		6.00
				Presentation Pack	9.50	

MAIL BOATS 1972

No.	Issued	Type		Colour	U/M	F/U
GY135	10/2/72	44	**2p**	Multicoloured	15	10
GY136		45	**2½p**	Multicoloured	20	15
GY137		46	**7½p**	Multicoloured	2.00	1.75
GY138		47	**9p**	Multicoloured	3.00	2.35
				Set of 4	4.75	4.00
				First Day Cover		4.75
				Presentation Pack	7.00	

Type 44

Type 45

Type 48

GUERNSEY CATTLE BREEDERS CONFERENCE

No.	Issued	Type		Colour	U/M	F/U
GY139	22/5/72	48	**5p**	Multicoloured	1.90	1.30
				Gutter Pair	£15	£15
				First Day Cover		1.75

INDEPENDENT POST OFFICE BOARD (continued)
Decimal Issues 1972

All the following issues were printed on unwatermarked paper.

No.	Issued	Type	Colour	U/M	F/U

Type 49

Type 50

Type 51

Type 52

Type 53

Type 54

Type 55

Type 56

WILD FLOWER SERIES

No.	Issued	Type		Colour	U/M	F/U
GY140	24/5/72	49	**2p**	Multicoloured	10	10
GY141		50	**2½p**	Multicoloured	12	12
GY142		51	**7½p**	Multicoloured	1.40	1.40
GY143		52	**9p**	Multicoloured	1.55	1.55
				Set of 4	2.85	2.85
				Set of gutter pairs	£20	£20
				First Day Cover		3.25
				Presentation Pack	4.75	

SILVER WEDDING AND CHRISTMAS 1972

No.	Issued	Type		Colour	U/M	F/U
GY144	20/11/72	53	**2p**	Multicoloured	10	10
GY145		54	**2½p**	Multicoloured	15	15
GY146		55	**7½p**	Multicoloured	80	80
GY147		56	**9p**	Multicoloured	1.05	1.05
				Set of 4	1.90	1.90
				Set of gutter pairs	£15	£15
				First Day Cover		2.00
				Presentation Pack	3.50	

INDEPENDENT POST OFFICE BOARD (continued)
Decimal Issues 1973

All the following issues were printed on unwatermarked paper.

No.	Issued	Type	Colour	U/M	F/U		No.	Issued	Type	Colour	U/M	F/U

Type 57

Type 61

Type 58

Type 62

Type 63

Type 59

Type 64

Type 65

Type 60

MAIL BOATS 1973

No.	Issued	Type		Colour	U/M	F/U
GY148	9/3/73	57	2½p	Multicoloured	10	8
GY149		58	3p	Multicoloured	15	10
GY150		59	7½p	Multicoloured	1.45	1.20
GY151		60	9p	Multicoloured	2.00	1.70
				Set of 4	3.35	2.85
				Set of gutter pairs	9.50	9.50
				First Day Cover		3.00
				Presentation Pack	4.25	

50TH ANNIVERSARY OF AIR SERVICE

No.	Issued	Type	Colour	U/M	F/U
GY152	4/7/73	61	2½p	Multicoloured	6	6
GY153		62	3p	Multicoloured	8	8
GY154		63	5p	Multicoloured	28	28
GY155		64	7½p	Multicoloured	55	55
GY156		65	9p	Multicoloured	85	85
			Set of 5	1.65	1.65
			Set of gutter pairs	5.75	5.75
			First Day Cover		1.80
			Presentation Pack	2.25	

INDEPENDENT POST OFFICE BOARD (continued)
Decimal Issues 1973 – 74

All the following issues were printed on unwatermarked paper.

No.	Issued	Type	Colour	U/M	F/U

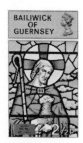

Type 66

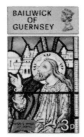

Type 67

Type 71

Type 68

Type 69

Type 72

Type 73

CHRISTMAS 1973

No.	Issued	Type		Colour	U/M	F/U
GY157	24/10/73	66	2½p	Multicoloured	10	5
GY158		67	3p	Multicoloured	15	10
GY159		68	7½p	Multicoloured	40	40
GY160		69	20p	Multicoloured	75	75
				Set of 4	1.25	1.15
				Set of gutter pairs	4.00	4.00
				First Day Cover		1.50
				Presentation Pack	1.50	

Type 74

Type 70

ROYAL WEDDING

No.	Issued	Type		Colour	U/M	F/U
GY161	14/11/73	70	25p	Multicoloured	70	70
				Gutter pair	3.00	3.00
				First Day Cover	95	
				Presentation Pack	1.40	

**150TH ANNIVERSARY OF ROYAL NATIONAL
LIFEBOAT INSTITUTION**

No.	Issued	Type		Colour	U/M	F/U
GY162	15/1/74	71	2½p	Multicoloured	6	6
GY163		72	3p	Multicoloured	7	7
GY164		73	8p	Multicoloured	28	28
GY165		74	10p	Multicoloured	30	30
				Set of 4	65	65
				Set of gutter pairs	3.00	3.00
				First Day Cover		1.20
				Presentation Pack	1.00	

INDEPENDENT POST OFFICE BOARD (continued)
Decimal Issues 1974 –

All the following issues were printed on unwatermarked paper.

Type 75

Type 76

Type 77

Type 78

Type 79

Type 80

Type 81

Type 82

Type 83

Type 84

Type 85

Type 86

Type 87

Type 88

Type 89

Type 90

Type 91

Type 92

INDEPENDENT POST OFFICE BOARD (continued)
Decimal Issues 1974 –

All the following issues were printed on unwatermarked paper.

No.	Issued	Type		Colour	U/M	F/U

3RD DEFINITIVE ISSUES
Printers: Delrieu in Photo. Perf. 13 x 13½ (20p–£1 only)

No.	Issued	Type		Colour	U/M	F/U
GY166	2/4/74	75	½p	Multicoloured	5	5
GY167	"	76	1p	Multicoloured	5	5
GY168	"	77	1½p	Multicoloured	5	5
GY169	"	78	2p	Multicoloured	5	5
GY170	"	79	2½p	Multicoloured	5	5
GY171	"	80	3p	Multicoloured	5	5
GY172	"	81	3½p	Multicoloured	6	6
GY173	"	82	4p	Multicoloured	7	7
GY174	29/5/76	83	5p	Multicoloured	9	9
GY175	2/4/74	84	5½p	Multicoloured	9	9
GY176	"	85	6p	Multicoloured	10	10
GY177	29/5/76	86	7p	Multicoloured	12	12
GY178	2/4/74	87	8p	Multicoloured	13	13
GY179	"	88	9p	Multicoloured	14	14
GY180	"	89	10p	Multicoloured	15	15
GY181	1/4/75	90	20p	Multicoloured	30	30
GY182	1/4/75	91	50p	Multicoloured	75	75
GY183	1/4/75	92	£1	Multicoloured	1.50	1.50
				Set of 18	3.40	3.40
				First Day Cover		
				(½p–10p)		1.75
				First Day Cover		
				(20p–£1)		3.00
				First Day Cover		
				(5p+7p)		45
				Presentation Pack		
				(½p–10p)	2.00	
				Presentation Pack		
				(20p–£1)	2.80	

Definitive Gutter Pairs

No.		Type		Colour	U/M	F/U
GY184		75	½p	Multicoloured	10	10
GY185		76	1p	Multicoloured	10	10
GY186		77	1½p	Multicoloured	12	12
GY187		78	2p	Multicoloured	16	16
GY188		79	2½p	Multicoloured	20	20
GY189		80	3p	Multicoloured	20	20
GY190		81	3½p	Multicoloured	24	24
GY191		82	4p	Multicoloured	24	24
GY192		83	5p	Multicoloured	28	28
GY193		84	5½p	Multicoloured	36	36
GY194		85	6p	Multicoloured	36	36
GY195		86	7p	Multicoloured	48	48
GY196		87	8p	Multicoloured	52	52
GY197		88	9p	Multicoloured	56	56
GY198		89	10p	Multicoloured	60	60

Booklet Panes & Strips

No.		Colour	U/M	F/U
GY199A		Strip of 8	15	15
		(5 x ½p, 3 x 2½p)		
		First Day Cover		75
GY199B		Strip of 5	15	15
		(1 x 5p, 2 x 2p, 1 x 1p)		
		First Day Cover		75
GY200		Pane of 16	50	50
		(4 x ½p, 6 x 2½p, 6 x 3p)		
		First Day Cover		1.50

Type 93

Type 94

Type 95

Type 96

CENTENARY OF UNIVERSAL POSTAL UNION

No.	Issued	Type		Colour	U/M	F/U
GY201	7/6/74	93	2½p	Multicoloured	10	10
GY202		94	3p	Multicoloured	12	12
GY203		95	8p	Multicoloured	30	30
GY204		96	10p	Multicoloured	40	40
				Set of 4	85	85
				Set of gutter pairs	3.00	3.00
				First Day Cover		1.00
				Presentation Pack	95	

INDEPENDENT POST OFFICE BOARD (continued)
Decimal Issues 1974 – 75

All the following issues were printed on unwatermarked paper.

No.	Issued	Type	Colour	U/M	F/U

Type 97

Type 98

Type 99

Type 100

RENOIR PAINTINGS
Printers: Delrieu in Photo. Perf. 13

No.	Issued	Type		Colour	U/M	F/U
GY205	21/9/74	97	**3p**	Multicoloured	6	6
GY206		98	**5½p**	Multicoloured	15	15
GY207		99	**8p**	Multicoloured	35	35
GY208		100	**10p**	Multicoloured	70	70
				Set of 4	1.15	1.15
				First Day Cover		1.30
				Presentation Pack	2.00	

Type 101

Type 102

No.	Issued	Type	Colour	U/M	F/U

Type 103

Type 104

GUERNSEY FERNS

GY209	7/1/75	101	**3½p**	Multicoloured	8	8
GY210		102	**4p**	Multicoloured	10	10
GY211		103	**8p**	Multicoloured	22	22
GY212		104	**10p**	Multicoloured	33	33
				Set of 4	65	65
				Set of gutter pairs	3.25	3.25
				First Day Cover		80
				Presentation Pack	85	

Type 105

Type 106

Type 107

Type 108

VICTOR HUGO

GY213	6/6/75	105	**3½p**	Multicoloured	7	7
GY214		106	**4p**	Multicoloured	8	8
GY215		107	**8p**	Multicoloured	20	20
GY216		108	**10p**	Multicoloured	25	25
				Set of 4	55	55
				Miniature sheet –	75	75
				(One of each value)		
				First Day Cover		75
				First Day Cover		1.00
				(Miniature sheet)		
				Presentation Pack	75	

INDEFENDENT POST OFFICE BOARD (continued)
Decimal Issues 1975 – 76

All the following issues were printed on unwatermarked paper.

No.	Issued	Type	Colour	U/M	F/U

Type 109

Type 110

Type 111

Type 112

Type 113

Type 114

Type 115

Type 116

CHRISTMAS 1975

Printers: Delrieu in Litho. Perf. 13

No.	Issued	Type		Colour	U/M	F/U
GY217	7/10/75	109	**4p**	Multicoloured	8	8
GY218		110	**6p**	Multicoloured	12	12
GY219		111	**10p**	Multicoloured	20	20
GY220		112	**12p**	Multicoloured	25	25
				Set of 4	60	60
				First Day Cover		75
				Presentation Pack	80	

LIGHTHOUSES

No.	Issued	Type		Colour	U/M	F/U
GY221	10/2/76	113	**4p**	Multicoloured	8	8
GY222		114	**6p**	Multicoloured	12	12
GY223		115	**11p**	Multicoloured	22	22
GY224		116	**13p**	Multicoloured	26	26
				Set of 4	60	60
				Set of gutter pairs	2.25	2.25
				First Day Cover		75
				Presentation Pack	75	

INDEPENDENT POST OFFICE BOARD (continued)
Decimal Issues 1976

All the following issues were printed on unwatermarked paper.

No.	Issued	Type	Colour	U/M	F/U

Type 117

Type 118

EUROPA 1976

No.	Issued	Type		Colour	U/M	F/U
GY225	29/5/76	117	**10p**	Multicoloured	80	80
GY226		118	**25p**	Multicoloured	1.40	1.40
				Set of 2	2.00	2.00
				First Day Cover		2.25
				2 Miniature sheets	£18	
				(each of 9 stamps)		
				Presentation Pack	2.25	
				(set of 2)		
				Presentation Pack	£20	
				(set of 2 + 2 Miniature sheets)		

Type 119

Type 120

Type 121

Type 122

No.	Issued	Type		Colour	U/M	F/U

VIEWS OF GUERNSEY

No.	Issued	Type		Colour	U/M	F/U
GY227	3/8/76	119	**5p**	Multicoloured	10	10
GY228		120	**7p**	Multicoloured	15	15
GY229		121	**11p**	Multicoloured	20	20
GY230		122	**13p**	Multicoloured	25	25
				Set of 4	65	65
				Set of gutter pairs	2.25	2.25
				First Day Cover		90
				Presentation Pack	90	

Type 123

Type 124

Type 125

Type 126

BUILDINGS

No.	Issued	Type		Colour	U/M	F/U
GY231	14/10/76	123	**5p**	Multicoloured	10	10
GY232		124	**7p**	Multicoloured	15	15
GY223		125	**11p**	Multicoloured	20	20
GY234		126	**13p**	Multicoloured	25	25
				Set of 4	65	65
				Set of gutter pairs	2.25	2.25
				First Day Cover		90
				Presentation Pack	90	

INDEPENDENT POST OFFICE BOARD (continued)
Decimal Issues 1977

All the following issues were printed on unwatermarked paper.

No.	Issued	Type	Colour	U/M	F/U

Type 127

Type 128

Type 131

SILVER JUBILEE

No.	Issued	Type		Colour	U/M	F/U
GY235	8/2/77	127	7p	Multicoloured	15	15
GY236		128	35p	Multicoloured	65	65
				Set of 2	75	75
				First Day Cover		1.50
				Presentation Pack	90	

Type 132

Type 133

Type 129

Type 134

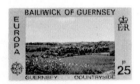
Type 130

EUROPA 1977

No.	Issued	Type		Colour	U/M	F/U
GY237	17/5/77	129	7p	Multicoloured	14	14
GY238		130	25p	Multicoloured	42	42
				Set of 2	50	50
				Set of gutter pairs	1.35	1.35
				First Day Cover		80
				Presentation Pack	80	

GUERNSEY PREHISTORIC MONUMENTS

No.	Issued	Type		Colour	U/M	F/U
GY239	2/8/77	131	5p	Multicoloured	10	10
GY240		132	7p	Multicoloured	15	15
GY241		133	11p	Multicoloured	20	20
GY242		134	13p	Multicoloured	25	25
				Set of 4	60	60
				Set of gutter pairs	1.60	1.60
				First Day Cover		90
				Presentation Pack	90	

INDEPENDENT POST OFFICE BOARD (continued)
Decimal Issues 1977 – 78

All the following issues were printed on unwatermarked paper.

No.	Issued	Type	Colour	U/M	F/U

Type 135

Type 136

Type 137

Type 138

Type 139

Type 140

Type 141

Type 142

CENTENARY OF ST. JOHN'S AMBULANCE ASSOCIATION

No.	Issued	Type		Colour	U/M	F/U
GY243	25/10/77	135	**5p**	Multicoloured	10	10
GY244		136	**7p**	Multicoloured	15	15
GY245		137	**11p**	Multicoloured	20	20
GY246		138	**13p**	Multicoloured	25	25
				Set of 4	60	60
				Set of gutter pairs	1.60	1.60
				First Day Cover		90
				Presentation Pack	90	

OLD GUERNSEY PRINTS
Printers: De La Rue in Litho. *Perf:* 14 x 13½

No.	Issued	Type		Colour	U/M	F/U
GY247	7/2/78	139	**5p**	Pale grn./grey/black	10	10
GY248		140	**7p**	Pale yel./grey/black	15	15
GY249		141	**11p**	Pale pink/grey/black	20	20
GY250		142	**13p**	Pale bl./grey/black	25	25
				Set of 4	60	60
				Set of gutter pairs	1.60	1.60
				First Day Covers		90
				Presentation Pack	90	

INDEPENDENT POST OFFICE BOARD (continued)
Decimal Issues 1978

All the following issues were printed on unwatermarked paper.

No.	Issued	Type	Colour	U/M	F/U

Type 143

Type 146

25TH ANNIVERSARY OF THE CORONATION

GY251	2/5/78 143	**20p**	Blue/grey	30	30
			Gutter pair	80	80
			First Day Cover		60
			Presentation Pack	45	

ROYAL VISIT

GY254	28/6/78 146	**7p**	Wedgwood grn./grey	15	15
			Gutter pair	35	35
			First Day Cover		40
			Presentation Pack	35	

Type 144

Type 145

Type 147

Type 148

Type 149

Type 150

EUROPA 1978

Printers: Questa in Litho. *Perf:* 14

GY252	2/5/78 144	**5p**	Multicoloured	10	10
GY253	145	**7p**	Multicoloured	15	15
			Set of 2	25	25
			First Day Cover		50
			Presentation Pack	45	

BIRDS OF THE BAILIWICK

GY255	29/8/78 147	**5p**	Multicoloured	9	9
GY256	148	**7p**	Multicoloured	13	13
GY257	149	**11p**	Multicoloured	18	18
GY258	150	**13p**	Multicoloured	20	20
			Set of 4	55	55
			Set of gutter pairs	1.50	1.50
			First Day Cover		90
			Presentation Pack	90	

INDEPENDENT POST OFFICE BOARD (continued)
Decimal Issues 1978 – 79

All the following issues were printed on unwatermarked paper.

No.	Issued	Type	Colour		U/M	F/U

Type 151 5p

Type 152

Type 153   Type 154

FESTIVE SEASON

No.	Issued	Type		Colour	U/M	F/U
GY259	31/10/78	151	5p	Multicoloured	9	9
GY260		152	7p	Multicoloured	13	13
GY261		153	11p	Multicoloured	18	18
GY262		154	13p	Multicoloured	20	20
				Set of 4	55	55
				Set of gutter pairs	1.40	1.40
				First Day Cover		80
				Presentation Pack	80	

Type 155

Type 156

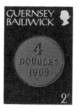

Type 157

Type 158

Type 159

Type 160

Type 161

Type 162

Type 163

Type 164

Type 165

Type 166

Type 167

Type 168

INDEPENDENT POST OFFICE BOARD (continued)
Decimal Issues 1979

All the following issues were printed on unwatermarked paper.

No.	Issued	Type	Colour	U/M	F/U

Type 169

Type 170

4TH DEFINITIVE ISSUES – (COINS)

No.	Issued	Type	Value	Colour	U/M	F/U
GY263	13/2/79	155	½p	New blue/bronze	5	5
GY264		156	1p	Dl.yel.green/bronze	5	5
GY265		157	2p	Bluish violet/bronze	5	5
GY266		158	4p	Light blue/bronze	6	6
GY267		159	5p	Yellow brown/silver	7	7
GY268		160	6p	Red/silver	10	10
GY269		161	7p	Dull green/silver	13	13
GY270		162	8p	Light brown/silver	14	14
GY271		163	9p	Slate blue/bronze	15	15
GY272		164	10p	Yellow green/bronze	16	16
GY273		165	11p	Reddish lilac/bronze	17	17
GY274		166	12p	Dp.tur.green/bronze	18	18
GY275		167	13p	Claret/bronze	19	19
GY276		168	14p	Dull blue/silver	20	20
GY277		169	15p	Olive sepia/silver	22	22
GY278		170	20p	Brown/silver	30	30
				Set of 16	2.00	2.00
				First Day Covers (2)		2.75
				Presentation Packs (2)	2.75	

DEFINITIVE GUTTER PAIRS

No.	Issued	Type	Value	Colour	U/M	F/U
GY283	13/2/79	155	½p	New blue/bronze	10	10
GY284		156	1p	Dl.yel.green/bronze	10	10
GY285		157	2p	Bluish violet/bronze	10	10
GY286		158	4p	Light blue/bronze	12	12
GY287		159	5p	Yellow brown/silver	14	14
GY288		160	6p	Red/silver	20	20
GY289		161	7p	Dull green/silver	26	26
GY290		162	8p	Light brown/silver	28	28
GY291		163	9p	Slate blue/bronze	30	30
GY292		164	10p	Yellow green/bronze	32	32
GY293		165	11p	Reddish lilac/bronze	34	34
GY294		166	12p	Dp.tur.green/bronze	36	36
GY295		167	13p	Claret/bronze	38	38
GY296		168	14p	Dull blue/silver	40	40
GY297		169	15p	Olive sepia/silver	44	44
GY298		170	20p	Brown/silver	60	60

MULTI-VALUE STRIPS

No.	Issued	Colour	U/M	F/U
GY303	13/2/79	Strip of 4 (6p+2p+1p+1p)	15	15
GY304		Strip of 5 (6p+8p+6p+8p+2p)	45	45

No.	Issued	Type	Colour	U/M	F/U

Type 175

Type 176

EUROPA 1979

No.	Issued	Type	Value	Colour	U/M	F/U
GY305	8/5/79	175	6p	Multicoloured	10	10
GY306		176	8p	Multicoloured	15	15
				Set of 2	25	25
				First Day Cover		40
				Presentation Pack	40	

Type 177

Type 178

Type 179

Type 180

PUBLIC TRANSPORT 1879–1979

No.	Issued	Type	Value	Colour	U/M	F/U
GY307	7/8/79	177	6p	Multicoloured	9	9
GY308		178	8p	Multicoloured	13	13
GY309		179	11p	Multicoloured	18	18
GY310		180	13p	Multicoloured	20	20
				Set of 4	55	55
				Set of gutter pairs	1.40	1.40
				First Day Cover		80
				Presentation Pack	80	

10TH ANNIVERSARY OF POSTAL INDEPENDENCE
To be issued 1/10/79

POSTAGE DUE ISSUES 1971 –

Printers: Delrieu in Photogravure   *Perf:* 12½ x 12   *No Watermark*

No.	Issued	Type		Colour	U/M	F/U
STERLING CURRENCY						
GYP1	1/10/71	1	**1d**	Reddish purple	1.00	80
GYP2			**2d**	Yellow green	1.25	1.10
GYP3			**3d**	Vermilion	2.00	1.65
GYP4			**4d**	Bright blue	3.00	2.20
GYP5			**5d**	Ochre	5.00	3.30
GYP6			**6d**	Turquoise blue	7.00	4.40
GYP7			**1/–d**	Chestnut	£25	£15
				Set of 7	£40	£25
				Presentation Pack	£50	
DECIMAL CURRENCY						
GYP8	15/2/71	2	**½p**	Reddish purple	5	5
GYP9	15/2/71		**1p**	Yellow green	5	5
GYP10	15/2/71		**2p**	Vermilion	5	5
GYP11	15/2/71		**3p**	Bright blue	6	6
GYP12	15/2/71		**4p**	Ochre	8	8
GYP13	15/2/71		**5p**	Turquoise blue	9	9
GYP14	10/2/76		**6p**	Purple	10	10
GYP15	7/10/75		**8p**	Orange	13	13
GYP16	15/2/71		**10p**	Chestnut	15	15
GYP17	10/2/76		**15p**	Grey	22	22
				Set of 10	85	85
	7/10/75			First Day Cover (8p)		60
	10/2/76			First Day Cover (6p+15p)		60
				Presentation Pack	1.00	
PERF: 13½ x 13						
GYP18	2/8/77	3	**½p**	Chestnut	5	5
GYP19			**1p**	Magenta	5	5
GYP20			**2p**	Orange	5	5
GYP21			**3p**	Scarlet	6	6
GYP22			**4p**	Turquoise blue	7	7
GYP23			**5p**	Yellow olive	9	9
GYP24			**6p**	Dp. turquoise green	10	10
GYP25			**8p**	Brown ochre	14	14
GYP26			**10p**	Blue	15	15
GYP27			**15p**	Violet	22	22
				Set of 10	85	85
				First Day Cover		2.50
				Presentation Pack	1.00	

Type 1

Type 2

Type 3

REGIONAL ISSUES 1958 – 73

Printers: Harrison & Sons in Photogravure   *Perf:* 15 x 14   *No Watermark* Unless marked MC = Multiple Crowns

No.	Issued	Type		Colour	Phosphor	Watermark	U/M	M/M	F/U
STERLING ISSUES									
Gum Arabic									
MX1	8/6/64	1	**2½d**	Carmine red		MC	1.00	65	65
MX2	18/8/58	2	**3d**	Reddish violet		MC	15	10	10
MX3	17/5/63	2	**3d**	Reddish violet (chalky paper)		MC	£22	£15	8.50
MX4	27/6/68	2	**3d**	Reddish violet	CB	MC	10	5	10
MX5	7/2/66	2	**4d**	Dull ultramarine		MC	1.00	65	15
MX6	5/7/67	2	**4d**	Dull ultramarine	2B	MC	20	15	15
PVA Gum – Unwatermarked Chalky Paper									
MX7	24/6/68	2	**4d**	Dull ultramarine	2B		10	5	10
MX8	4/9/68	2	**4d**	Sepia	CB		25	15	15
MX9	26/2/69	2	**4d**	Vermilion	CB		75	50	25
MX10	4/9/68	2	**5d**	Deep blue	2B		1.00	65	15
DECIMAL ISSUES									
OCP/PVA									
MX11	7/7/71	3	**2½p**	Magenta	CB		25	15	10
MX12	7/7/71	3	**3p**	Dull ultramarine	2B		20	15	10
MX13	7/7/71	3	**5p**	Bright violet	2B		35	25	30
MX14	7/7/71	3	**7½p**	Chestnut	2B		50	35	50
FCP/PVA									
MX15	–/3/73	3	**2½p**	Magenta	CB		60	40	15
MX16	–/7/73	3	**3p**	Dull ultramarine	2B		3.00	2.00	1.00
Presentation Pack									
	7/7/71			4 stamps Nos. MX11 – 14			2.25		

Type 1

Type 2

Type 3

Multiple Crowns

INDEGENDENT POSTAL AUTHORITY ISSUES
Inaugurated on 5th July, 1973

All the following issues were printed on unwatermarked paper.

Type 4

Type 5

Type 6

Type 7

Type 8

Type 9

Type 10

Type 11

Type 12

Type 13

Type 14

Type 15

Type 16

Type 17

Type 18

Type 20

Type 19

Type 21

INDEPENDENT POSTAL AUTHORITY (continued)
Issues 1973 – 75

All the following issues were printed on unwatermarked paper.

No.	Issued	Type	Colour		U/M	F/U

DEFINITIVE ISSUES
Printers: Courvoisier on Granite paper Perf: 11½

No.	Issued	Type	Colour		U/M	F/U
MX17	5/7/73	4	**½p**	Multicoloured	5	5
MX18	5/7/73	5	**1p**	Multicoloured	5	5
MX19	5/7/73	6	**1½p**	Multicoloured	5	5
MX20	5/7/73	7	**2p**	Multicoloured	5	5
MX21	5/7/73	8	**2½p**	Multicoloured	5	5
MX22	5/7/73	9	**3p**	Multicoloured	5	5
MX23	5/7/73	10	**3½p**	Multicoloured	6	6
MX24	5/7/73	11	**4p**	Multicoloured	7	7
MX25	8/1/75	8	**4½p**	Multicoloured	8	8
MX26	5/7/73	12	**5p**	Multicoloured	9	9
MX27	28/5/75	9	**5½p**	Multicoloured	9	9
MX28	5/7/73	13	**6p**	Multicoloured	10	10
MX29	28/5/75	7	**7p**	Multicoloured	12	12
MX30	5/7/73	14	**7½p**	Multicoloured	13	13
MX31	8/1/75	14	**8p**	Multicoloured	13	13
MX32	5/7/73	15	**9p**	Multicoloured	14	14
MX33	5/7/73	16	**10p**	Multicoloured	15	15
MX34	29/10/75	17	**11p**	Multicoloured	17	17
MX35	29/10/75	18	**13p**	Multicoloured	20	20
MX36	5/7/73	19	**20p**	Multicoloured	30	30
MX37	5/7/73	20	**50p**	Multicoloured	75	75
MX38	5/7/73	21	**£1**	Multicoloured	1.50	1.50
				Set of 22	4.00	4.00
	5/7/73			First Day Cover		6.50
	8/1/75			First Day Cover		45
	28/5/75			First Day Cover		45
	29/10/75			First Day Cover		45
				Presentation Packs (6)	5.00	

Booklet panes & Strips

No.		Colour	U/M	F/U
MX39		Pane of 1 x ½p	10	10
MX40		Pane of 2 x ½p	1.75	1.75
MX41		Pane of 4 x ½p	50	50
MX42		Strip of 4 x ½p	10	10
MX43		Pane of 2 x 1½p	10	10
MX44		Pane of 2 x 2p	2.00	2.00
MX45		Pane of 3 x 2p	20	20
MX46		Pane of 2 x 2½p	40	40
MX47		Pane of 2 x 3p	65	65
MX48		Pane of 4 x 3p	60	60
MX49		Pane of 4 x 3½p	1.25	1.25
MX50		Strip of 4 x 3½p	35	35
MX51		Pane of 3 x 5p	35	35
MX52		Pane of 3 x 5½p	35	35

Type 22

INAUGURATION OF POST OFFICE
Printers: Harrison in Photo. Perf:14

No.	Issued	Type	Colour		U/M	F/U
MX53	5/7/73	22	**15p**	Multi. (brown gum)	1.25	1.25
MX54		22	**15p**	Multi. (white gum)	1.50	1.50
				First Day Cover		1.75
				Presentation Pack (brown gum)	2.00	
				Presentation Pack (white gum)	2.25	

Type 23

Type 24

Type 25

Type 26

STEAM RAILWAY CENTENARY
Printers: Harrison in Photo. Perf:15 x 14

No.	Issued	Type	Colour	U/M	F/U
MX55	4/8/73	23	**2½p** Multicoloured	10	10
MX56		24	**3p** Multicoloured	15	10
MX57		25	**7½p** Multicoloured	1.75	75
MX58		26	**9p** Multicoloured	2.25	1.25
			Set of 4	3.75	2.00
			First Day Cover		2.25
			Presentation Pack	5.00	

INDEPENDENT POSTAL AUTHORITY (continued)
Issues 1973 – 74

All the following issues were printed on unwatermarked paper.

No.	Issued	Type		Colour	U/M	F/U

Type 27 · Type 28

GOLDEN JUBILEE OF MANX GRAND PRIX
Printers: J. Waddington in Litho. Perf:14

No.	Issued	Type		Colour	U/M	F/U
MX59	4/9/73	27	**3p**	Multicoloured	28	22
MX60		28	**3½p**	Multicoloured	33	33
				Set of 2	55	50
				Set of gutter pairs	6.00	6.00
				First Day Cover		65
				Presentation Pack	1.00	

Type 29

ROYAL WEDDING
Printers: De La Rue, Recess & Litho. Perf: 13½

No.	Issued	Type		Colour	U/M	F/U
MX61	14/11/73	29	**25p**	Blue/grey	1.25	1.25
				Gutter pair	£18	£18
				First Day Cover		1.40
				Presentation Pack	1.75	

Type 30 · Type 31

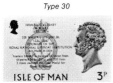

Type 32 · Type 33

150TH ANNIVERSARY OF ROYAL NATIONAL LIFEBOAT INSTITUTION
Printers: Courvoisier on Granite paper, Photo. Perf: 11½

No.	Issued	Type		Colour	U/M	F/U
MX62	4/3/74	30	**3p**	Multicoloured	10	10
MX63		31	**3½p**	Multicoloured	10	10
MX64		32	**8p**	Multicoloured	35	35
MX65		33	**10p**	Multicoloured	45	45
				Set of 4	90	90
				First Day Cover		1.20
				Presentation Pack	1.50	

Type 34

Type 35

Type 36

Type 37

ISLE OF MAN TOURIST TROPHY RACES
Printers: De La Rue in Litho. Perf: 13 x 13½

No.	Issued	Type		Colour	U/M	F/U
MX66	29/5/74	34	**3p**	Multicoloured	10	10
MX67		35	**3½p**	Multicoloured	10	10
MX68		36	**8p**	Multicoloured	30	30
MX69		37	**10p**	Multicoloured	30	30
				Set of 4	70	70
				Set of gutter pairs	6.00	6.00
				First Day Cover		90
				Presentation Pack	1.20	

INDEPENDENT POSTAL AUTHORITY (continued)
Issues 1974 – 75

All the following issues were printed on unwatermarked paper

No.	Issued	Type	Colour	U/M	F/U

Type 38

Type 39

Type 40

Type 41

HISTORICAL ISSUE 1974
Printers: Questa (3½p & 10p)
J. Waddington (4½p & 8p) in Litho. Perf: 14

No.	Issued	Type		Colour	U/M	F/U
MX70	18/9/74	38	3½p	Multicoloured	8	8
MX71		39	4½p	Multicoloured	9	9
MX72		40	8p	Multicoloured	25	25
MX73		41	10p	Multicoloured	30	30
				Set of 4	65	65
				Set of gutter pairs	4.00	4.00
				First Day Cover		80
				Presentation Pack	90	

Type 42

Type 43

Type 44

Type 45

BIRTH CENTENARY OF SIR WINSTON S. CHURCHILL
Printers: Courvoisier on Granite paper, Photo. Perf: 11½

No.	Issued	Type		Colour	U/M	F/U
MX74	22/11/74	42	3½p	Multicoloured	6	6
MX75		43	4½p	Multicoloured	9	9
MX76		44	8p	Multicoloured	25	25
MX77		45	20p	Multicoloured	30	30
				Set of 4	85	85
				Miniature sheet – single of each value	1.00	1.00
				First Day Cover – 4 stamps		1.00
				First Day Cover – miniature sheet		1.25
				Presentation Pack – 4 stamps	1.00	
				Presentation Pack – miniature sheet	1.20	

Type 46

Type 47

Type 48

Type 49

MANX PIONEERS TO CLEVELAND, OHIO
Printers: Courvoisier on Granite paper, Photo. Perf: 11½

No.	Issued	Type		Colour	U/M	F/U
MX78	14/3/75	46	4½p	Multicoloured	8	8
MX79		47	5½p	Multicoloured	15	15
MX80		48	8p	Multicoloured	25	25
MX81		49	10p	Multicoloured	35	35
				Set of 4	75	75
				First Day Cover		1.00
				Presentation Pack	1.00	

INDEPENDENT POSTAL AUTHORITY (continued)
Issues 1975

All the following issues were printed on unwatermarked paper.

No.	Issued	Type	Colour	U/M	F/U

Type 50

Type 51

Type 52

Type 53

TOURIST TROPHY RACES 1975
Printers: J. Waddington in Litho. Perf: 13½

No.	Issued	Type	Colour	U/M	F/U
MX82	28/5/75	50	**5½p** Multicoloured	11	11
MX83		51	**7p** Multicoloured	15	15
MX84		52	**10p** Multicoloured	20	20
MX85		53	**12p** Multicoloured	24	24
			Set of 4	65	65
			Set of gutter pairs	3.00	3.00
			First Day Cover		85
			Presentation Pack	90	

No.	Issued	Type	Colour	U/M	F/U

Type 54

Type 55

Type 56

Type 57

SIR GEORGE GOLDIE, FOUNDER OF NIGERIA
Printers: Courvoisier on Granite paper, Photo. Perf:11½

No.	Issued	Type	Colour	U/M	F/U
MX86	9/9/75	54	**5½p** Multicoloured	11	11
MX87		55	**7p** Multicoloured	15	15
MX88		56	**10p** Multicoloured	20	20
MX89		57	**12p** Multicoloured	25	25
			Set of 4	65	65
			First Day Cover		80
			Presentation Pack	80	

Type 58

Type 59

Type 60

Type 61

BICENTENARY OF MANX BIBLE
Printers: Questa in Litho. Perf: 14

No.	Issued	Type	Colour	U/M	F/U
MX90	29/10/75	58	**5½p** Multicoloured	10	10
MX91		59	**7p** Multicoloured	12	12
MX92		60	**11p** Multicoloured	22	22
MX93		61	**13p** Multicoloured	28	28
			Set of 4	65	65
			Set of gutter pairs	2.75	2.75
			First Day Cover		80
			Presentation Pack	80	

INDEPENDENT POSTAL AUTHORITY (continued)
Issues 1976

All the following issues were printed on unwatermarked paper.

No.	Issued	Type	Colour	U/M	F/U

Type 62

Type 63

Type 66

Type 64

Type 65

Type 67

Type 68

Type 69

BICENTENARY OF AMERICAN REVOLUTION
Printers: J. Waddington in Litho. Perf:13½

No.	Issued	Type		Colour	U/M	F/U
MX94	12/3/76	62	5½p	Multicoloured	10	10
MX95		63	7p	Multicoloured	12	12
MX96		64	13p	Multicoloured	24	24
MX97		65	20p	Multicoloured	38	38
				Set of 4	75	75
				Set of gutter pairs	3.25	3.25
				Miniature sheet–Perf. 14	2.50	1.50
				single of each value		
				First Day Cover –		1.00
				4 stamps		
				First Day Cover –		1.75
				Miniature sheet		
				Presentation pack –	1.00	
				4 stamps		
				Presentation Pack –	3.00	
				miniature sheet		

DOUGLAS HORSE TRAMS CENTENARY
Printers: Courvoisier on Granite paper, Photo. Perf:11½

No.	Issued	Type		Colour	U/M	F/U
MX98	26/5/76	66	5½p	Multicoloured	11	11
MX99		67	7p	Multicoloured	15	15
MX100		68	11p	Multicoloured	20	20
MX101		69	13p	Multicoloured	25	25
				Set of 4	65	65
				First Day Cover		80
				Presentation Pack	75	

INDEPENDENT POSTAL AUTHORITY (continued)
Issues 1976 – 77

All the following issues were printed on unwatermarked paper.

No.	Issued	Type	Colour	U/M	F/U

Type 70

Type 71

Type 72

Type 73

Type 74

Type 75

EUROPA '76 CERAMIC ART
Printers: Courvoisier on Granite paper, Photo. Perf: 11½

No.	Issued	Type		Colour	U/M	F/U
MX102	28/7/76	70	**5p**	Multicoloured	25	25
MX103		71	**5p**	Multicoloured	25	25
MX104		72	**5p**	Multicoloured	25	25
MX102/4				Se-tenant strip 3 x 5p	2.00	2.00
				Miniature sheet 9 x 5p	7.50	–
MX105		73	**10p**	Multicoloured	20	20
MX106		74	**10p**	Multicoloured	20	20
MX107		75	**10p**	Multicoloured	20	20
MX105/7				Se-tenant strip 3 x 10p	1.25	1.25
				Miniature sheet 9 x 10p	4.00	–
				Set of 6 in 2 strips	3.25	3.25
				First Day Cover		5.50
				Presentation Pack	5.50	

Type 76

Type 77

Type 78

Type 79

CENTENARY OF MOTHERS' UNION
Printers: Questa in Litho. Perf: 14½

No.	Issued	Type		Colour	U/M	F/U
MX108	14/10/76	76	**6p**	Multicoloured	12	12
MX109		77	**7p**	Multicoloured	15	15
MX110		78	**11p**	Multicoloured	22	22
MX111		79	**13p**	Multicoloured	25	25
				Set of 4	65	65
				First Day Cover		80
				Presentation Pack	75	

Type 80

Type 81

Type 82

SILVER JUBILEE
Printers: De La Rue, Recess & Litho. Perf: 13 x 14

No.	Issued	Type		Colour	U/M	F/U
MX112	1/3/77	80	**6p**	Multicoloured	10	10
MX113		81	**7p**	Multicoloured	11	11
MX114		82	**25p**	Multicoloured	45	45
				Set of 3	60	60
				Set of gutter pairs	3.50	3.50
				First Day Cover		1.50
				Presentation Pack	75	

INDEPENDENT POSTAL AUTHORITY (continued)
Issues 1977

All the following issues were printed on unwatermarked paper.

No.	Issued	Type	Colour	U/M	F/U

Type 83

Type 84

EUROPA '77 LANDSCAPES
Printers: Questa in Litho. Perf: 14½

No.	Issued	Type		Colour	U/M	F/U
MX115	25/5/77	83	6p	Multicoloured	9	9
MX116		84	10p	Multicoloured	18	18
				Set of 2	23	23
				Set of gutter pairs	80	80
				First Day Cover		50
				Presentation Pack	50	

Type 85

Type 86

Type 87

No.	Issued	Type	Colour	U/M	F/U

Type 88

LINKED ANNIVERSARIES
Printers: J. Waddington in Litho. Perf: 13½

MX117	25/5/77	85	6p	Multicoloured	12	12
MX118		86	7p	Multicoloured	15	15
MX119		87	11p	Multicoloured	22	22
MX120		88	13p	Multicoloured	25	25
				Set of 4	65	65
				Set of gutter pairs	1.65	1.65
				First Day Cover		80
				Presentation Pack	75	

Type 89   *Type 90*

Type 91   *Type 92*

BICENTENARY OF JOHN WESLEY'S VISIT
Printers: Courvoisier on Granite paper, Photo. Perf: 11½

MX121	19/10/77	89	6p	Multicoloured	12	12
MX122		90	7p	Multicoloured	15	15
MX123		91	11p	Multicoloured	22	22
MX124		92	13p	Multicoloured	25	25
				Set of 4	65	65
				First Day Cover		80
				Presentation Pack	75	

INDEPENDENT POSTAL AUTHORITY (continued)
Issues 1978

All the following issues were printed on unwatermarked paper.

No.	Issued	Type	Colour	U/M	F/U

Type 93

Type 94

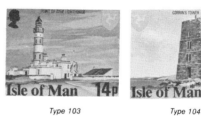
Type 101   *Type 102*

Type 95

Type 96

Type 103   *Type 104*

Type 105

Type 97   *Type 98*

Type 99   *Type 100*

NEW DEFINITIVE ISSUES – LANDMARKS
Printers: Questa in Litho. *Perf:* 14

No.	Issued	Type	Value	Colour	U/M	F/U
MX125	28/2/78	93	½p	Multicoloured	5	5
MX126		94	1p	Multicoloured	5	5
MX127		95	6p	Multicoloured	10	10
MX128		96	7p	Multicoloured	12	12
MX129		97	8p	Multicoloured	13	13
MX130		98	9p	Multicoloured	14	14
MX131		99	10p	Multicoloured	15	15
MX132		100	11p	Multicoloured	17	17
MX133		101	12p	Multicoloured	18	18
MX134		102	13p	Multicoloured	20	20
MX135		103	14p	Multicoloured	20	20
MX136		104	15p	Multicoloured	25	25
MX137		105	16p	Multicoloured	25	25

INDEPENDENT POSTAL AUTHORITY (continued)
Issues 1978

All the following issues were printed on unwatermarked paper.

No.	Issued	Type	Colour	U/M	F/U

Type 106 20ᴾ **ISLE OF MAN** *Type 107* 25ᴾ **ISLE OF MAN**

Type 108 50ᴾ **ISLE OF MAN** *Type 109* £1 **ISLE OF MAN**

NEW DEFINITIVE ISSUES – LANDMARKS (continued)

Printers: Courvoisier on granite paper, Photo. *Perf:* 11½

No.	Issued	Type		Colour	U/M	F/U
MX138	18/10/78	106	**20p**	Multicoloured	30	30
MX139		107	**25p**	Multicoloured	45	45
MX140		108	**50p**	Multicoloured	75	75
MX141		109	**£1**	Multicoloured	1.50	1.50
				Set of 17	4.50	4.50
				First Day Covers (4)		6.00
				Presentation Packs (4)	5.25	

Type 110

Type 111

Type 112

Type 113

ROYAL AIR FORCE – DIAMOND JUBILEE

Printers: J. Waddington in Litho. *Perf:* 13½ x 14

No.	Issued	Type		Colour	U/M	F/U
MX153	28/2/78	110	**6p**	Multicoloured	10	10
MX154		111	**7p**	Multicoloured	13	13
MX155		112	**11p**	Multicoloured	18	18
MX156		113	**13p**	Multicoloured	20	20
				Set of 4	55	55
				Set of gutter pairs	1.25	1.25
				First Day Cover		85
				Presentation Pack	75	

Type 114   *Type 115*

Type 116   *Type 117*

Type 118   *Type 119*

EUROPA '78 – MANX CROSSES

Printers: Courvoisier on granite paper, Photo. *Perf:* 11½

No.	Issued	Type		Colour	U/M	F/U
MX157	24/5/78	114	**6p**	Multicoloured	10	10
MX158		115	**6p**	Multicoloured	10	10
MX159		116	**6p**	Multicoloured	10	10
MX157/9				Se-tenant strip 3 x 6p	35	35
				Miniature sheet 9 x 6p	1.10	–
MX160		117	**11p**	Multicoloured	18	18
MX161		118	**11p**	Multicoloured	18	18
MX162		119	**11p**	Multicoloured	18	18
MX160/2				Se-tenant strip 3 x 11p	60	60
				Miniature sheet 9 x 11p	2.00	–
				Set of 6 in 2 strips	90	90
				First Day Cover		1.20
				Presentation Pack	1.00	

INDEPENDENT POSTAL AUTHORITY (continued)
Issues 1978

All the following issues were printed on unwatermarked paper.

No.	Issued	Type	Colour		U/M	F/U

Type 120

25TH ANNIVERSARY OF THE CORONATION
Printers: Questa in Litho. *Perf:* 14

MX163	24/5/78 120	**25p**	Multicoloured	40	40
			Gutter pair	90	90
			First Day Cover		70
			Presentation Pack	60	

Type 121

XI COMMONWEALTH GAMES – EDMONTON 1978
Printers: J. Waddington in Litho. *Perf:* 13½

MX164	10/6/78 121	**7p**	Multicoloured	13	13
			Gutter pair	30	30
			First Day Cover		35
			Presentation Pack	30	

Type 122

Type 123

JAMES K. WARD – MANX PIONEER IN CANADA
Printers: J. Waddington in Litho. *Perf:* 13½

MX165	10/6/78 122	**6p**	Multicoloured	10	10
MX166		123	**13p**	Multicoloured	20	20
			Set of 2	30	30
			Set of gutter pairs	75	75
			First Day Cover		45

No.	Issued	Type	Colour		U/M	F/U

Type 124

50TH ANNIVERSARY NORTH AMERICAN MANX ASSOCIATION
Printers: J. Waddington in Litho. *Perf:* 13½

MX167	10/6/78 124	**11p**	Multicoloured	18	18
			Gutter pair	40	40
			First Day Cover		35
			Presentation Pack	65	
			(includes MX165/6)		

Type 125

CHRISTMAS 1978
Printers: J. Waddington in Litho. *Perf:* 13½

MX168	18/10/78 125	**5p**	Multicoloured	10	10
			Gutter pair	30	30
			First Day Cover		35
			Presentation Pack	30	

INDEPENDENT POSTAL AUTHORITY (continued)
Issues 1979

All the following issues were printed on unwatermarked paper.

No.	Issued	Type	Colour	U/M	F/U

Type 126

Type 127

Type 132

Type 133

Type 128

Type 129

Type 134

Type 135

NATURAL HISTORY & ANTIQUARIAN SOCIETY
Printers: Questa in Litho. Perf: 14

No.	Issued	Type		Colour	U/M	F/U
MX169	27/2/79	126	**6p**	Multicoloured	9	9
MX170		127	**7p**	Multicoloured	13	13
MX171		128	**11p**	Multicoloured	18	18
MX172		129	**13p**	Multicoloured	20	20
				Set of 4	55	55
				Set of gutter pairs	1.40	1.40
				First Day Cover		70
				Presentation Pack	70	

Type 136

Type 137

THE MILLENIUM OF TYNWALD 979–1979
Printers: J. Waddington in Litho. Perf: 14

No.	Issued	Type		Colour	U/M	F/U
MX175	16/5/79	132	**3p**	Multicoloured	5	5
MX176		133	**4p**	Multicoloured	7	7
MX177		134	**6p**	Multicoloured	10	10
MX178		135	**7p**	Multicoloured	13	13
MX179		136	**11p**	Multicoloured	18	18
MX180		137	**13p**	Multicoloured	20	20
				Set of 6	70	70
				Set of 5 gutter pairs (incl.3px2,4px2 with gutter between)	1.75	1.75
MX175/176				Se-tenant pair (vert.)	13	13
				First Day Cover		1.00
				Presentation Pack	90	

BOOKLET PANES

MX181	Pane of 6 (3px2,4px2,3px2)	30	30
MX182	Pane of 6 (4px2,3px4)	30	30

Type 130

Type 131

EUROPA 1979 – HISTORY OF POSTAL SERVICES
Printers: Questa in Litho. Perf: 14½

No.	Issued	Type		Colour	U/M	F/U
MX173	16/5/79	130	**6p**	Multicoloured	9	9
MX174		131	**11p**	Multicoloured	18	18
				Set of 2	27	27
				First Day Cover		45
				Presentation Pack	45	

CHRISTMAS 1979
To be issued in October 1979

POSTAGE DUE STAMPS

Printers: Questa Colour in Lithography   *Perf:* 13½ x 14   *Unwatermarked Paper*

No.	*Issued*	*Type*		*Colour*	*U/M*	*F/U*

FIRST PRINTING – "1973" (Printed at base of stamps)

No.	Issued	Type	Denom	Colour	U/M	F/U
MXP1	5/7/73	1	½p	Multicoloured	1.10	80
MXP2			1p	Multicoloured	65	50
MXP3			2p	Multicoloured	65	55
MXP4			3p	Multicoloured	75	65
MXP5			4p	Multicoloured	1.10	75
MXP6			5p	Multicoloured	1.65	1.35
MXP7			10p	Multicoloured	4.40	2.65
MXP8			20p	Multicoloured	9.75	7.00
				Set of 8	£18	£13
				First Day Cover		£28
				Presentation Pack	£19	

Type 1

SECOND PRINTING – "1973 A" (Printed at base of stamps) ★

No.	Issued	Type	Denom	Colour	U/M	F/U
MXP9	10/9/73	1	½p	Multicoloured	3.00	2.00
MXP10			1p	Multicoloured	1.25	45
MXP11			2p	Multicoloured	20	15
MXP12			3p	Multicoloured	25	15
MXP13			4p	Multicoloured	35	20
MXP14			5p	Multicoloured	40	20
MXP15			10p	Multicoloured	75	50
MXP16			20p	Multicoloured	1.50	1.00
				Set of 8	7.00	4.00
				First Day Cover		£90
				Presentation Pack	7.50	
MXP17	8/1/75	2	½p	Multicoloured	5	5
MXP18			1p	Multicoloured	5	5
MXP19			4p	Multicoloured	8	8
MXP20			7p	Multicoloured	12	12
MXP21			9p	Multicoloured	13	13
MXP22			10p	Multicoloured	15	15
MXP23			50p	Multicoloured	75	75
MXP24			£1	Multicoloured	1.50	1.50
				Set of 8	2.50	2.50
				First Day Cover		3.75
				Presentation Pack	2.75	

Type 2

★ Collectors are warned that the 'A' has been known to be fraudulently removed from this second printing.

THE GREAT BRITAIN PHILATELIC SOCIETY

From modest beginnings in November 1955 and with a founder membership of twenty-eight people, the Great Britain Philatelic Society has grown and developed until, at the end of 1978, the membership stood at over seven hundred and fifty.

This membership is drawn from all parts of the United Kingdom, but it is not limited only to this country, there being a sizeable contingent from such countries as France, Switzerland and Australia among others.

Although there is plenty of opportunity for specialisation and deep study, it would be a misconception to assume that this Society caters only for specialists. Anyone at all who is over the age of sixteen and who has any interest whatsoever in the collection of British stamps or Postal History is a most welcome member, subject to the provision of suitable references; and because the range covered by study circles is so varied it would be hard for him or her not to find something of absorbing interest.

The majority of meetings are held in London, but the committee make a point of arranging a certain amount of provincial meetings each year.

With such a society, it is understandable that many members find it impossible to attend all meetings, of which there are approximately sixteen a year, and therefore a large amount of its resources are devoted to the publication of the G.B. Journal, specialist books and booklets which are offered to members at reduced prices, and a monthly Newsletter. The former is a vehicle for the publication of new discoveries in the field of philatelic research and carries articles especially relating to Great Britain which are not general enough for inclusion in the national philatelic press. By the means of the Newsletter many collectors have been put in touch with one another, individual difficulties have been solved and queries answered.

The study circles cover every reign from Queen Victoria to Queen Elizabeth, the latter evoking more and more interest with each new issue. The interests of Postal Historians and collectors of Postal Stationery and Stamp Booklets are catered for by further circles, and members in several counties have benefited by the formation of local groups.

The Society possesses a library from which books may be borrowed upon the payment of a charge to cover post and packing and small fee to the Society, and there is also a photocopy service which is proving most useful. An exchange packet is available to those members living in the United Kingdom, and the regular auction sales add a further valuable source for the collection of material.

There are opportunities for every member to display to the rest of the Society, and talks are given on the art of exhibiting and displaying at all levels.

The annual subscription, which entitles members to receive the Journals and Newsletters, and to participate in all the activities is £10.00 and any other details of membership can be obtained from:
Mrs KF Goodman
"Ingledene"
5 Oakwood Road
Highcliffe
Christchurch
Dorset BH23 5NY

Acclaim for Stoneham '79!

The 1979 edition of this catalogue was awarded a bronze-silver medal at Stampex in March 1979.

The Press Reviews said:-

"A stop-press with the most recent price changes demonstrates the sincerity which underlines this publication"

– Robson Lowe
in the Philatelic Journal of Great Britain

"the 'Stoneham' bids fair to become a popular standard reference work as the only comprehensive, single volume catalogue of G.B., including the Channel Islands and the Isle of Man"

– Kenneth Chapman in the Philatelic Magazine

"The clear print and layout makes the book a pleasure to use, and the prefacing notes are first class. Altogether a very good buy at £3.75"

– The Post Office Philatelic Bulletin

"This edition of the catalogue is a worthwhile and well produced volume which will no doubt be as successful as the first edition"

– Mike Jackson in the Philatelic Review

"Pricing is more accurate than might be expected with the current state of the market"
– Stamp Magazine (February 1979)

"this book remains without doubt a valuable addition to the current catalogue scene and those of you who have not yet made its acquaintance would be well advised to do so"
– Dr. A.K. Huggins in the G.B. Journal

"Stoneham offers unmounted, mounted and fine used quotations for issues from 1887. For the earlier issues the book, sensibly, divides the used column into 'fine' and 'average' with the latter category averaging about half the price of the former. The distinction is an important aid in establishing true values"
– 'Watchman' in Stamp Collecting Weekly (14 Dec. 78)